ESSEX

MARCUS CROUCH

ESSEX

B. T. BATSFORD LTD
LONDON

First published 1969

© Marcus Crouch 1969

Text printed in Great Britain by Northumberland Press Ltd,
Gateshead, Co. Durham. Plates printed and books bound by
Richard Clay (The Chaucer Press) Ltd, Bungay, Suffolk,
for the publishers
B. T. Batsford Ltd, 4 Fitzhardinge Street, London W1

7134 0063 3

For J. J. Tufnell of Langleys

Contents

Illustrations

Grateful thanks are due to Edwin Smith for permission to reproduce Plates 1, 13, 18, 19, 21-24, 26, 27, and 35-37. All the other photographs are the author's.

CHAPTER ONE

The Essential England

'This country is a part of the real England,' says that admirable patriot and incompetent pioneer motorist Mr Britling in Wells' half-forgotten novel. Today, as in 1916 when they were written, the words come as a surprise. For most people the type of the English landscape may be Devon lanes and red fields or the golden-grey of a Cotswold village but surely not the mud and leaden skies of an Eastern county.

No county has been less understood than Essex. 'Flat, isn't it?' is the common reaction, a modern variant of Waller's 'cursed Essexian plain'. The flatness of Essex is a legend which persists in face of all the evidence, a legend growing from half-remembered trips to Southend or Clacton. I got to know the county in boyhood from the saddle of a bicycle and I found much of it anything but flat. Although the land nowhere rises to 500 feet, the greater part of it rolls gently. Height is relative. The Red Queen could doubtless show us hills, in comparison with which the highest in Essex would be called a valley, but in the context of the Eastern counties Danbury (at 380 feet) is a high hill, and Donald Maxwell, a most genial guide to this country, once called Laindon (387 feet) the nearest mountain to London. These two eminences impress because they overlook the levels of great estuaries. The highest points of the county, towards the Hertfordshire and Cambridgeshire borders, command less dramatic prospects and give no such feeling of height.

Essex is indeed a large and complex county which cannot be summed up in a single word. It is no more 'flat' than Sussex is 'pretty' or County Durham 'industrial'. What quickly impresses the sensitive explorer is its variety. This despite a comparatively un-complicated geological structure. The ground plan is a large shallow chalk bowl. The north-west rim of this makes the characteristically down-like hills around and beyond Saffron Walden. The southern rim appears briefly in the Thames valley at Purfleet, where the approach road to the Dartford Tunnel cuts deeply into it, and the great cement works spread an even layer of chalk dust indiscriminately over fields and houses. The great part of the chalk bowl is filled with sedimentary deposits, notably the vast acres of London clay which covers much of the south and east of the county. North of this is an area of boulder clay, giving a lush landscape and fields of wheat and barley. Around the estuaries of Thames, Crouch and Blackwater are the dead levels of recently deposited alluvium, producing the least appreciated and perhaps the most fascinating of the Essex scenes.

Landscape is geology shaped by history. History, it needs to be remembered, is not only the military commander throwing up his dykes across the approaches to Camulodunum and building his Martello towers along the vulnerable coast; it is the farmer marking the land indelibly with his plough and clearing the ancient forest, and the engineer holding back the tides to gain a few precious yards of soil.

As much as any county Essex is man-made. Travellers along the A 13 out of London will not question this statement. Man has made the brick wildernesses of Barking and Dagenham and gashed the earth to feed the greedy mouths of cement works. Man, too, planted the elms which give character to this Thameside scene and soften the harsh lines of pylons and tower-flats. Man won back Canvey from the sea and then disfigured it with a bungaloid rash.

For some of the present-day charms of Essex we have to thank the Norman and Angevin Kings. The fragments surviving from the royal Forest of Essex which they kept for their pleasure held back the tide of London long after much of the northern Home Counties had disappeared under bricks and mortar. Only in the last 30 years has suburbia penetrated beyond Epping Forest and even now central Essex has escaped the fate of Middlesex and southern Hertfordshire. Just how much of mediaeval Essex was forest is still perhaps in doubt. In theory at least virtually the whole county was under forest law, but there were doubtless many exceptions in practice. Place-names give a useful, but not infallible, guide to the age in which forest settlements were established. The term 'forest' does not of course necessarily imply woodland. Dense thickets existed ertainly, but for the royal sport open country and heathland were also needed. It was not uninhabited country. There were plenty of villages in clearings of the forest, the inhabitants of which enjoyed vastly fewer privileges than the pampered deer. Gradually through the centuries of the Middle Ages the forest shrank, as the feudal system weakened and landowners and burgesses gained power. The Forest of Essex became the Forest of Waltham, then Epping Forest, with the neighbouring fragments of Hainault Forest and Hatfield Forest. Even the last five and a half thousand acres of Epping Forest would have been whittled away but for the vigorous action of the Corporation of the City of London, which won a protracted legal battle in 1882 and so preserved this priceless area for ever to be the first (but not in name) of our National Parks.

This thin eleven-mile strip of woodland and plain served for a surprisingly long time as a *cordon sanitaire*. Forty years ago I used to walk from my crowded northern suburb through the glades of Epping Forest and out into a country seemingly untouched by the twentieth century. Chigwell, roughly as far from central London as Edmonton, was a village. Ongar, 24 miles from Charing Cross, might have been two hundred. All this has changed now. Chigwell gives its name to an Urban District. Ongar is a commuter town. And yet the change is not fundamental. Chigwell still keeps its village character; Ongar High Street has the air of a country market-town, remaining somehow aloof from the traffic thundering through it.

Although the great forests of Essex have almost completely gone and have not—thank heaven—been replaced by the regimented acres of the Forestry Commission, trees play a vital part in the landscape of modern Essex. Those who believe, with a contemporary State Governor in America, that when you have seen one tree you have seen the lot, need not make the journey into Essex. It is trees—individual elms punctuating the precise furrows of a newly ploughed field, copses of oak or beech focusing the eye on a low-swelling hill—which make the Essex scene memorable. It is, for those whose sensitivity is tuned to its deceptively low key, a deeply satisfying countryside. It never bludgeons the visitor into awareness of its beauty. Its surprises, of which there are many, are so subtle as to be missed altogether by those who hurtle through the county in search of more dramatic scenes. It is a landscape to be enjoyed slowly and at leisure, to be tasted and savoured. The gobbler must go elsewhere.

There are no deserts in Essex, if one excepts the saltings of the coastal levels. There is no waste. This is a countryside for use, and the acres earn their keep. Surprisingly, in land so tamed and geared to production, it is nevertheless rewarding to the walker. No county is better provided with footpaths, well indicated by signposts sufficiently robust to resist the onslaught of the idiot one-per-cent of our youth. These paths exist and are duly recorded on the Planning Department's maps. They are not always visible on the ground. In some parts, and too often, neglect has encouraged the farmer to obliterate rights-of-way. Tracks which start out optimistically lose heart in ploughed earth—and deep mud of the authentic Essex texture—or knee-high corn. For those who persevere the paths lead to enchanting places and to a proper understanding of this elusive countryside. Beside the field-tracks Essex is provided generously with 'green lanes', roads of mediaeval and later date which have been by-passed by the twentieth century.

No one can get to know Essex without enjoying the leisurely pleasures of walking. The country nevertheless has much to offer the resourceful motorist. I know no more congested and unlovely trunk-roads than these—nor any drivers more ill-mannered and homicidal than those who use them. Beyond the terrors of A 11, A 12 and A 13, however, lies a network of well-made and astonishingly peaceful byways. Even today, and within 40 miles of Charing Cross, it is possible to find roads which seem to belong to an earlier age of motoring. This is not quite true of summer week-ends, but on weekdays and in unpopular—but not unlovely—seasons an enterprising motorist may recapture pleasures which he had believed to be gone for ever.

It is a country of contrasts. The less attractive aspects of modern civilization seem a degree or two worse here. The new housing estates are meaner and get shabby more quickly. The cement-dust lies more thickly over roofs and hedges. Wires proliferate, not just the super-grid, which has its own kind of grandeur, but a mass of minor festoons which ruin the visual impact of almost every village in the county. There is a suburban dreariness about some parts which is profoundly depressing. This, one feels, is a county which has lost heart. Against this sad picture must be set the other, of fruitful

2   *Hobs Aerie, Arkesden*

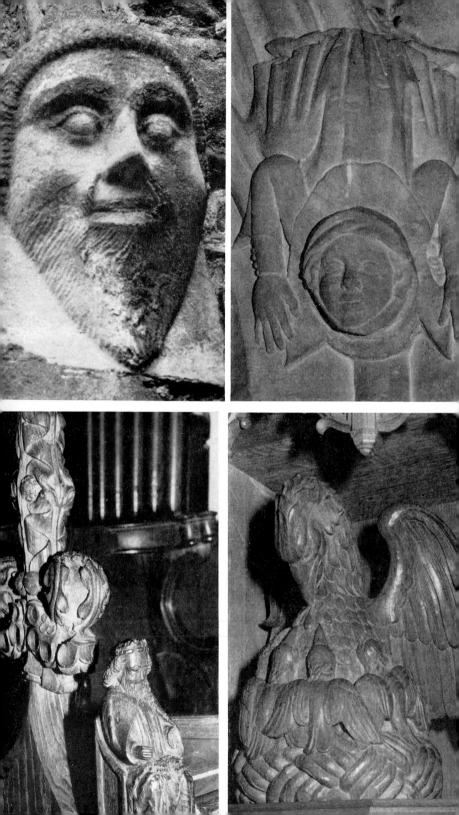

fields, fine trees, lovely houses of all sizes from great mansions to exquisite cottages, village churches which are mostly homely and quite remarkably matched to their environment. Here is a landscape which imitates, or inspires, art; part of the country which made Constable a painter.

It is no disparagement to insist that Essex is a county of minor pleasures. Out of the sum total of these comes the major pleasure of living. There is quiet pleasure here for the connoisseur of landscape, as for the botanist and the bird-watcher. Innumerable small delights await the amateur ecclesiologist. Collectors of absurd, evocative and meaningful place-names will find rich opportunities for indulging their hobby, as Edward Thomas did once in a charming poem. Havering and Clavering, Fingringhoe and Fobbing, Wivenhoe and Wix: the roll-call can be extended indefinitely. Then there are the 'families' of villages: the Rodings, the Easters, the Woodhams, the Lavers. Meeting them on the map one is enchanted by their euphony; meeting them on the ground it is a delight to find that they can be as lovely as their names. A place-name may hint at the origin of the village—as Mersea; or a stage in its history—as Stansted Mountfitchet. Others, like Messing and Mucking, are memorable by reason of their incongruity. Occasionally one comes upon a real oddity; my favourite of this kind is Shellow Bowells, a name so hugely improbable that one looks at the signpost in flat incredulity.

As history goes in these islands that of Essex is comparatively brief. Dense forest and treacherous marsh made it inhospitable country for early invaders, and of the oldest prehistoric cultures only slight remains have been found—Paleolithic in the Lea Valley, Neolithic around Clacton and Walton, where there was a flourishing flint-industry. Bronze Age settlers penetrated as far as Braintree where they established a lake-village of the Glastonbury pattern. It is necessary to visit museums—the British Museum and remarkable local collections at Colchester and Saffron Walden—to see the evidence on which our fragmentary knowledge of these remote Essex men is based. I don't much care for museums myself, and I am happier looking for the next wave of invaders—the Celtic tribes of the Iron Age—among their defensive works, at Colchester, in Epping Forest and on the banks of the Stort.

By the time Julius Caesar turned his attention to Britain, partly to demonstrate Roman might, partly to discourage the British Celts

3-6   Church details: Canewdon (top left), Stebbing (top right), Belchamp St Paul (bottom left), Margaretting (bottom right)

from sending military aid to their cousins in Gaul, Essex had become
a major centre of Celtic life. The Belgic tribe of Trinobantes had
their capital at Camulodunum (roughly the modern Colchester
under a formidable warlord called Cassivellaunus. Although the
Trinobantes submitted to Caesar at the end of his campaign of
54 BC they remained supreme in south-east Britain. Cunobelin, who
was Shakespeare's Cymbeline, established a Romanized capital at
Colchester. It was a dynastic dispute here which gave the Emperor
Claudius an excuse for the invasion of AD 43 which led to the Roman
conquest of Britain.

The Trinobantic chief who led the opposition to Claudius's army
was the famous Caractacus. In spite of his heroic resistance, which
he continued in a series of actions while retreating to the west, the
Trinobantes were forced into surrender, and Aulus Plautius chose
a site alongside the tribal capital for a Roman colony, to be a permanent settlement for discharged legionaries. British taxes paid for
this and for the huge temple erected to the glory of Claudius the
God. Eighteen years later this building was destroyed in Boadicea's
uprising and never rebuilt.

After the defeat of Boadicea—probably in Essex—there was a
long period during which the British farmers and traders enjoyed
the benefits of the Roman Peace. Roads were built, based on Colchester, and prosperous Romanized natives put up great houses in
which they copied the style of living of their conquerors and
adapted it to the chills and damp of east-coast Britain. But Romanized Essex was limited to fairly well-defined areas. The great centre
of activity was Colchester, and there were minor centres at Chelmsford and Great Chesterford, but much of the country was cut off
from these civilizing influences by forest and marsh.

With the decline of Roman power Essex began an era of violence
which was to give the county its name and lay down the pattern
of its villages. The first onslaughts of the barbarians were merely
raids, designed to collect loot and slaves. It was not until richer and
more hospitable parts of the country had been settled that the
Saxons came to Essex for good, evolving the Kingdom of the East
Saxons of which London was to become the principal city. In
population, it was still compared—say—with Kent, a fairly small
kingdom. The family settlements—the names of their founders still
recalled in -*ings* such as Feering and Ulting—spread along the river

valleys and the clearances made by Roman road-builders. The dark forests and the damp marshes alike were shunned at first, to be opened up later when land-hunger proved stronger than fear.

The forests of Essex, like those of Sussex, insulated the country from civilization and delayed the return of Christianity. It is true that in 604 St Augustine made his lieutenant, Mellitus, Bishop of London with the express task of converting the East Saxons, but this mission was disastrously unsuccessful and that doughty and gouty bishop had to escape overseas. It was left to St Cedd, nearly 50 years later, to establish the Christian church in Essex.

For over a century the kingdom existed in peaceful obscurity, enjoying nominal independence although dominated first by the kingdom of Kent and later by that of Wessex. But the indented coastline which had attracted the original Saxon pirates now drew the attention of still more savage invaders. This was ideal campaigning country for the Danes, whose longships penetrated the estuaries, from which raiding parties could sack towns and monasteries. Such country was hardly defensible, however much the defenders hit back. Essex was a battleground for much of the period of the Danish wars, until the death of Edmund Ironside and the remarkable transformation of Canute from pirate chief into statesman-king brought peace to the country again.

At the Norman Conquest the Saxon lords were dispossessed with exceptional thoroughness. Their lands were given to favourite followers of the Conqueror, notably his steward Eudo Dapifer, Geoffrey de Mandeville who, contrary to William's usual cautious practice, got a large concentrated estate, and Aubrey de Vere who made his headquarters at Hedingham. They and their heirs left their mark on Essex in place-names and in the castles and abbeys they built. The largest of all Norman castles—at Colchester—belongs to the immediate post-Conquest period, and Castle Hedingham, which was built during the stormy reign of Henry II, is the most perfect of surviving Norman keeps. But of the great abbeys which the Norman barons founded at Earls Colne and Walden, in thanksgiving for victory or as insurance for the welfare of their souls, hardly a trace remains.

Essex suffered during the period of anarchy which followed William's firm rule. In the civil wars of Stephen's reign, Geoffrey de Mandeville, whose grandfather had been rewarded by the Conqueror, played power politics with a cynical disregard of honour and loyalty. The Essex barons were united in resistance to King John. Four of their number were appointed guardians of Magna Carta, and in the subsequent civil war the King devoted his energies especially to the subjugation of Essex. Not for the first time it was the ordinary people of the county who suffered most as the King's men and the Barons' and the French army looted and burned.

In the brief intervals of peace the King and his Court hunted in the diminishing Forest of Essex. Meanwhile the towns began to prosper from their traffic in wool from Essex sheep. The first towns to gain royal charters, however—Maldon and Colchester—owed their success to the sea, and Essex wool was exported to bring wealth to the Low Countries.

Vigorous action to restrict these exports was taken by Edward I, and as a result a native cloth industry was deliberately created. Expert craftsmen were brought in from Flanders to set up their mills on the Stour, the Colne and the Blackwater. From this time dates the prosperity of the new industrial towns of Braintree, Halstead and Dedham, and Colchester found a new source of wealth in the making of Colchester russet.

The devastation caused by the Black Death in 1349 upset the balance of rural economy, and from this grew the discontents which came to a head in the Peasants' Revolt of 1381. Essex was deeply committed to this cause. The spokesman for the peasants, John Ball, was an Essex man, and the refusal of Thames-side fishermen to pay poll-tax touched off the revolt north of the Thames at just the time that Wat Tyler called out the Kentish peasants. In the reaction following the death of Wat Tyler and the dispersal of his followers, savage reprisals were taken on them. A last resistance near Billericay was defeated with great slaughter. John Ball suffered a traitor's, or a martyr's, death.

During the civil wars which put an end to mediaeval England and to the villeinage against which the peasants had revolted Essex was left largely alone. While in distant counties the great Essex noblemen killed one another in the Yorkist or Lancastrian cause, the citizens of Essex got on with the business of making money. Fine houses and noble churches survive as witness to their success.

The Tudor age saw the rise of a new gentry and aristocracy, canny experts in survival like Petre, ruthless go-getters like Rich, who built their great houses out of the profits, and sometimes the materials, of the dissolved monasteries. Essex became a popular place in which to live. Anne Boleyn lived in New Hall at Boreham which the King delighted to call his Beaulieu. The unhappy Princess Mary was perhaps least unhappy here. Elizabeth made several progresses through the county to the cost of her involuntary hosts.

While the great families trimmed their sails carefully to the winds of religious change, the people on the whole inclined towards reform. Essex had rather more than a fair share of Marian martyrs, and in the following reign the county welcomed, and benefited from, a new influx of migrants from the Low Countries, this time Protestant refugees from the savagery of Alva. Through the energies and technical skill of these industrious people the cloth trade of northern Essex received a useful shot in the arm: this despite a good deal of racial dissension, of a kind familiar enough to us today, which intensified as the trickle of immigrants grew into a flood when conditions in Holland became more and more intolerable.

The east-coast ports, which had played their part in the semi-piratical naval actions of the Hundred Years' War, sent out their contribution to the fleet against the Spanish Armada, and Essex took briefly the centre of the national stage when the Queen reviewed her land forces at Tilbury and addressed them in words of unforgettable magnificence.

The traditional non-conformity of Essex continued into the seventeenth century. The Pilgrim Fathers assembled in the county and sailed under an Essex captain. The county was fairly solidly for Parliament in the Civil War, and it is ironic that the one great event of the war in Essex—the Siege of Colchester—sees a Parliamentary force attacking a Royalist stronghold. The siege was disastrous for Colchester and for much of northern Essex. The cloth trade was damaged beyond effective repair and prosperity declined alarmingly. A dispirited town and countryside were ill-prepared to resist the plague which hit Essex in the same year as the more notorious, but not proportionately more damaging, Great Plague of London.

It was an unhappy ending to a long story of prosperity. In the following century the great landowners increased their wealth through the enclosure of common lands, and the rural labourers became poorer and poorer. The eighteenth century, which saw the rebuilding of magnificent houses and the creation of landscaped parks which are still the glory of the Essex countryside, was an age of desperate poverty and unrest. Farm workers became a charge on the poor rate or went off to the new industrial cities of the north.

Meanwhile London had begun to spill over its borders into south-eastern Essex. The process was accelerated by the growth of the London docks along the north shore of the Thames and the development of riverside industries on a large scale. There was an industrial revival too in the old cloth-working areas of central north Essex, where George Courtauld had set up his first silk factory in 1798.

Essex, in common with other south-eastern coastal counties, returned to the glare of national history in the Napoleonic Wars. In the expectation of invasion great military camps were set up, at Danbury, Lexden and elsewhere, and coastal defences were strengthened with the huge Martello towers which still survive on the coast between Stour and Colne.

The familiar process of urban growth and rural depopulation continued through the nineteenth century and up to the end of the Second World War. Communications, notoriously bad ever since Roman times, improved with the building of the railway between London and Colchester in the 'Forties'. Other lines were added through the century. The 'navigation' from Maldon to Chelmsford alone remains as evidence of the canal craze which swept the country in the eighteenth and early nineteenth centuries.

Recent history has seen the acceleration of urban growth and the reversal, for different reasons, of the depopulation of the rural county. Essex has become a popular county with commuters, some housed in not-very-lovely newly built estates along the main railway lines, some bringing new life to neglected country halls and cottages. There has been on the one hand substantial loss of amenity, on the other solid benefit through the injection into the county of new money and new enthusiasm. The man who can afford to put a new hat of thatch on his cottage may not have his roots in the country but his heart is there. Meanwhile the soil, where it has been spared from brick and concrete, grows its barley and cabbages vigorously. As to the towns we may, perhaps with profit, contrast the architectural anarchy of Dagenham and Romford with the controlled experiments in communal living of the New Towns of Basildon and Harlow.

Essex architecture makes a splendid virtue of necessity. Of good native building stone there is none. A very few patrons could afford to import stone from Normandy, and in parishes on navigable waterways one may find that Kentish rag has been brought down the Medway and across the Thames for use in church towers. But for the most part local materials have been used, flint, conglomerate masses of various constituents, timber, and later brick. To venture into dogma: Essex has the best roses and the best brick in the country. (Walkers might be inclined to add a third distinction— the finest mud.) For the former, no traveller through the county in high summer is likely to forget the splendour of the colours blazing in every cottage garden. As for brick, Essex can show the earliest examples since Roman days, and can meet the challenge of any other English county with Layer Marney, Leez Priory, Faulkbourne Hall and a host of incomparable church towers of which Ingatestone and Sandon are only *primi inter pares.*

In the course of the Essex journeys which follow I mention in passing some of the hundreds of fine houses which are among the wonders of the county. Even to mention them all would produce an unmanageably long book, and the monumental report of the Royal Commission on Historical Monuments was hard put to it to do justice to them. Audley End, only a fragment of its original mansion, is still among the greatest of English houses. Layer Marney Tower is a fragment, too, not like Audley End, because of later demolition but because its grandiose plan was never completed. Buildings like these are of national importance. Some visitors may find, as I do, as much or more satisfaction in more modest houses, gracious halls like those of Belchamp or Langham which grew out of a conscious feeling for symmetry and proportion, or humbler examples of vernacular architecture, whose charm comes not from professional skill or cultivated taste but from sound native craftsmanship and an honest respect for local materials. There is hardly a village in Essex which lacks a house of this kind, and many are full of them.

The most characteristic feature of the Essex countryside is the 'hall', almost invariably accompanied by the parish church, the group more often than not remote by a half-mile or so from the modern centre of the village. Our spokesman on Essex matters, Mr Britling, says: 'All the old farmhouses are moated—because of the wolves.' Whatever the reason Essex has more moated homestead sites than any other county. Sometimes the original hall has vanished, leaving the moat as a damp depression among the wheat or the nettles. Often part of the ditch has been filled in. The old defences—against human and animal enemies or against flood—are now the home of ducks and geese, including some exotics. I must confess to an extreme and quite uncritical affection for these halls. Whether half-timbered, colour-washed or brick, they provide high-lights in the flat fields of the low country and tuck snugly into the folds of the rolling hills. They call insistently for the attentions of the photographer and still more the water-colourist.

No hall seems complete without its neighbouring church, and if this is missing as likely as not its foundations lie among the weeds beyond the farm-yard or beneath the ploughed field. The two buildings made up the basic unit of each original Saxon or mediaeval settlement.

As to the churches themselves, these are not often of the highest architectural quality, judged by the exacting standards of East Anglia or Somerset or the Cotswolds. The great churches of Saffron Walden and Thaxted, and to a lesser extent Dedham, are obvious exceptions to a general rule. The typical Essex church is a small building, on a simple plan of aisleless nave and choir, with a brick or timber porch and a shingled spire or bellcote. It is scarcely 'architecture', but it has great antiquarian interest and still more visual charm. Few village churches fit more perfectly into their settings. If they lack finely patinated stone, such stone as they have is often carved with vigorous grotesques. The timber belfries are masterpieces of rustic carpentry; indeed the intricate skeletons of spires like Blackmore and Margaretting are primitive but effective engineering. Throughout the areas of former forests the woodwork is of high excellence. There are nobly designed roofs like those of High Easter and Stebbing. At Stock the windows have wooden tracery. There is even a wooden font at Marks Tey.

As in other parts of England most of these churches are survivors from mediaeval times. Essex, however, is unusually rich in post-Reformation churches. These, so long neglected by antiquarians, are now, and rightly, in fashion. At Woodham Walter there is a remarkable example of Elizabethan work. In this reign it was more common for churches to fall into ruin, but here is a delightful brick building, authentically 'Gothic' in feeling despite its stepped gables, which was put up in the first years of Elizabeth under the patronage of Thomas, Earl of Essex. From the end of the same reign comes the sturdy elegance of Theydon Mount. There is good Georgian work at Shellow Bowells—traditional—and Ingrave—eccentric—and an exquisitely remodelled interior of the same period at Lambourne. The restrained good manners of these homely buildings contrast nicely with Adams' exuberant towers at Mistley. From the Gothic Revival there is Bodley's tower at Epping, and Great Warley has an extraordinary interior in the Art Nouveau manner. There is not much to show, outside the New Towns and the London fringe, for the modern age; some visitors will be pleased, as I am, with the traditional post-war rebuilding at Little Horkesley.

In mediaeval times Essex was generously provided with religious houses. The destruction following the Dissolution was exceptionally thorough. Of the great abbey churches only Waltham and St Botolph's in Colchester were spared for parochial use, and the latter was later ruined during the Civil War. The 'new men' of the age, who found Essex convenient for access to the capital and the Court, bought up the deserted conventual buildings and demolished the churches for their materials. Hardly a trace remained of the premier convent in the country at Barking. The search for fragments of the buildings which once provided Essex with its schools, hotels, art centres and social services can be most absorbing, but with a handful of notable exceptions it does not lead to major discoveries. Visitors to this county must not expect the romantic beauty and the aesthetic satisfaction which the monastic remains of more remote places give.

In the essential Essex, from which I exclude places like Clacton, one gets a strong impression of self-sufficiency. The visitor is unnecessary. This is not to say that the county is unwelcoming. In my wanderings I have not gone out of my way to seek human contacts, being interested to a fault in trees and buildings rather than in people; I have nevertheless met everywhere with the greatest and most unforced friendliness, from the owners of great houses and the cleaners of country churches, from parsons and publicans. The tourist, however, is not important here, as he is in areas less economically self-contained. There is a sufficiency of good hotels and restaurants but not an industry based on visitors. The visitor comes and is greeted courteously, but when he goes he has the impression that the county is ready to get back to its own affairs without delay.

Similarly the good Essex farmer would rather grow corn on his land than caravans. This self-interest might be dangerous were it not so often allied to pride and good taste. Fine old houses are preserved, and handsome new ones built in traditional styles, not to attract the tourist trade, but because a good environment is essential to good living. When this environment is threatened by alien forces the people of Essex unite in formidable opposition. The battle of Stansted is a magnificent example of this, a concerted protest at an intolerable proposal which gave arrogant autocracy its biggest shock since the War.

Another manifestation of this inturned spirit, so surprising in a county so near to London and so much a reception area for immigrants from the cities, is the strength of tradition. The county changes, certainly, from day to day under the pressures of the century, but some things go on persistently. In no other Home County are the old crafts practised so effectively and so unselfconsciously. There are not so many bearded and sandalled potters, producing affectedly primitive wares for undiscriminating visitors. But in the country you will find craftsman bricklayers at work and craftsman plumbers, expert in skills which have not changed fundamentally in four centuries. The woodcarver leaves his mark on houses and churches. The most characteristic of all Essex crafts —pargetting—can be studied not only in ancient buildings but in those going up today. When on your travels you see a frontage decorated exquisitely with stars and moons, heron or horse or geometrical shapes, what you admire may spring from the mind of an artist dead these 200 years or from one who has just knocked off for his tea-break. The new work is not less good than the old and not basically different in technique. There is a timelessness about these country crafts, so far removed from the olde-worlde puerilities familiar in some other places, which seems appropriate in a county where the man glimpsed strolling through a park may be living in a house his ancestor built in the reign of the first Elizabeth.

Essex lives for itself. To take an example: there are probably more beautiful and historic houses here than in any county of comparable size. Only 10 are opened regularly to the public, compared with 45 in Kent. This is not just selfishness or lack of friendliness. These houses are homes, not Stately Homes. The same self-sufficiency is met in the towns and villages. These may be immensely attractive

7   *Dukes, an Essex hall at Roxwell*

but—with a few exceptions—they do not set out to attract. Go into a village shop and you will be served with the greatest courtesy, but you will see that the shop is there to serve the villagers and only incidentally you and your like. In any other county a village as exquisite as Clavering would be full of gifte shoppes and tea-houses. Here you will find not even an antique shop.

This book has been in some ways a sentimental pilgrimage for me. I spent my boyhood in one of the brick deserts of North London. The River Lea was the boundary of a promised land, a land of trees and fields. From my unlovely suburb I explored, first on foot, later extending my range by bicycle, the forests and the dusty lanes of Essex. In them I learnt one of the most precious lessons of my life, that deep personal satisfaction can come from close experience of nature and that history is to be read not only in books, but in the patterns of fields and the texture of buildings. Now I am again living in a neighbouring county and the Dartford Tunnel has become the gateway not only to the cement wilderness of Purfleet, but to a host of delightful and unexpected pleasures. In preparing my book I have recreated and extended the discoveries of my boyhood and confirmed my belief that, notwithstanding the ruins wrought by twentieth-century folly and greed, this is still a most lovely and characteristic landscape.

There are without question many people native to Essex or steeped in its history whose knowledge makes them infinitely better qualified to write about the county. I must plead in my justification, partly that the outsider may sometimes be more sensitive to impressions than those familiar with every detail, partly that I yield to no one in my affectionate appreciation of this country. In putting down these impressions I pay most joyfully my boyhood debts.

My book remains one of impressions. There is room for a new history of Essex, and the materials for this are being assembled in what is, by common consent, the foremost of County Record Offices. There may even be a case for a fresh evaluation of Essex buildings, for readers who find the Royal Commission's volumes intimidating and Professor Pevsner's handbook laconic. It would certainly be good to see a book on Essex churches as authoritative and affectionate as the late Kenneth Wickham's on those of Somerset. These books must find their own authors. I hope that there is still a place for a book like mine, which aims merely at sharing pleasure in the

8-11 *Mills: Felsted (top left), Witham (top right),*
Aythorpe Roding (bottom left), Mountnessing (bottom right)

delights of landscape and architecture and in the peculiarly happy blending of these two elements which makes up the Essex scene.

Essex does not lend itself readily to topographical treatment. Its geology is not varied enough to provide the pattern for a book, as does, for instance, that of Kent or Devon. The catchment areas of the towns are not sufficiently self-contained or satisfactory. One seeks a pattern based on nature and history. The best answer seems to lie in the rivers. On the ground these appear, apart from the estuaries, to be comparatively insignificant. The motorist crosses Chelmer and Pant without noticing that they are there. Yet these little streams have been the key to history through all the centuries. They have provided the highways for invasion and civilization.

I have based my book, therefore, on the exploration of the river-valleys of Essex. I begin with the Thames, whose estuary forms the southern boundary of the county. Thameside is for many people the typical Essex countryside, flat, industrialized, grossly over-developed. It is rich in history, however, and full of surprises. Then there are the four east-flowing rivers which give Essex its deeply indented coastline. Of these Colne is the richest in history, while Stour has the most softly lovely landscape and Chelmer-Blackwater the largest and most varied basin. Roding flows south through the heart of Essex and unveils that heart to the discerning visitor. Lastly there are the rivers of the western border, ranging from the clean chalk downs of the north to the industrial wastes of London-side.

Journeys through these valleys will take the visitor to a great many delectable places, as well as to others less obviously attractive but essential to a proper view of the county. They will leave un-visited other parishes equally charming and historic. Any topo-graphical book, if it is not to be intolerably long, must select, and the self-imposed sacrifice of many places dear to me has been pain-ful. How could I bear to leave out the breezy uplands of the extreme north-west? or the peninsula between the Colne and Stour estuaries? I have no regrets about missing out Clacton, but what of the bird-haunted lagoon of Hamford Water? or the noble church of Great Bromley, which I last saw on a sunny Easter morning, with the flag of St George high on the flint tower and the faithful flocking to prayer? These, and many other delights, must be the object of explorations not guided by me. The journeys I have outlined briefly in the following pages are the bare bones of fuller and richer journey-ings through the lanes and fields of a lovely county. Those who go on to make their own discoveries, hunting out still more tall-chimneyed halls and discreetly hidden churches, will in their personal way come to the heart of this 'essential England'.

CHAPTER TWO

Thames

Barking—Rainham—Aveley—Orsett—Tilbury—
Laindon Hills—Canvey—Hadleigh—Southend

My aim in this book is twofold: to try to define what seems to me the individual quality of Essex, and to help visitors to find landscape and buildings which are rewarding for their beauty and for their capacity for evoking the past. The routes I follow will be often enough far from the usual tourists' haunts, of which there are in any case few in this county. I must, however, resist the temptation towards mere perversity, which might convince us that a place is interesting or attractive just because it is neglected.

This risk is particularly high in this first journey beside the tidal waters of the Thames. The crowded streets of London-in-Essex are not normally visited by tourists for the sound reason that there is not enough here to attract them. This is not to say that the new London boroughs lack interest. A wealth of history lies hidden here, but it awaits the archivist rather than the topographer.

I intend therefore, with only a token feeling of guilt, to deal inadequately with much of Thameside Essex, neglecting large areas in favour of getting beyond the range of the City and into open country. So we shall ignore the densely populated districts between the Lea and the Roding, and all the fascinations of dockland, foregoing the detective pleasures of seeking out the village hearts of East and West Ham, and leaving undiscovered the site of Stratford Abbey, where Chaucer's Prioress learnt her French. We will regard the Roding as our starting point, and Barking Abbey our first objective.

This was the earliest nunnery to be founded in Essex and throughout its long history it was pre-eminent in the whole country. It was
founded about 675 by the saintly Earconwald (or Erkenwald),
Bishop of London, a man of such holiness that—according to Bede
—even the carriage in which he travelled was able to perform
miracles. He appointed his sister Ethelburga to be the first abbess,
a formidable ruler of her house and a woman of unquestioned sanct-
ity; Bede said that 'no person who knew her ought to question
but that the heavenly kingdom was open to her'. Under the Normans
the abbey was reorganized in the Benedictine rule. The abbess of
Barking held rank as a peer throughout the Middle Ages; she had
precedence over all other abbesses in the kingdom and lived in the
style appropriate to a great noble. The abbey retained its wealth
and vitality right up to the Dissolution. It was an efficiently managed organization, still doing good work in the education of young
ladies from the best houses of Essex, and having many noblewomen
among the nuns, which in 1539 surrendered to the King's Commis-
sioner, Doctor William Petre (whom we shall meet again more than
once in the course of our journeys). The destruction was systematic.
Of the vast complex of buildings just east of Barking Creek, where
the abbey mill ground corn, only one fragment remains. The rest:
cathedral-sized Norman church, cloisters, living quarters for the
sisters and their army of retainers, the palatial house of the abbess;
all have vanished. The surviving fragment is the present entrance to
the churchyard, a tall gatehouse with chapel above, its proportions
lost with the demolition of the wall which once flanked it on either
side. This was one of the newer buildings of the abbey and was put
up around the close of the fourteenth century to give access to
the cemetery of the sisterhood. If you stand in the arched entrance,
you may imagine the east end of the great abbey church straight
in front of you, while away on your right stretched the infirmary
and all the other buildings needed to keep the complicated organization in being. On your left, beyond the parish church, was the great
gatehouse.

A little of the importance of the abbey is reflected in the parish
church, a large stone building which belongs largely to the thirteenth
and the fifteenth centuries. Some of the fabric may be re-used
material from the abbey. It is interesting rather than beautiful, and
there is much detail which calls for examination. As a good town-

church should, it contains a great many monuments to past notables mostly of seventeenth- and eighteenth-century dates, although the finest is also the oldest, a slab commemorating the first vicar of 1328. There is an especially delightful memorial to Sir Charles Montague who died in 1625. This shows him sitting outside his tent on the eve of battle.

It would be a mistake to think that the churchyard, a green haven down towards the river with no through-road immediately adjacent is typical of Barking. It is not, although I find the new town hall almost opposite, has a little of the right kind of panache; it might inspire some city father to unconventional enterprise. For the rest the houses press down on the traveller. If you follow the road east and south away from the town hall, heading towards the Southend Road you will pass near and with good navigation may reach a most surprising building. In the precise centre of a housing estate which seems to epitomize all the dreariness of its kind there is an Elizabethan manor house. The National Trust, whose beneficent work we usually expect to meet in noble parks or city squares or on windswept cliffs or moors, here preserves a house of around 1570, in brick, and having that blend of formality and homeliness which is so much the hall mark of the age. Eastbury House is used for communal activities and can hardly fail to exert an uplifting influence on those who come to it from these dismal Barking streets.

We are now coming up to Dagenham. A genial radio journalist once claimed that, compared with Dagenham, Slough looked like an Area of Outstanding Natural Beauty, and one sees his point. Let us be fair. Some of the newer housing is worth the attention of students of contemporary community problems and their architectural solution. Right in the middle of the new town a tiny village is trapped, old Dagenham with its mediaeval church and Georgian accretions and some old houses. Not everyone is prepared to face the hazard of traffic in order to find this astonishing survival. Those who play for safety will continue down the main road past the wide acres of the Ford Motor Works. These enclose the waters of Dagenham Gulf, a large lake which resulted from a breach of the river defences early in the eighteenth century. This land lies perilously low and has always been subject to flooding. Throughout the middle ages the maintenance of the river wall was a duty of Barking Abbey. When the abbey was destroyed no one thought seriously enough about the mplications. The wall was patched up in Elizabeth's reign, but it was reached again less than 30 years later, when the famous Dutch ngineer Vermuyden was called in to direct the repairs. His work eld until 1707, and then the wall collapsed in a great storm. The uthorities argued for 15 years about what should be done. By that ime some of the land was lost for ever and it took a vast sum to pay or repairs. Today some people still feel that this part of Thameside is he soft underbelly of London's defence against flood.

On these busy roads there are not many reminders of the natural tructure of scenery on which these houses and factories have been uperimposed. Even the Thames, a mile away, is mostly out of sight. Ve have a reminder of the river in two small tributaries which we ross quite close together between Dagenham and Rainham. The first f these is the Beam River, or the River Rom, which rises near Nave-tock, within a mile of the Roding, and flows past the former royal nanor of Havering-atte-Bower and through the densely urban area f Romford. The other is the Inglebourne Brook. This too rises in the ong ridge of Navestock, but takes an opposite course, south-east.)ne of the earlier feeders is a brook coming out of Weald Park. This s too far off our route to justify a visit now, but a later trip to South Veald would be well rewarded. The village, despite the nearness of 3rentwood, is quite unspoilt, and the group of inn, cottages and hurch is as charming as we shall find anywhere in Essex. The church tands on a mound, obviously artificial, in a corner of Weald Park. he hall which stood here had been a home of Princess Mary during he long unhappy years following King Henry VIII's repudiation of er mother. It was demolished after the Second World War, and the ark was acquired by the County Council as an open space. It is a reezy area, with views and, on the lower ground, a chain of lakes reated out of the brook in an eighteenth-century landscaping. The rook manages to avoid the main built-up area of Upminster, touches he fringe of Hornchurch—where a magnificent town-church has ne unique feature, a bull's head with horns sheathed in copper, vhich gives the parish its name (or was it the other way round?)— nd reaches the Thames on Rainham marshes.

Happily Rainham is by-passed by the main Southend Road. This 1as not spared it from becoming rather a messy little town—or large village—but it has made possible the survival of a genuine village entre at a road junction. Here, surrounded by squalid houses, stands

an almost perfect Norman church with a Georgian hall beside i
which is even nearer to perfection.

We shall see so much of the work of Norman architects and
masons in Essex that we may be in danger of thinking it common
place, but we shall find no church so completely of Norman work
manship as this. It is a large building, rather gloomy because of close
neighbours, stained glass and—one suspects—a coating of grime, bu
we should not be deterred from looking closer. The work belongs to
the end of the Norman period. It was, perhaps, completed just abou
the time when the Archbishop of Canterbury lay murdered in hi
cathedral. The decoration of the massive pillars, used with economy
for this is an austere building, belongs to this late phase. The chance
arch is of the same period. Larger windows were inserted in the wal
of the choir a century later, but more of the original Norma
windows have survived throughout the church than is common. Al
in all, a sombre building of great dignity and strength; the weight o
the centuries seems to bear down upon it.

Among the vicars of Rainham was Charles Churchill, and his son
another Charles, was curate here in 1756. It was not a seemly ap
pointment and Charles soon went off to London to live it up in the
company of the wits and to write in *The Rosciad* a highly popula
satire of the stage, in which not even Garrick escaped injury. Per
haps Churchill was thinking of his Rainham days when he wrote
about the effect of his sermons:

Sleep at my bidding crept from pew to pew.

Rainham Hall, in what we shall come to see as the characteristic
Essex pattern, stands just beside the church. This is not, as Essex
halls mostly are, a country mansion in a park, but essentially a town
house. It would not look out of place in Queen Anne's Gate. Rainham
Hall belongs to the first stage of the Georgian age. A conservative
building, it has some features of the earlier age. It is in a dark red
brick, five symmetrical bays, three storeys high, with attics above
lit by dormers almost hidden by the parapet. The one external
extravagance is the porch, an exquisite arched portico supported on
Corinthian columns, but even this is gravely splendid rather than
exuberant. The railings and gates are contemporary iron-work and
very fine. This lovely house is now safe in the keeping of the National
Trust. It is not normally open but may be seen by appointment.

In Rainham we are still within the influence of London, but this is weakening. Along the minor road to Wennington there is just a first hint of rural Essex. Wennington itself, if you see it from a distance across the fields, might be mistaken for a real village. Close to, the signs of suburbia cannot be ignored, although Wennington church—locked, alas—is a typical village church of the riverside country, near enough to the water to justify bringing in stone by barge for its sturdy western tower.

The Thames is still well away to the south. If you want a close view, you may get down to the river at Purfleet, but the industrial traffic is so great that this cannot be recommended. Some of the buildings, old like the gunpowder magazine or new factories, would be worth seeing if one had but the time and the freedom of movement. I like best in Purfleet the splendidly fictional derivation of its name. Queen Elizabeth watched the little ships sailing down river to tackle the Invincible Armada and exclaimed: 'Oh, my poor fleet!'

At Purfleet the Mardyke joins the Thames. This is a stream, too creek-like in its last miles of independence to be attractive, which flows out of the higher country to the north-east. One of the head-streams rises in the Laindon Hills, the other in wooded country beyond the New Southend Road. Should you be tempted that way, you would find a uniquely decorated church at Great Warley, with an interior given over unreservedly to the Art Nouveau fashion of the Edwardians. But I should be reluctant to take the responsibility of sending you so far out of your way.

Our course is by way of Aveley, which may be reached by continuing through Purfleet to a road junction almost under the shadow of the Tunnel Approach Road, and then straight across to the Southend Road and again across this. The view here is punctuated with the chimneys of the cement works, an exciting skyline visually, although the grandeur of this industrial architecture would not reconcile me, if I lived this way, to the rain of cement dust which covers everything with a grey-white film. Coming up to Aveley village, we cross the Mardyke and then have a brief taste of the country. To the right Aveley Hall stands well beside the church, and elms stride across a ploughed field to make a characteristic Essex scene.

As usual Aveley church has the hall for partner. The hall was outshone in Tudor times by a great mansion to the north of the village. This was Belhus (or Bellhouse), rebuilt on an old site some time before 1526 by John Barrett. His family had been here for a century and more already, and Belhus remained with the Barretts—later the Barrett-Lennards—until after the First World War. The Tudor house was brought into fashion from time to time by additions and re-shapings, including a phase of Strawberry Hill Gothic, until it became a fascinatingly eccentric hotchpotch. By the beginning of the Second World War it was in poor shape and the military completed its dilapidation. Afterwards the house was demolished. Housing estates encroach on either side of the park and the new Aveley By-pass cuts across its lower edge, but the County Council have preserved part of what is left as an open space. 'Capability' Brown had been responsible for laying out the park under the patronage of Lord Dacre, not the happiest of partnerships for the noble Lord had been driven to fury by Brown's casual approach to the job which was extended over eight years. Of his work sadly little remains, but the woods to the north of the landscaped park are still lovely.

Some Barrett-Lennard monuments are to be seen in Aveley church. The old village is so shabby, and the new so brash, that hopes of a good church are not high, but this is in fact a remarkably interesting building. The nave is Norman, of a singularly gaunt kind but impressive. The font is of this date too; it has not worn too well and the decorative arcading is now indistinct. Perhaps the best of the fittings is the handsome Jacobean pulpit with its sounding-board, a perfect stage for the eloquence of a Donne or an Andrewes—but what standard of preacher came this way?

The country around Aveley, when it has not gone under houses, is largely taken for quarrying and gravel working, but little pockets of genuine rural Essex survive miraculously. In one of these there is a farm—Bretts—which is linked by tradition with the de Bret who was one of the murderers of Thomas Becket, but proof is lacking.

At Aveley we are in the Urban District of Thurrock, which is largely rural and which lacks the unifying characteristics which would make it a district. It includes the industrial tangle down by the river at West Thurrock—where the mediaeval parish church has been cut off from the community it serves by railway and factories, and the crowded housing estates of Grays, as well as genuine villages like Orsett and Bulphan. I intend, not altogether reluctantly, to lay aside my brief for a while and to stay inland from the river, believing that, for every visitor to Essex whose heart leaps up at the sight of a towering block of flats or a belching chimney, a dozen will prefer elm trees against the sky or a mellowed brick mansion in the contrived landscape of its setting.

Let us go north out of Aveley, then, on the Upminster road, a country lane still with woodlands left over from the Belhus estate. The first lane right will bring us to North Ockendon, but we will turn south again before this to enter the new housing area on the northern fringe of South Ockendon. The village has been filled in, at least on one side of the main road, but by a happy chance, or by vigorous protective action, the old village heart of South Ockendon still beats, albeit fitfully. A little square beside the road has on one side an exceedingly attractive inn, the Royal Oak, long and low with a gable at either end, carrying its three centuries with an air. Side on to this is the church, the first of six which we shall see in Essex with round towers. These towers, which are confined almost exclusively to this eastern eighth of the country, have aroused a good deal of speculation. They all appear in stoneless parts of England, and flint certainly lends itself to this form of construction. It has been said that the round towers were defensive in origin, and this was true of most early towers built in districts subject to disorder or raid. This, however, does not altogether explain that some at least of the round towers were afterthoughts. The tower at South Ockendon may be of this kind, for it is appreciably later than the late Norman nave to which it is joined; it might of course have replaced an earlier tower of a similar kind. It is a spectacular example of the use of flint, the split blue surface glossy and apparently indestructible. The battlements are finished in brick and were added later. The best of the church is its south doorway, a rich example of late Norman work enriched with conventional ornament.

The illusion of rural Essex, which is convincing enough if we stand with our backs to the main road, might be maintained longer by a walk through the gate beside the Royal Oak, along the drive of South Ockendon Hall and then by fieldpath to Bulphan. This would be worth doing if only for the sheer incongruity of this charming scenery in the middle of an urban district. The hall is a Victorian rebuilding, but it occupies part of a typical moated site of a kind with which we shall become very familiar.

A diversion on this scale and on foot will take time, and we ought perhaps to press southwards through the new development of South

Ockendon, noticing, just before we cross the Mardyke, the dignified façade of Ford Place among trees on the left. Then comes the village street of Stifford, with its ancient church (locked) and some good houses. Just past the best of these we resist the pull of the main road going down towards Grays and turn left—in effect we keep straight on, but along a minor road—through a curious mixture of urban and rural. On the left the country is unspoilt for miles. On the right —but let us not dwell on it! Further along not even the huge bulk of a new hospital can disguise the fact that Orsett maintains, in the face of considerable pressures, its essential village character.

The first evidence of this is a glorious mansion: Orsett House, standing back on the left among trees, a singularly covetable building in brick with a sober and flawless front belonging to the middle of the eighteenth century. This is a minor house. The hall is further east, in a large and beautiful park, and cannot easily be seen from the road. Between the two is the village, entered past a little green on which stand the pound and the lock-up as evidence that even in so delectable a place animals and humans might still go astray. Here you might turn north to see some undistinguished earthworks which tradition claims to be the foundations of Bishop Bonner's Palace. Orsett belonged to the Bishops of London from the Conquest to the reign of Elizabeth, when the queen acquired it from Bonner, that dedicated burner of heretics, when the wheel had turned and he was himself in disgrace and peril.

It is better in Orsett to remember lesser and nicer men than Bonner. There is Sir John Hatt, Lord of the Manor during the Commonwealth, who lies not too comfortably on his elbow in the north chapel of the parish church. He has his tomb to speak for him:

> *Free'd from the worlds disturbances I keepe*
> *His sacred bones, who does within mee sleepe*
> *His soule the heavens, his name the world containes*
> *For charity a prince, a judge for braines*
> *His body resst within my silent wombe*
> *Till death shall dy, and I shall be no Tombe*
> *Then his refined soule to's body must*
> *Returne, and live wn I am dead & duste*

I like too a memorial to a later owner of the Hall, Richard Baker who, dying in 1827, is commemorated by an allegorical illustration of the text: 'Thou shalt come to thy grave in a full age like as a shock of corn cometh in his season.' This sensitive sculpture is by Sir Richard Westmacott.

These memorials, and a great many others, are in a large church, entered through a Norman door, which illustrates the whole range of architecture and ornament from Norman times to the present day.

It is more sumptuous than most, but much of the more recent introductions, from the Italian wall panels to Sir Charles Nicholson's metalwork on the screen, is comely and harmonious. I like one reminder that history is a continuing process; knightly helms are a commonplace among trophies, but Orsett has a tin-hat from a more recent conflict, a trophy, unlike most ceremonial helmets, meant for use.

Beyond the church and its neighbouring cottages the road bends past an inn bearing the badge of the Whitmores, most recent owners of the hall, whose late representative, Sir Francis, did spectacular service in two World Wars. He won his DSO in a fantastic episode of the Battle of Arras. Then the road skirts the lovely grounds of Orsett Hall and crosses the main Brentwood road to continue towards Horndon-on-the-Hill.

Of the Essex Horndons this has the most distinctive character. This is partly a matter of position, for the 'Hill', though only just above the 100-foot contour, is appreciably hilly; the centre, moreover, where the lane from Orsett joins the main street at a narrow junction whose picturesqueness has somehow not yet been improved out of existence, is most attractive.

The main street is evidence of much greater importance in the past. The Bell Inn was not built on this scale for the sake of purely local trade, and beyond this is the market hall. Even the most tragic episode in Horndon's story is in a way a confirmation of the village's standing. A Horndon farmer, Thomas Higbed, was arrested on a charge of heresy in 1555, tried and condemned. Most of the judicial bonfires of Mary's wretched reign were lit in towns, but Higbed was sent home to suffer in his own parish, behind—it is said—the Bell. An admirable local church-history quotes the martyr's final address to his judges: '. . . do what ye will you will do no more than God will permit you to do and with what measure you measure to us, look for the same at God's Hands.'

There were several manors in Horndon, of which the most considerable was Arden (or Ardern), a half-mile east of the village. This
was the home of the Shaa family, two of whom became Mayors of
London. They were involved in the wool trade on which local and
national prosperity was based in the fifteenth century.

The church stands back from the Orsett road, with a lime avenue
to the door. It is highly picturesque. The style is largely Early
English of the early thirteenth century, less common in Essex than
in some other southern counties. There is a severity about the nave
arcades and the deep-cut clerestory windows which is pleasing after
a surfeit of extravagant later Gothic work. The complicated wooden
framework inside the nave which supports the weight of the belfry
is a fascinating exercise in primitive engineering. It is a later addition
to the church and quite independent of the original structure. This
is the first example we have so far met of one of the characteristic
architectural features of Essex churches, and one of the best.

The immediate neighbourhood of Horndon-on-the-Hill is pleasing.
Just to the north, between the village and Malgraves where Thomas
Higbed's persecutor, Sir John Tyrell, lived, the views to the west are
quite unspoilt. Seen in winter, when the anatomy of the trees can
best be enjoyed, the landscape has an unemphatic beauty which is
deeply satisfying.

Our immediate course however is south. We reach the Southend
Road on the outskirts of Stanford-le-Hope. The name is so delightful
that the reality, an ancient village submerged under modern houses,
is a sad blow. The growth is quite recent. Joseph Conrad, who came
here in 1897, living first in a 'damned jerry-built rabbit hutch' of a
villa, moved later to a remote Tudor farmhouse, Ivy Walls, and here
finished *The Nigger of the Narcissus* and worked on *The Rescue*.
By the time Stanford broke its banks and spilt over into the fields,
Conrad had long been dead and his house demolished.

I am not going through Stanford-le-Hope just yet, however, because a lane goes right just beyond the Southend Road and I must
go to Mucking. This is largely on account of the name, which seems
to suggest all that Essex means to those who have never been there.
Beyond the village lie Mucking Marshes and Mucking Flats, with a
promise of wide acres of mud and muck. We must in fact accept the
indisputable fact that Mucking is no more mucky than Messing,
further north in the county, is messy. It was the settlement of Saxons

tracing their line back to a savage old pirate named Mucca. Muck-ing, although it has not yet been 'developed', has lost the mystery and end-of-the-worldness which Donald Maxwell captured so success-fully in the drawings he did during the Twenties. It is still an end-of-the-road village. A lane crosses the railway and comes to an end at a typical Essex pair of neighbours, hall and church. The church looks not much older than its Victorian tower, but it has one memorable feature. From the capital of a pillar in the nave looks a face entwined in stiff thirteenth-century carved leaves. A spray of these emerges from his mouth. Here, unashamedly on view in this holy place, is a pagan Green Man, linking the ceremonies of the church with his rites of an older religion.

Mucking is essentially a riverside settlement. A stream near the church quickly joins a Thames creek among inaccessible flats. The road goes past Linford and then right through the great factory complex of Bata's at East Tilbury. Factories have a visual place in the scene, and here the setting is right and the buildings suitably confid-ent and dominant. The road comes to the old village of East Tilbury and peters out at the river. For the first time we have a close view of the Thames, a mile wide and backed by the low hills of Kent. The road is closed by a granite blockhouse, Coalhouse Fort. This was originally one of Henry VIII's coastal fortresses put up during the invasion scare of 1539. This was reinforced during the Napoleonic Wars, and rebuilt in the present form following a report on coastal defence in 1860. The engineer for the work was Charles George Gordon, enjoying a brief quiet interlude in his stormy life.

This was a late stage in the story of East Tilbury. It began some time in the first century when a settlement was established at a crossing of the river. The foundations of a group of huts used to be visible on the foreshore. This place could be the 'Tilaburg' on the banks of the Thames where St Cedd, the missionary of Essex, built a church in 653. It used to be the custom to point to an old coffin slab in East Tilbury church as his, but he went north when the conver-sion of the East Saxons had been safely accomplished and died in Yorkshire.

The little church, which is almost on the shore, looks extremely odd. This is because the Dutch destroyed the tower when they raided up the Thames in 1667 to the discomfiture of the English Navy, and attempts to rebuild it—started, it is said, by bored soldiers from the garrison of Coalhouse Fort during the First World War—were not pursued as far as roof height. It is an attractive little building inside, mostly of the late twelfth and thirteenth centuries. A large Georgian tomb, of unusual shape for this date, has low-relief baroque carving on its sides, displaying among other things a flight of thoughtful, not to say disconsolate cherubs. There is one pleasing new feature. In the floor of the chancel a mosaic forms that primitive symbol of Christianity, the fish.

West Tilbury is on higher ground and its church tower is a landmark. There is quite an appreciable escarpment here, not a hundred feet high, but steep by comparison with the dead flat of the marshes. At Gun Hill there is a fine view, not less impressive for the towers and pinnacles of Tilbury Power Station which give a needed touch of drama to the scene. Here, unlike West Thurrock, the industrial buildings have elbow-room; they rise out of undeveloped marsh and enjoy a setting in scale with their bulk. To the right there is the large area of Tilbury Docks. Our road goes in that direction, but stops short of the former car-ferry to Gravesend. An embankment, vaguely reminiscent of the riverside at the Tower of London, runs along the face of Tilbury Fort.

The Thames narrows here, and this must always have been a place of at least potential strategic value. In the crisis year of 1539 a strongpoint was built here, as at Coalhouse Point, as part of a complex system of coastal defences. The threatened invasion came to nothing at that time, but in 1588 Tilbury became the base camp for the land forces mustered against the Armada. Elizabeth came down river on the 8th August, to review the troops marshalled by her old favourite Leicester. All through her reign she had lived in danger of assassination, but she went among the host without a bodyguard, saying 'Let tyrants fear'. Her devious nature, and the pathological dislike of decision which experience had produced in her, made her a mistress not easy to serve, but here for once she matched the occasion with fitting action and word. The Elizabethans loved a grand gesture and she gave it to them magnificently:

'I am come amongst you, as you see, at this time, not for my recreation and disport, but being resolved, in the midst and heat of the battle, to live and die amongst you all; to lay down for God, for my kingdom, and for my people, my honour and my blood,

even in the dust. I know I have but the body of a weak and feeble woman; but I have the heart and stomach of a King, and of a King of England too, and think it foul scorn that Parma or Spain or any Prince of Europe, should dare to invade the borders of my realm; to which, rather than any dishonour should grow by me, I myself will take up arms, I myself will be General, Judge, and Rewarder of every one of your virtues in the field.'

Of the Tudor coastal fortress nothing can now be seen. It was transformed in the reign of Charles II after the Dutch fleet had demonstrated the inadequacy of English defences in the Thames. The new work was in the hands of the king's Chief Engineer, a man of genius, Sir Bernard de Gomme. Sir Bernard was a Dutchman who had been on the Continent with Charles during the Commonwealth and who had studied in the same school as Louis XIV's Vauban. He favoured the geometrical fortifications which gave a garrison formidable advantages in defence and attack. The work was long and costly, and could hardly be said to have been justified in use, for the fort was never tested in action. Its chief interest is that, despite a great deal of addition and repair work spread over the succeeding centuries, including the present, this is a largely unaltered example of seventeenth-century military architecture, and certainly the finest in this country.

For visitors the principal eye-catcher is the Water Gate, now the main entrance. This is a dignified piece of ceremonial architecture in the pseudo-classical manner. Charles II's arms are displayed in stone, with a niche below obviously lacking the figure of the gay and resourceful monarch himself. On either side are splendid trophies of arms. All this pomp makes an impression, but this is the only extravagance in a grimly utilitarian building. Inside there are some visually attractive things, the chapel block and still more the Georgian officers' barracks, but everything is very much for use. Amateur tacticians will enjoy a walk around the ramparts to study the complicated line of fire of the batteries and the skilful use of water and earthworks in the defensive system. But romantics will find here nothing to evoke pictures of an heroic past.

Our way back to the Southend Road is through Chadwell, a place of small attractions. The name, seemingly derived from a warm (*chaud*) spring hereabouts, has become confused with Cedd's saintly

13 Cottages on the shore, Leigh-on-Sea

brother Chad, the missionary to the Mercians. There seems no reason to suppose that Chad came this way, although Cedd almost certainly did, but his name is established here once and for all.

A turn left will bring us to the main road on a corner called Dane-holes. Beside the road, surrounded by new houses, a little piece of woodland has been preserved, making a welcome oasis. If you walk here you will find that fences have been placed around several holes in the ground. An underground plan of the area would disclose a whole network of pits and passages. These are the mysterious dene holes, the most accessible examples of a phenomenon which recurs in the chalk on both sides of the Thames. No problem has produced more conflicting theories among antiquarians. The holes are around 80 feet deep. They are obviously artificial and ancient, although guesses at their age vary widely. As to their purpose, guesses are permissible where authorities disagree. It seems rather more probable that they were chalk-mines than grain-stores, refuges from Danish pirates, oubliettes or subterranean shrines.

So much of Thurrock is unlovely that one should note here, with pleasure, how much trouble is taken to turn roadside verges and islands into gardens. In this respect at least the Urban District earns full marks.

There is at this point no escape from a spell on the main road, a dismal experience relieved only by a glimpse of a Georgian farm-house near Orsett—Whitecrofts—and a little beyond this a characteristic South Essex scene, composed of elms, ploughed fields, tower blocks of flats, and pylons. Curiously the effect is more pleasing than anything else.

At Stanford-le-Hope we go straight ahead through the village, past a church whose mediaeval work scarcely shows through the coating provided in a more than usually ruthless Victorian restoration. Instead of going immediately left into Corringham we should continue towards Coryton to see a most astonishing transformation of the Essex marshes. An area perhaps four miles long by one-and-a-half deep is covered with the oil refineries of Thames Haven. This may not sound attractive. The architecture of oil, like that of the wind-mill, is based on entirely practical considerations, but I find the refineries, like the mills, quite extraordinarily beautiful. In sunlight these domes and pinnacles sparkle and glow; they lurk in a winter fog with more than a touch of mystery; evening light turns them to fantasy. I can well understand that the technician sees in these buildings the perfection of pure mathematics. The layman, seeing them without understanding, can still enjoy a rare aesthetic experience.

There is an experience of a different kind at Corringham. The new housing estates that have grown up recently, largely to serve the workers in the oil industry, stop just short of the old village which was built on a low but steep hill above the marshes. So at Corringham there is the strange juxtaposition of new and old, each keeping to its own territory. The village consists of church, hall, inn and a handful of cottages grouped around a green, a singularly perfect unit. It is dominated by the church tower. In this county we shall find many Norman towers, plain, massive, even bald. Corringham church is of this kind and one of the earliest. Its distinctive feature is a blind arcade around the top of the tower, too simple to be called ornament, but just providing the relief which the eye needs.

Height is relative. Fobbing church stands just within the 50-foot contour. It seems to stand on a great height with Essex, Thames and Kent laid out below it. So dramatic a position would commend itself to primitive people, and it would not be surprising to discover that this has been a sacred site from the earliest times. The present building is largely of the fifteenth century. The design belongs to Kent rather than Essex; the tower with its corner turret has a multitude of relatives across the water.

Fobbing has a place in history. In 1381, when the grievances of the English villeins were building up to an intolerable pitch, an arrogant steward named Thomas Bampton came into Essex to supervise the levy of the new Poll Tax. The people of Fobbing told him roundly that they had already paid the tax and would pay no more. They rallied their neighbours in Corringham and Stanford-le-Hope, and chased Thomas back to London. Out of this minor incident grew the insurrection of the commons of Essex. The fire spread into East Anglia while a similar rebellion was on the boil in Kent. The men of Essex were to suffer for their part in the Peasants' Revolt—a misleading name for the rebels included many of a higher rank than villein—but their action has disclosed the cracks in the rickety structure of feudalism. It would be no bad thing to have a memorial to the commons of Fobbing on this high point.

The little square beside the church has some style, and there are a few good houses further up the village, including some examples of thatching. The road climbs steadily for a mile and then drops gently to the main road at Vange roundabout.

Straight ahead is Basildon New Town. We shall be visiting Harlow later, and one New Town is enough for any county, so we shall not look at this mixture of imaginative design and commonplace. Without going to the town centre, however, we might pay a brief visit to the Laindon Hills, on the lower slopes of which much of the town has been built. The hills are the highest in South Essex, although they provide less expansive views than one might expect because much of the upper slopes are wooded. Most happily several tracts of these upland woods have been preserved for public enjoyment, and they are the more precious because of the densely populated areas immediately to the north. A number of delightful short walks may be had, especially pleasing from late autumn to spring when it is possible to look out from the woodlands to the undulating country to the west and to the Essex plain below.

At the roadside and backing on to the woods is a large church, an effective neo-Gothic building from the eighteen-seventies. This has, regrettably, replaced the old church of Laindon Hills which is just down a lane to the west. It is well worth this short journey to see this charming and typical Essex building in its pretty setting. It is very quiet here after the main road and you will probably have a robin for company on a sunny day. The church is early Tudor with some fittings of the Stuart period and the Royal Arms of Charles II painted over the chancel arch. This exceptionally attractive building is in a sad state. It seems doomed to become quite ruinous unless drastic remedial action is taken. But who will take it? The spectre of redundancy haunts this church, a historic monument and a work of art but with its employment gone.

While we are in this melancholy mood we may as well endure the grim miles of the Southend Road. There are houses on both sides of the road for most of the way and the traffic is heavy during all the hours of the day, and there will be little opportunity, even if there is an inclination, for lingering. We pass two mediaeval churches on the right, at Vange and Pitsea, each on its distinctive knoll overlooking the marshes. A third, at Bowers Gifford, lies well off the road, and a visit may offer brief respite from the clamour of traffic. There is a break in the continuous urban development here, and the

hurch stands alone beside the railway with marshes and creeks be-
ond. A little further on a road right goes through South Benfleet,
eavily built-up and with a handsome church in a key position
bove the river, to that remarkable phenomenon, Canvey Island.

I hesitate to take you this way, for not even its most devoted
dmirer would say that Canvey is rich in architecture or natural
eauty. This, however, is so fascinating an example of man's tri-
mph over nature that it should not be missed. There is not much on
anvey which is more than ten feet above sea level, and much of the
sland is below the level of high tide. Through the centuries it has
uffered at best from intermittent flooding and on occasion there
ave been major disasters. So urgent has been the demand for land,
owever, and so persistent man's refusal to accept the inevitable that
uring most of the centuries of history Canvey has remained in-
abited. The islanders have made a bleak living out of salt-panning
—producing the characteristic Red Hills along the shore where they
umped the debris of their industry—sheep grazing and arable
arming. The last occupation became practicable early in the seven-
eenth century, when Dutch businessmen and engineers contracted
o build effective defences against the sea, in return for which they
ained possession of one-third of the island. The newly recovered land
vas let to Dutch immigrant farmers who during the next century
naintained a separate community and culture on their part of the
sland. The whole of this extraordinary story is told by Basil E.
racknell in his *Canvey Island: the History of a Marshland
Community* (1959).

One phase of Canvey history came to an end with the economic
ollapse of Essex farming in the 1880s, and the land was bought
heaply by a man with plans to turn it into a major holiday island.
The plan failed, but farming was finished and Canvey became an
sland of holiday huts and bungalows. Out of this grew the present
argely residential town. The people of Canvey may have forgotten
heir ancient history, but they were reminded of it abruptly on 31st
anuary, 1953, when a combination of gales and spring-tides brought
he sea spilling through breaches in the sea-wall. Fifty-eight people
ied on Canvey in that night, and by morning most of the houses
vere uninhabitable.

The scars of this recent disaster have vanished now, and the visitor
vill see only the commonplaces of a modern seaside community,

half resident, half holiday, with nothing exceptional or even particularly pleasing in its buildings or their setting. The best of the island to the eye is the shoreward side by the bridge from the mainland, which has an authentic marshland character. Two cottages alone survive from the century of the Dutch occupation. They are charming little buildings, round—more correctly octagonal—and with thatched roofs. One is now a museum of island antiquities. At Hole Haven, in an area now given up largely to oil, there is an inn which may perhaps be older than these, dating from Elizabethan times. This inn, the Lobster Smack, comes into the closing stages of *Great Expectations*, when Pip makes his bid to smuggle the doomed convict out of the country. The action may, to sophisticated tastes, seem melodramatic, but the landscape painting is superb, conjuring up the essence of these muddy flats.

Returning to the mainland and turning right in South Benfleet village we have a stiff climb up to Round Hill where a water-tower disguising its function as such buildings tend to do, sits dramatically at the highest point. Here is the wide view which we have so far lacked on this journey, looking across the tumbled hills to Thames mouth. There is still some green country here, but bricks take over very soon. Beyond the Southend Road is Thundersley, which has no attractions apart from the name. This is one of the rare village names which recall pagan England when the Saxon settlers still worshipped the savage gods of their homeland. Thunor among them, in a sacred grove on this ridge.

A mile from the Thundersley cross-road the Southend Road comes to Hadleigh. The one-time village exists uncomfortably among new buildings of a rather shrill kind. Right in the middle stands a small but singularly perfect Norman church, complete with apse. It looks, if one can ignore the surroundings, quite charming. Alas, the Church authorities have lost the battle against vandalism and the building remains locked between services. Pilgrims are thereby prevented from seeing its treasures, which include a wall-painting of Thomas of Canterbury, possibly the earliest representation of England's most popular mediaeval saint to escape the campaign of destruction which accompanied the Reformation.

A road past the east end of the church goes south for the best part of a mile and then comes to an end at a gate leading to the ruins of Hadleigh Castle. Essex, which has the largest Norman keep in the world and also the finest surviving keep in England, is otherwise poorly off for castles. Mostly they were ransacked for their building materials—particularly valuable in this stoneless county—and only the earthworks remain. Such ruins as survive at Hadleigh, which might be despised on the Welsh Marches or the Border, are correspondingly precious here. The site has natural advantages. A spur of the hills above the Thames thrusts out to form almost a peninsula in the marshes. Here Hubert de Burgh, Earl of Kent, built a strongpoint in 1231, in the last days of his power. Hubert de Burgh was a remarkable man. In an age of ruthless power-politics his actions were dictated consistently by loyalty. He supported King John against the barons, and acted as Judiciary and, in effect, regent during the minority of Henry III. The barons hated him as much for his integrity as his low birth, and within a year of the building of his castle they at last succeeded in causing his downfall. But Hubert was as admirable in disgrace as in power. His castle passed to the Crown and was developed in the Edwardian age; most of the buildings still remaining belong to Edward III's reign. What we see are the battered remains of a curtain wall, following the contours of the land on three sides but tumbled on the south where the land has slipped. The most exciting buildings are two angle towers on the east, the southern one standing still three storeys high. It is built right on the edge of the escarpment, with the marshes and river gleaming below. It was this aspect that captured Constable's imagination during a visit in 1814, maturing in his mind and emerging in one of his most miraculous paintings 15 years later.

The castle is in the care of the Ministry of Public Buildings and Works and is very well kept, with less than usual of this department's clinical tidiness.

After Hadleigh there is no escape from Southend. This must sound ungracious, because the County Borough has taken in a number of ancient parishes and many of their treasures remain intact. There are moreover a number of modern buildings of character, notably churches belonging to the Gothic Revival and after. The long seafront from the Crow Stone to Thorpe Bay is unique in Essex. All these things are good, but my heart sinks at the thought of all those streets and all those people, including holiday-makers ruthlessly seeking fun.

However, Southend is in its way as much a part of the essential

Essex as Greensted and Thaxted, and we must not flinch from it

Southend itself is modern, the south end of the ancient parish of Prittlewell. There was little here before the latter part of the eighteenth century, for fishing, the native industry apart from oyster breeding, was concentrated in the more sheltered harbourage of Leigh. Its tentative progress as a watering-place was accelerated after a visit by Queen Caroline in 1804. A pier was built in 1830 for the use of packets and pleasure-craft. The town grew rapidly after the arrival of the railway in 1856. By the end of the nineteenth century the famous iron pier stretched more than a mile and a half out to sea. Originally Southend had been a place of fashion, but in time nearness to London and quick communication made it essentially the objective of a day trip. It still has this function today although it is also a residential town with a population of nearly 166,000.

There is a convincing picture of the town in its early days in a remarkable novel—ostensibly for children but of much wider appeal —*The Maplin Bird* by K. M. Peyton (1964).

It is not easy to suggest an itinerary in Southend because in the matter of holiday resorts tastes vary sharply. Some may wish to seek out the relics of the Victorian and even the Georgian town where these have escaped the developer. Others may be fanciers of such diverse expressions of the holiday spirit as hotels, bandstand and pleasure-garden ironwork, or entertainment arcades. Some may even come for the sea, or for that strange manifestation of Pop Art, the 'Lights'.

One way of seeing a little of all these things would be to turn right outside Hadleigh, dropping down towards the front, but kept from it by the railway, at Leigh. There is little to be seen of the one-time fishing village. In the main street, a flight of steps leads to the old parish church, magnificently placed and still, in its much restored state, splendid. After this comes Westcliff, at one time the favoured residential part of Southend—and it may well be so still— which has no obvious charms for the casual visitor. Southend proper comes next, with some buildings around the pier which might repay examination. Certainly everyone should go to the end of the pier, by tramway or—preferably—walking. Out of the season and on a foggy day this can be an eerie experience, for the walker seems to be in a world apart, not quite of the sea, but by no means of land.

14   *Hawkwell Church*

Beyond the pier is Southchurch, with the Kursaal as a choice example of the Edwardian architecture of pleasure. Inland from this the late mediaeval hall has survived and may be visited. Next comes Thorpe Bay with its beach huts, and then the road is deflected inland by War Department land on the promontory of Shoebury Ness. Here, it is said—but the Army is in possession and they cannot be seen—are the remains of a fortress built by the Danes in 894 when Hasten was ravaging the outposts of King Alfred's Wessex. The town of Shoeburyness is depressing beyond words, and beyond lie the forbidden wastes of Foulness which have long been closed to civilians and now await fateful decisions.

There is some danger of despair in this sad, disheartened country at the end of Essex. We might gain heart a little by going inland and west again to end the journey in some style in the parent village of Southend, Prittlewell. This is trapped in the town now, but the church is the splendid building of a prosperous village, exuberant in its gleaming ragstone and chequered battlements. A little north of this is the source of Prittlewell's ancient fame, the Priory. This was a Cluniac house, subject to Lewes, founded in or about 1110 and enlarged in two stages, once in Henry II's reign and again a century later. By the end of the middle ages the priory was in decline and it was suppressed with the minor houses in 1536. The church was demolished and the monks' quarters turned into a house. Parts of this have been preserved and now belong to Southend Corporation as a home for an excellent local museum. In the pleasant gardens the outline of the priory church has been set out in concrete in the grass. The finest surviving feature is the door from the cloister into the refectory, which is excellent Transitional Norman work, enriched with zigzag ornament. The refectory itself has been greatly restored, but is nevertheless a finely proportioned hall. The other original work is in the Prior's Room, at first floor level, which has a very fine kingpost roof.

Although Prittlewell Priory is surrounded by the noise and clutter of a large town which grew too quickly for good planning, it stands apart in its little park, insulated from the modern age which, here at least, does not put its best face foremost. The Thames, which we have followed none too diligently, is out of sight, but in the priory garden we shall find one reminder of it, the old Crow Stone which once stood beside the shore at Chalkwell, between Leigh and

CHAPTER THREE

Crouch

Ingrave—the Bursteads—Billericay—Stock—the
Hanningfields—Battlesbridge—Canewdon—
Fambridge—Dengie Hundred—Burnham

The Crouch illustrates in an extreme form one of the curiosities of the tidal rivers of Essex. The estuary is the finest, in terms of navigable depth; the river above the tidal waters is the most inconspicuous. Of its kind there is no finer sight than the river at Burnham or Fambridge, the water alive with sailing craft of every class. Above Battlesbridge it calls for alertness and a sharp eye to notice the Crouch at all, and only the most tolerant of critics would call it picturesque. Nevertheless there is much that is interesting in its little valley and considerable charm in those parts of the landscape through which it flows which have so far escaped development; while the landscape of the tidal river is often most distinctively beautiful. Between Battlesbridge and Burnham the land undulates, rising at its highest to around 170 feet on the northern side. The altitude would make a cragsman or even a downsman smile, but in the estuary these are appreciable hills, giving a clearly defined quality to the landscape. Beyond Burnham are the marshes, rarely rising above ten feet and, in the right season and weather, quite uncannily beautiful. Once desolate, they are now drained by a spiders-web of channels and the land makes fine pasture. Green fields, dead flat to the horizon, are patterned with the black and white of Friesians in numbers beyond easy counting. Other fields are heavy with wheat.

I must add that mine is a landsman's Crouch. To the yachtsman this is a confession of inadequacy, for this strange country is half water and that half the more important. While readily granting the superiority of sail over any form of land transport, I hope that my landbound view, lit by sincere affection for the valley in all its moods, will have some validity for others who perforce travel by road.

It is indeed rather difficult to get this journey started at all. The source of the Crouch is beyond the long low ridge which travellers on the New Southend Road, if they can take their eyes off the traffic, see running to the north of the road and roughly parallel with it. The actual source may be in a pond behind Stockwell Hall at Little Burstead. Another of the head-streams begins close to the pretty by-road from Herongate to Burstead, and yet another rises close by the cloverleaf junction on the Southend Road at Dunton. None of these has quite the style to make a proper jumping-off place for a memorable journey. Perhaps we might begin right on the watershed which at Ingrave attains a height of 283 feet.

Two distinguished architectural critics, separated by nearly a half-century, illustrate the change in attitude towards the achievements of Georgian England. Dr Charles Cox, in 1909, says of Ingrave: 'an unsightly church.' Dr Nikolaus Pevsner's view, in 1954, is: 'The most remarkable C18 church in the country.' Travellers may take their choice between these extremes. It is not a church to overlook, although many of those who come up from Tilbury to Brentwood mistake it for the waterworks. One distinction of this tall brick tower is that it makes uncompromising use of its material. In other places brick is employed, most ingeniously, as if it were stone. The anonymous architect at Ingrave makes no such pretence. For the rest, the church is very plain with none of the ornamental bravura of, for example, later Georgian work at Wanstead.

The church was built in 1735 under the patronage of Lord Petre whose principal residence was at Thorndon Hall. The Petres, as we shall see later, had settled at Ingatestone in Henry VIII's reign. John Petre, the son of the founder of the family's greatness, had acquired an old house at West Horndon in 1575 and had rebuilt this on a very lavish scale over the next 20 years. The eighth Lord Petre who re-built the church had plans for remodelling the house early in the eighteenth century and he had employed the celebrated Palladian architect, Leoni, to carry them out. His early death put a stop to the work, and by the time his son, the ninth Baron, was old enough to take over, fashions had changed. He therefore commissioned James Paine to build an entirely new mansion on a site a mile away. Paine also favoured the Palladian style, but used it with less discipline than Leoni. The old house was gutted to provide materials, and a huge mansion arose beyond the Brentwood road and within sight of Ingrave tower. It consisted of a massive central block linked with two slighter wings. 'Capability' Brown made a noble landscape design to frame the house. The setting has lasted longer than the hall which suffered a disastrous fire in 1878 and can still be seen as a gaunt shell from the road.

The hall and park are private, but a footpath crosses the park and the neighbouring woodlands on its way to Childerditch. This, you may remember, was to be part of Edward Thomas's poetic legacy to his elder daughter—but Thomas died in the mud of Flanders before he could ever grow rich.

A mile south of Ingrave church, the main road passes the hamlet of Herongate, where the tide of suburbia is held at bay by a pretty little green backed by attractive houses and an inn with a good sign. The village sign is even more delightful. The hamlet grew up at the gate of Heron Hall, the home of a distinguished family, the Tyrells. They were connections of the Petres. William Petre had married a Tyrell of a cadet branch and on her death had married the widow of John Tyrell of Heron Hall. The house, which was rebuilt at the end of the eighteenth century, occupies an ancient moated site just over the watershed towards Brentwood and can be taken in as part of a circular footpath walk from Ingrave.

From Herongate a lane with more up and down than is customary in central Essex leads most pleasantly to Little Burstead. This is now part of the Urban District of Basildon, but at present it retains its village character intact. There are several fine houses grouped around the main road-junction, but the best, Stockwell Hall, is a little to the north. Its clock tower, which gives the house its local name of Clock House, is conspicuous. The Georgian façade hides an earlier, probably late Tudor or Jacobean, building. The church is all alone, half a mile to the south and right on the edge of a ridge with wide views to the Laindon Hills and beyond into Kent. It is a pretty little building of a typically Essex kind, with nave, chancel with a lower roof, and the wooden bell turret with broach spire. It looks particularly well from the floor of the valley below. The interior is pleasantly plain. The nave roof is supported on crudely carved corbels; there are a few monuments, notably of the Walton family—the most famous was Admiral Walton who smashed the Spanish fleet up off Cape Passaro in 1718—and some nice Flemish glass.

Anyone with a taste for contrasts might try a little walk here, starting by a path immediately opposite the approach to the church, where the road makes an uncomfortable double bend. The track goes across fields and crosses the infant Crouch in a wooded valley, coming out beside the road up to Great Burstead. The scene changes in a moment from rural to suburban.

The tide of houses, held in check by some Canute of the Planning Department at Little Burstead, has flooded into Great Burstead. In the immediate neighbourhood of the church alone has the village survived in a precarious fashion. This was the original parish out of which the town of Billericay grew. A slim spire rises through fine trees quite dramatically. This is indeed an impressive church, having, it would seem, some standing in the late fourteenth or early fifteenth century when ragstone was imported at considerable cost for the western tower. The church was Norman, but most traces of the original work have vanished in successive improvements. The main entrance is on the north, through a doorway with square head and flying angels filling the spandrels. The label stops have crowned heads, and there is a fairly well-preserved stoup. Altogether an impressive composition, executed when the tower was being built. The fittings are an interesting mixture, with Georgian sanctuary rails and carved mediaeval benches. Collectors of church chests will find a massive example dug out and bound with iron.

Just beyond the church the new housing estates take over and it is houses, houses all the way to Billericay. A decision about routes must be taken here. The Crouch flows south of Great Burstead, making its humble way through the Ramsden country to Wickford and so to the tidal waters at Battlesbridge. This is clearly the correct and the shortest way. It is also the dullest. Of the Ramsdens, Ramsden Cray has unexciting new developments along the main road, while the hall stands beside the river to the north. The church, mostly Victorian, has been abandoned. There is more to see at Ramsden Bellhouse, but not enough to call for a special journey. Here the church is another Victorian rebuilding, but the old wooden porch and belfry spire were retained. Wickford is now a largish town and dormitory area which resembles, to an uncanny degree, other towns of its kind. The best of this route is undoubtedly Runwell, on the northern outskirts of Wickford, where some good houses survive uncomfortably beside the busy road and the handsome and interesting church is set finely among trees. This is worth a pause, if the press of traffic will allow it.

On the whole, however, I would recommend that we give up this slavish tracing of the river and approach the estuary by a northern diversion. This journey will be much longer and, taking in as it does a part of the Brentwood-Southend road, not always attractive, but there is reward in the shape of one very attractive village and a good deal of quietly pleasing country.

The first objective is Billericay, a place of some importance from the earliest times and now largely a commuter town. It has some charm, although nothing which quite comes up to the individuality of its strange name. This seems so far to have defeated the place-name experts. Billericay has its moments of excitement at general elections, for it is usually the first result to be announced, and, traditionally, this result is taken to be prophetic of the electoral trend.

Such architectural interest as the town has is contained in High Street, with Chapel Street entering it behind the church. This was indeed a chapel until the formation of the parish in 1844. By that time the town was many times larger than the parent parish of Great Burstead. The church is a curious building reflecting this strange history. Flush with the High Street is a low brick tower, early Tudor, of unusual design; more of an elaborate tall porch than a tower. Much of the rest of the building is Georgian and later, and this gives the building its predominant character.

Hereabouts are most of the town's best houses, although some of them have suffered from the competing demands of the twentieth century. There is a charming building towards the southern end of the High Street, the Shambles, which has an exceptionally good wrought-iron sign. Mostly the frontages are Georgian plasterwork, but with a mixture of brick and half-timbering.

Of the last, the most spectacular example is the Chantry House, now a restaurant. This is part of a large town house of about the same date as the church tower just across the road. The Chantry has a small place in Anglo-American history. Christopher Martin, who worked with Cushman in making the final arrangements for the emigration of the Pilgrim Fathers and who was himself Governor of the Mayflower, was of Billericay, and a persistent tradition—if it is no more—says that the English contingent assembled here before embarking.

Minor roads go east out of Billericay through pleasant wooded country. Our way is north along the Chelmsford road, reaching in three miles one of the prettiest of Essex villages, Stock. If there is a blemish, it is a touch of self-consciousness. A notice as one comes in appeals: 'Keep Stock a tidy village', and, my goodness, it *is* tidy even to excess. The presiding genius, one feels, is Mrs Ogmore-Pritchard. But this is ungracious. So delightful a place has every need to keep itself so.

The village stands on rising ground and the road swings into the main street through wooded country. There is a wide green in front of the church, and across the road stands a pretty group of alms-houses, the foundation of a sturdy Essex man, Richard Twedye of Boreham, in Elizabeth's reign. In the church is his memorial brass, with a record of his exploits 'against the Engleshe foes'.

The church stands in an immaculate churchyard, chequered with flagstone paths which dare the weeds to grow along them. It has one of the familiar wooden belfry towers of Essex and one of the finest of the kind. Even the tracery of the tower windows is in wood. This superb work, equally commendable as craftsmanship and engineering, is supported on an elaborate web of massive timbers. It masks the old west-front with its fifteenth-century doorway. A timber porch on the south side was perhaps put up at the same time as the tower. In general the building had the architectural and antiquarian interest knocked out of it in a nineteenth-century restoration and rebuilding, but I must admit to a strong liking for the modern rood. It is clearly now a church in competent and appreciative hands.

Most of the village lies north of the church around a complex junction of roads. Here are a couple of inns and some old houses which deserve study. We take the right-hand road and go through an area of recent and inoffensive development to the east. On the edge of the village this way stands a fine tower windmill. It is masked to some extent by the houses around, but enough can be seen to show that this is among the best—perhaps the best—of tower mills in Essex, where those that survive are mostly post-mills, and in very good condition.

Roads to the east of Stock are affected to some extent by the flooding of thousands of acres to form Hanningfield Water, a new reservoir. Unlike the larger Abberton Reservoir near Colchester, this man-made lake cannot be well seen from the road, except where a lane from Stock to Wickford touches one arm of the lake, and access to the shore is by permit. Like Abberton, Hanningfield has proved an irresistible attraction to birds and has become, involuntarily, an important nature reserve. It is a pity that there are no convenient public viewing points.

There are three Hanningfield villages. East Hanningfield is away on the other side of the Southend road, a neat village with green, inn and modern church. The old church, gutted by fire and abandoned, lies in ruins near the hall. South Hanningfield is close to the reservoir. The Norman church stands back from the road beside its attendant hall. West Hanningfield is the least attractive village. There is much new housing, not all of it sightly, and the setting has been much impaired by the long high embankment containing the reservoir. This village has however one of the most interesting and evocative churches in this part of the county, and this certainly calls for a visit.

Remarkably in this semi-suburban country West Hanningfield retains the atmosphere of a village church of Georgian time. This is partly on account of the architecture, notably the debased Gothic tracery of the windows, and the fittings, but this cannot be the full explanation. The building seems to have got off lightly in the Victorian restoration. Some of the furnishings are good, fine Jacobean altar rails, a battered carved font, an enormous dug-out chest, and a benefactions' board carved in low relief with a representation of the Pelican in her Piety. This is eighteenth century, surely a late date to find so essentially mediaeval a symbol of Christ. The artist had never seen a pelican in the life! The principal interest of West Hanningfield church lies in the tower. Several of the timber belfry towers of Essex have a cruciform structure, masked by rectangular weatherboarding. This tower, however, is externally cruciform, an effect at once curious and impressive which is accentuated by a strange curved projection at the level of the bell-chamber, presumably some mediaeval experiment in acoustics.

I hope that this remarkable building alone will have justified our diversion. From here there is now no reasonable alternative to making a dash down the Southend road, pausing, if at all, at Rettenden church, almost isolated on the west side of the road for a glimpse of an extraordinary monument. A 30-foot pile of marble with figures and all the customary trimmings commemorates Edmund Humphreys, who died in 1727. What this baroque magnificence has to do with the faith which prompted the mediaeval builders of this church and kept it open through eight centuries is not clear.

We reach the Crouch at Battlesbridge, which is not quite as attractive as in the commercial heyday of the river, when the wharves were busy with traffic. Now the old tide-mills are dilapidated, picturesque still but sadly anachronistic. The name is commonly associated with the battle about which we shall hear shortly at Ashingdon. This seems to me highly improbable; it is, to my mind more likely that the bridge was named after some local worthy perhaps Ben Battle, who lived nearby or who perhaps was in charge of building a new bridge.

Just across the bridge, our way lies left along a narrow lane which makes its unremarkable way for some miles. A great deal of building has taken place at Hullbridge, where a road goes down to the Crouch. The name confirms a tradition that there was an ancient bridge over the river here. If this was so, it argues considerable traffic between, say, Maldon and Rayleigh to justify so costly an engineering operation. There is a similar mystery further down stream at Fambridge. In our affluent days no bridge crosses the Crouch between Battlesbridge and the sea, and the country further east is quite remarkably isolated, to our present benefit.

There is no particular attraction to take us down the side road to South Fambridge. Ashingdon, almost opposite the opening of this lane, has 'enjoyed' much modern development, and only the little hilltop church remains to remind us of the old village. This, however, looks out across the new houses to the marshes and the river which improvements have not so far reached. It would be pleasant to believe that the church is pre-Conquest, but all the visible evidence is to the contrary. It may nevertheless be accepted that this is the successor on the same site—which would have commended itself to early planners—to the minster built 'of stone and lime' by order of Canute at the scene of his greatest victory. This was in 1020. The first priest was Stigand, later to become the over-politic archbishop of Canterbury.

By this time Canute had been King of all England for three years. His success had been assured in 1016 when he met King Edmund Ironside 'on the down called Assingdon'. 'All England', said the Chronicler, 'fought against him', all, that is, except Edric, the habitually treacherous Alderman of Mercia, who deserted with his force early in the battle, most probably by pre-arrangement with the Danes. The two greatest military leaders of the age met in the battle. Edmund had the advantage in numbers and, apart from treachery, it is not clear what went wrong, but 'all the nobility of the English nation were there undone'. England was afterwards divided between the two nations at a treaty in Gloucestershire, but Edmund died shortly afterwards—helped, it is said, to this end by Edric, and the Witan had no one to choose but Canute. It was no bad choice. Canute was a ruthless opportunist, but the end of strife gave him the chance to develop remarkable powers of statecraft, and the former warlord became one of the greatest of English kings. The centuries-old struggle with the Danes came to an end on the low hills of Ashingdon above the wide and treacherous waters of the Crouch which penetrated at high tide right to the foot of the church hill.

There is, in all this country, a clear definition of contours which makes it possible to read the past history of the river and to see how it used to spill over the tidal flats. In the next three miles the road climbs steadily until it reaches at Canewdon church its highest point of nearly 130 feet. On this eminence above the marshes the tall tower of Canewdon has a touch of the dramatic rare indeed in this country.

Not surprisingly this height is known as Beacon Hill. It is said to have been the Danish command post before the battle and a formidable one it must have been. The church, which occupies the top of the hill, is architecturally the finest in the Crouch valley, and its tower is splendid in a way almost unknown elsewhere in southern Essex. It is a ragstone, probably brought by water from the Medway. The date is early in the fifteenth century, and it is associated, on the strength of heraldic shields on the west face, with King Henry V. These shields are now almost indecipherable, but Dr

Cox, writing in 1909 when the air was less polluted, identifies them
as the arms of England and France, Bohun, Mowbray and Warren—
a roll-call of mediaeval chivalry. This noble tower, the building o
which must surely commemorate some great occasion, might jus
possibly be a memorial to the Hundred Years War; at least, in th
absence of positive evidence, romantic speculation of this kind i
not quite out of order.

Much of the outside of the church is of the same period. There i
a very handsome battlemented porch, and several of the window
have carved heads as label-stops. Not all of these are grotesques. On
at least is a sensitive portrait-head. Some of the detail inside suggest
that an earlier church is encased in the fifteenth-century walls. Th
two best fittings are borrowed. The font, square on columns and wit
decorated faces, came from the parish church at Shopland—toward
Southend—when this was demolished not long ago. The pulpit is *
splendid example of late seventeenth-century work, its panel
framed with carved leaves and fruit and with cherubs above. If w
came across this in the City of London, we should think at onc
of Grinling Gibbons, and our sense of period at least would not b
at fault. The pulpit was brought here from a lost Wren church
St Christopher-le-Stocks, which had been demolished to make way
for the Bank of England. It is said—but I have not attempted to dis
cover whether this is true—that the churchyard is still there, hidde
in the Old Lady's bosom.

The best of Canewdon is around the church. The village stree
comes up to the east end of the church, and here is the little villag
lock-up. There has been much building nearby, good of its kin
but not really congruous. From the churchyard there are fine view
to the river and beyond.

The road past Canewdon crosses a creek and comes to an end i
the cultivated emptiness of Wallasea Island. It may not seem wort
coming so far to so little purpose, but Wallasea, a true island be
tween the Crouch and the Roach, is so characteristic of one kin
of Essex that it should not be missed, even though the road goe
no further and no public paths cross the watery flats.

Here the exploration of the southern shore of the Crouch ough
to end. I am, however, unwilling to go away without a look at on
more village and that one of my favourites. To reach Paglesham w
double back halfway to Canewdon and then turn left, near a fin

imbered house, to come up to Church End past the elegant West Hall. This is the—relatively—dry end of Paglesham. Sailing folk know the East End on the Roach better. This is, or was, oyster country, the breeding ground for, according to Defoe, 'the best and nicest, though not the largest oysters in England'. At Church End there are no oysters, only one of the most delightful groups of buildings in the country. As usual the road ends beside the hall and the church, but before this we pass an exceedingly attractive row of cottages, brick and plaster with steep red roofs, and a surprisingly small weatherboard inn, the Punch Bowl. Opposite the church there is a pond with some exotic duck on it, a pretty scene; here I met a satisfyingly fat child named Deborah who discussed the points of the mandarins in friendly and knowledgeable fashion. The church is rather like a slightly poor relation of Canewdon. The tower, for instance, is flint, not stone, but much on the Canewdon pattern. The rest of the church is Norman, much altered and with mostly renewed windows. It is set well among trees.

We are here squarely in the middle of the peninsula between Crouch and Roach and need to get back to explore the northern shore of the former river. We can hurry back by the way we came, or go due west to Hawkwell—where there is a pretty little church well away from the new sprawl of houses—and Hockley. This is sad country, its charms submerged under tons of brick and mortar. The road, built up all the way, comes at length to Rayleigh, where something of the old market town survives around the church and the mound which marks the site of one of the earliest of Norman castles. To find this, you may navigate by the tower-mill on top of the hill, now capped in a mildly comical way with battlements. Beyond this the main road leads by way of Rawreth—church in extravagant Victorian Gothic a little off the road—back to Battlesbridge.

On the northern side of the Crouch the hills come down closer to the shore and the scenery is rather more exciting. Sometimes this country can be uncomfortably dramatic. I was caught one evening in the eye of a thunderstorm here, and within half an hour every one of these innocent-seeming lanes had become an impassable torrent. On a spring day, with the sun soft among drifting cloud, such an experience seems to belong to some other planet. The beauty of this country, indeed, depends more than in most places on the weather. It is a landscape which is more than half sky and on leaden day it is flattened into insignificance.

At first we are well north of the river. Keeping to the main roa the first village is Stow Maries. The name is more attractive tha the place and recalls, not the Virgin and the Magdalen, but th family of Marisco. The church, down a side road which is on ou route, is of the fifteenth and sixteenth centuries, so much enriche and tidied up within the last century that all feeling of antiquit has vanished. It has attracted many gifts in this period which som how just fail to coalesce; one example of this is the illuminate cross on the spire. This is a reminder of a link between Stow Marie and the Royal Air Force and is of genuine historical significanc how sad that it should be so out of scale with the homely littl wooden spire.

The lane past the church comes shortly to a minor road t Burnham, and we take this for two miles when a side road goes righ to North Fambridge. This will give us the best impression to dat of the tidal river. Fambridge is a minor yachting centre, minor, tha is, in terms of size, not importance. Here you may sit and enjo the unceasing movement of the river and, at low tide, smell tha most evocative of all odours, river mud. If time allows and yo are suitably shod, you might try a muddy stroll along the river wa for a mile or so to get, so far as a landsman can, the feel of the rive The bank is the familiar muddle of boats living, dying and long dea a sight which would in any other context be depressing, if not objec tionable. Just behind the sea wall there is a weatherboard inn, th Ferry Boat, a picturesque and welcoming sight especially to sailin men after a long day.

Back on the Burnham road, we have a few miles of very deligh ful country, quite unspoilt. Elms stride purposefully across th sloping fields and the river shines a hundred feet below. Here th wide channel is broken by an island—Bridgeman Island—which i an object lesson to those who may be tempted to neglect the se defences. Its once-fertile acres are now criss-crossed with salt-wate channels.

It is worth stopping for a tiny mediaeval building beside the roa The old church of Latchingdon was abandoned when a new on was built higher up in the village and left to fall gently into ruit Later the nave was patched up and made weather-proof. The frag

nent has a certain sad appeal, and it is not difficult to recognize
he modest charms of the original building.

By the time we reach Althorne another suburban influence, this
ime from Burnham, can be felt and the old village is all but lost.
'he church stands back from the road and the traveller, who has
ιad an almost unrelieved diet of these buildings during this journey,
ηay be tempted to keep going. I should regret this, because Althorne
'hurch, besides having a fine tower rather like the one at Canewdon
owards which it looks across the river, has a font which, for all
)r Pevsner's strictures, I find most attractive. It is octagonal, Per-
)endicular, of an East Anglian pattern. There are the usual support-
ng angels and the eight sides are carved, perhaps crudely, certainly
vith vigour. Among the scenes represented is a baptism, at just
uch a font as this. On another panel St Andrew is bound to his
'ross—the church is dedicated to him—and nearby there is a very
'eathery, but headless, angel.

There is really nothing now to prevent a final dash to Burnham,
·o conclude this journey on the most celebrated quay in the county.

have a personal fancy to linger in the marsh country of Dengie
Iundred. This is quite different to any other part of Essex. Many
)eople, including some who are sensitive to landscape and not irre-
rievably committed to the picturesque, will dismiss this scenery
ιs dull, flat, empty. It is certainly flat. East of the Burnham-Bradwell
·oad, only a few places rise above 50 feet and in the marshes the
ιverage is below ten. Dull? Perhaps, on an utterly cheerless day with
he clouds down solidly and no spark of light. Empty? Never. The
ηarshes are full of their own life; especially at those seasons when
here are few human visitors, the flats are alive with the restless
ηovement of countless birds. If you want to taste every kind of
:ssex, therefore, you must try this strange country, walking round
he sea wall or sampling one of the narrow roads which run so
)urposefully across the levels and then stop suddenly in the middle
)f nowhere in particular. You will discover the difference between
he reclaimed marsh and the saltings and the distinctive population
)f each. Here is richly productive land; here too some of the loneliest
:ountry—in human terms—in southern England.

How strange then that I associate this country, in which more
:han in most I find satisfaction in the absence of human beings, with
:hat most humane of writers, S. L. Bensusan. Mr Bensusan, who sees

and captures the peculiar essence of Essex better than any othe
writer of this or any other century, is equally at home in th
marshes and in the rolling wheat-fields of the northern chalk. I se
him most clearly among the flats of Dengie Hundred, not watchin
birds or seeing the dawn sky over the North Sea—although he
sharply aware of such things—but listening in pub or cottage to th
rough music of the Essex tongue. His books are essential readin
for those who hope to reach the heart of this country.

In Dengie Hundred the villages hug the one main road and yo
will see them all, except Dengie, on a simple drive from Burnha
to the Blackwater estuary at Bradwell. They are in fact of no ver
great interest. (I except from this, of course, Bradwell itself whic
we shall meet on a later journey.) The largest is Southminster, whic
I find a rather drab and disappointing place. Even the churc
which is large, roughly cruciform, and of a variety of styles, gives
muddled impression. Only the porch, with its distinctive ston
decoration, is worth stopping for. Despite the name, this was nc
monastic. 'Minster' here seems to mean no more than 'church', bι
'south' of what? Bradwell seems the obvious answer today, bι
both Asheldham and Tillingham are ancient settlements and so
Dengie. Asheldham is on a complex series of road bends. These aι
folded around an old earthwork which can just be seen—helped b
the eye of faith—on the right. I would not be rash enough to gue
at the date. The church is along a side road with the hall behin
it. It is a good-looking sturdy building with a low tower, set we
among trees, but quite unexceptional in architecture or fittings. .
little further along this road we come to Dengie, which gives i
name to the Hundred but it is now much the smallest place in it. 1
amounts to little more than hall, church and a farm or so. Th
church is suitably diminutive, a plain building but with som
extremely jolly carving below the belfry. I have no doubt that it 1
no older than Victorian, but I like its humour and spirit, especiall
a happy lion with mane like the rays of a formalized sun. The la
village in this direction is Tillingham. This is larger and altogethe
very pleasant. There is a little square beside the church, framed wit
good cottages, which has real style. The church is unexpectedl
splendid, partly as a result of restoration. The chancel, early thi
teenth century, has a soaring quality. The tower is of the ne
century. The stair turret is unexpectedly square, and has battlemen

and gargoyles. These latter look like renewals. They are so well done, however, that we need not quibble but be content to enjoy the ferocity with which they leer down at the motorists who clutter up the village green.

If we return along the Burnham road we shall come first to Church End where Burnham parish church, in Essex fashion, stands a long mile from the town centre. In some parts of the country this might be taken as evidence that the maritime history of the town had begun after the middle ages. In Essex it merely means that the lord regarded the church as his personal province and so he put it next to his hall. Burnham church belonged to Dunmow Priory from the twelfth century to the Dissolution, and this may account in part for the unusual scale and splendour of the church. By the time the present building came to be erected, or modelled from the earlier one, however, Burnham was flourishing as a wool-port, and some of the lavish details are a mirror of civic dignity, others a reflection of the pride of Thomas Ratcliff, Lord Fitzwalter, whose family had been patrons of Dunmow Priory from the beginning and who inherited the manor in Henry VIII's reign. The south porch is very fine. It bears the date 1523 and has a set of four heraldic shields linking the church with the Priory, Fitzwalter and Ratcliff and so providing a shorthand summary of its history. The building is more imposing outside than in, but it has an exceptionally lovely stone niche in the north aisle. This is enriched with intricate decoration and must have been designed to frame an image of the Virgin. It could not have been originally in this position, and from its design and materials might have been intended for an exterior setting. Was it taken down and hidden after the suppression of the parent Priory?

Between Church End and Burnham High Street lies modern Burnham, about which little should be said, although much could. It is not the most successful grafting of new on to old. The best of the old is in the rectangle formed by the high street and the river front. The centrepiece is a brick clock tower of mid-Victorian origin. It has no architectural quality, yet somehow it strikes almost the right note in a street which falls somewhat short of distinction. The best house is almost opposite this, and there is a scattering of Georgian and Victorian brick and weather-boarding, pleasant rather than admirable. If the High Street is disappointing, the Quay is

correspondingly heartening. Here, for the first time and perhaps th
last in Essex, land and water meet with a proper sense of occasion
There is an atmosphere, and not one just composed of fish and muc
The river is about half a mile wide, and at most times of the yea
and day you will soon tire of trying to count the craft. This is th
premier sailing base on the east coast, and you are not likely to b
able to forget it. Dropped alongside, and not excessively shipshape
is a row of cottages, grouped casually around the hotel. It is a highl
successful example of no-planning. The architectural tones are low
which is just right because it is the river that matters here and an
forceful landward accent would be distracting.

The Crouch has been an elusive river. Too small to see in th
upper waters, cut off by wide marshes in the tidal reaches, it come
into its own at Burnham, and here, lacking the boat to follow th
last five roadless miles, we must leave it in all its beauty and purpose
ful activity.

CHAPTER FOUR

Roding

Broxted—Canfield—the Rodings—Fyfield—
Ongar—Greensted—Navestock—Lambourne—
Chigwell—Wanstead

Of all the rivers which impose their character on the countryside
the Roding is the most insignificant. For half its length one notices
it only by a conscious effort. From Fyfield to Wanstead it makes
more of a mark, but is still never more than a stream. In its last
miles it becomes the insalubrious Barking Creek and meets the
Thames under the towers of the Barking Power Station.

Why then waste a chapter on the Roding? By one of the strange
ironies which one meets so often in Essex this negligible trickle of
water is the unifying factor in a most characteristic and attractive
valley. It gives its name to a group of charming villages. If one were
to name one district which has an individual Essex character this
might be the choice; it would be mine. But here, more than anywhere else in this county, it is difficult to define the precise quality
of a landscape which is entirely without highlights or any hint
of drama.

The Roding rises below the ridge which runs across western Essex
between the Stort and Chelmer valleys. The ridge rises to 375 feet,
but the source of our stream is 30 feet or so below this. It is an
attractive bit of breezy upland country, and before picking up the
source of the river one might linger briefly on the ridge at Broxted,
right on the watershed. It is a place of wide views and spectacular
sunsets. To the south and east the country is open; to the north there
are woods with the little spire of Chickney church—remote and

ancient—peeping out. There is not much in Broxted village, except Church Hall, which can be glimpsed over the churchyard wall, the Elizabethan gabled house quite overwhelmed by its great barn.

Just along the road beyond the church is one of the loveliest of modern gardens. Hill Pasture is open to the public now and again during the summer and richly rewards the visitor. The house is modern and so is the garden, created by the artist owner. There are only three acres, yet so cunningly is it laid out that one gets the impression of a very extensive garden. Woodland paths and formal yew-lined walks are punctuated by statuary, old and new, and some very handsome lead cisterns of the seventeenth century. One of these is huge. A rose garden on formal wrought-iron frames like Gothic tracery opens into a view across rolling farmland. In another corner a picture of flagstones and round pond is trapped enchantingly in a large brick moon-door. This garden, varied and sensitively arranged, has its horticultural interest but appeals more strongly because of its architectural quality; it has been set on the ground as a conscious work of art.

A minor road out of Broxted runs steeply south to Brick End and then to Molehill Green. Here those who enjoy purposeful exercise may abandon their cars and seek by footpath the source of the Roding. With plenty of time to spare they may even follow it by green lanes and muddy tracks for its first few miles until it passes Little Canfield Hall and flows under the busy Dunmow road. The same point can be reached less eventfully by road from Molehill Green. Little Canfield village straggles uneasily along the main road. The church—lavishly restored—stands alone near the river, with a tangled complex of footpaths around to tempt the traveller astray. If one resists these, the road goes south from the main road, winding sharply by way of Bacon End Green and Bacon End to Great Canfield. What appears to be a drainage ditch beside the road is the Roding.

An arm of the river in mediaeval times formed part of the defences of a castle here. This is so much overgrown now that it is difficult to form a clear idea of its nature. Beyond the churchyard and in the private grounds of the hall, is a huge mound densely covered with trees. A moat filled from the river surrounded this and also the double fortified bailey which, while no doubt accessible to the archaeologist's spade, can be identified by the casual visitor only with the eye of faith. This motte-and-bailey castle, typical

hough bigger than some in this county, seems to have been one
of the emergency fortresses thrown up immediately after the
Conquest, and to have been a stronghold of the powerful De Vere
family, later to become Earls of Oxford.

Perhaps the same family was responsible for building the church,
which is sufficiently near to the castle to suggest a close association.
By the time the church was built, however, in Henry II's reign fashion
favoured more sophisticated fortifications than these. Whatever its
origin Great Canfield church is a remarkably fine building and, but
for its Victorian restoration, remarkably of a piece. Basically it is
late Norman work with a magnificent chancel arch and richly
ornamented north and south doors. The latter has swastika ornaments and carved capitals. The restorers were guilty of some terrible
crimes here, destroying the old font and pulpit and providing new
and distressingly gorgeous replacements. Out of the restoration came,
however, the church's noblest possession and one of the great artistic
treasures of Essex. Behind the altar, and symmetrically between the
two little Norman east windows, was a seventeenth-century monument (now in the nave). When this was taken away an arched recess,
a little larger than but matching the twin windows, was revealed.
Under the plaster at the back of this was found a mural painting of
the Virgin and Child. Restored discreetly, this now glows most
beautifully above the altar. The Virgin, crowned, looks down ten-
derly at a rather overgrown Babe, a little old for the breast she is
offering. The whole composition, dated by Professor Tristram at
about 1250, is most moving. Although, as usual, the artist probably
used as his copy-book a contemporary illuminated manuscript, the
painting has an architectural quality which is exactly right for its
setting. It dominates the lovely building of which it is the crown.

This is the threshold of the area known as the Rodings (or Rooth-
ings, an alternative and probably less authentic variant). Eight
villages take their surname from the river which makes the valley
in which they are set, although only two of them can truly be
said to stand on the river. These little villages have a fascination
which increases as acquaintance grows into knowledge. Dr Cox,
the Edwardian guide to this county, said rather testily: 'There is
not an old camp, castle or monastery, or even a good monument
or brass among them. The churches are small and of no architectural
merit'. The strictures may be justified but the old antiquarian took

no account of atmosphere or charm. The Rodings have these in abundance. This is country not to be hurried, and it is a pity that two roads (Ongar to Dunmow, and Chelmsford to Sawbridgeworth) which pass through the Rodings now carry such a heavy load of traffic making lingering a hazardous business. The by-ways and the green lanes are still undisturbed.

High Roding is first on our route. 'High' does not refer to altitude but to status or possibly position on the high road. Apart from church and hall High Roding consists of a double row of houses flanking the main road. Despite a few unworthy buildings the general effect is most satisfying. No house is of the first importance but there is much variety—black-and-white, plaster, thatch and tile —and a characteristic blending of different façades, levels and periods. You are clear of the village before the by-road to the church goes off right. This, although the least interesting of the Rodings is still worth a visit for the peace of its setting among arable fields with the narrow wooded belt of the river beyond. The church itself is humble enough, apart from some ostentatious Victorian corbels. The best of it is the weathered south porch.

In visiting all the Rodings—and I should be reluctant to miss one —it is not easy to avoid retracing steps. The next on the list is Aythorpe Roding where a good deal of modern housing, not bad of its kind, has grown up around a very fine post-mill, recently restored and now in excellent condition. This stands on a private road but is accessible on foot. It makes a feature in the view from many points around, notably from the church which, as usual, stands well away from the village. Apart from a later wooden belfry and spire, this is entirely of the thirteenth century with a simple and handsome three-lancet east window. Unfortunately the building appears to be kept locked.

If the lane giving access to the church is followed it quickly crosses the Roding at one of the few points where the charm of the little stream can be appreciated. It is best seen early in the year; in high summer the waterway tends to become choked with reed and weed. Just beyond the river there is a glimpse up a farm-track on the right of a huge Tudor barn. The lane turns left, still giving most pleasing views across the valley, and in a mile passes Lucas's Farm, an exceptionally fine example of a timber-framed house, its austere lines broken by a projecting two-storeyed porch. With its mellow brick wall and wrought-iron gate, and with some handsome farm buildings to the side, Lucas's makes a most satisfying picture.

This is in White Roding parish, and the village is not far away, most of it along a minor road. It is possibly the least attractive of the Roding villages, its best houses hidden away along farm roads and its tower mill half ruined. The church however—whose white-washed exterior gave the village its distinctive name—is a building of some distinction with a tall battlemented flint tower. The best of it is the south door which still has its ancient ironwork and the massive Norman font with primitive geometrical ornament. The east window has good tracery and sets off a dignified plain reredos. The rood stairs are a curiosity; instead of being set in a wall-turret in the almost invariable manner they simply stride up the wall in full view.

There is a good house—Mascallsbury—on the winding road to Abbess Roding, two miles away. The name derives from Barking Abbey, which owned the church in mediaeval times. There is some new housing here of an undistinguished kind. The church has a flint tower (Victorian) and slim spire somewhat in the Hertfordshire fashion. It is nicely situated and makes a pleasing picture in its bower of trees, especially if the village is approached from the Laver road. The screen has, for Essex, quite elaborate tracery, but the most noticeable feature of the interior is the pulpit with a splendidly lavish hexagonal sounding-board. An hour-glass in wrought-iron frame stands nearby to measure out the preacher's eloquence. Two Jacobean wall-monuments are excellent of their kind, ornate yet restrained.

Abbess Roding is not far from the main Ongar road, where you will find a fine old farmhouse almost straight ahead. A little down the road and to the left is the village of Beauchamp Roding, such as it is. There is not much of it and that of no particular attraction, except for the church which, unusually, stands quite alone in fields a quarter-mile from the nearest house. Its slim tower is a feature in all the views around. One reaches it by footpath or by a rough track from the Ongar road. This is the kind of rural building which one too easily dismisses as uninteresting. It has no claim to architec-tural quality, and the fittings and monuments are nothing special. But such analytical evaluations take no account of atmosphere. This little, lonely church, standing remote on its hillock, is immensely appealing. It is quiet, contained, timeless (despite an inevitable tendency to decay). And for collectors of the grotesque there is a corbel which presents the kind of zoological puzzle dear to such antiquarians. Snouted like a pig, maned like a lion, it has a benignity all its own. A long tongue dangles whitely.

If we are to gather up the missing Rodings we have to double back here by a side road to Birds Green—the inn here has a charming sign—then across the river and north again by a narrow lane noisy in season with building rooks, and so to the farm road up to Berners Roding. Like Beauchamp Roding this takes its distinguishing name from a former owner. Berners Roding is the smallest of the Roding family. There is really no village at all, just the hall (eighteenth-century red brick) with its farm and the miniature church. This must be among the very smallest in the county and the plainest. No tower or steeple, only a little box, no monuments to speak of, just enough architectural detail to hint at a date around the early sixteenth century; is it worth the journey? I would say yes with no hesitation at all. It is one of the joys of the Essex countryside that tiny social units like this can survive intact, with no self-conscious archaism, into the modern age.

Back to the road, it is a mile and a half north again to the busy Chelmsford road, with Margaret Roding a little to the left. It is hardly bigger than Berners Roding, but the hall is rather more stately and the church much richer. Access to both involves crossing the line of traffic into a short side road, an extremely hazardous business but worth the risk. On most counts this is the best of the Roding churches. It may not look much. It is small and the plain line of nave and choir is broken only by a little modern stone belfry. In a moment the south door comes into sight and all doubts disappear. This compares with the best Norman work in the county. It is massive and elaborately carved with conventional zigzag decoration. A flatter version of the same ornament appears on the outermost of the shafts of the doorway. The door itself has ironwork roughly contemporary with the building. This church, whose dedication to Margaret of Antioch gives the village its name, is in fact late Norman with little later addition. Several details are interesting to the ecclesiologist: sedilia contrived by lowering the sill of a south-east window; an enigmatic recess in the north wall, its carved crocket battered and incomplete; a vast dug-out chest, with iron clasps and

locks remaining as witness to the skill of some rustic blacksmith. This is the best thing in the church. Next comes the font, octagonal with heraldic shields—now blank. Despite the stately bowl and elaborate column, it seems incomplete; surely flights of stone angels should be bearing it up, as they do similar fonts in other parts of the county.

There is one Roding still to go, Leaden Roding—a descriptive name, as is White Roding; the church was roofed in lead in the days when mostly they were thatched, and the village sits around the junction of the Sawbridgeworth and Dunmow roads. It is an uncomfortable position, and most travellers are too much occupied with negotiating the traffic to notice its quality. The church, just beyond the cross-roads and very near to the river, is extremely picturesque. A wooden belfry with spire is just too small for the rest of the building; aesthetically a blemish which nevertheless gives the church an endearing quaintness. The work seems to be mainly Norman, but a locked door prevents one from checking the impression from within. A very conspicuous east window, if it is original—and it does not look like restoration work—belongs to the beginning of the fourteenth century and is of intriguing design.

It is now necessary to cover some of the ground again. To keep this to the minimum we might endure a mile or two of the main Ongar road, turning off, as before, at Beauchamp Roding, but going right after crossing the Roding beyond Birds Green. This road, narrow and attractive, will lead to Willingale—more correctly to Willingale Doe and Willingale Spain. For as long as I can remember—and before I thought of coming here—I have known of these two parishes, because of a distinction which, although not I believe unique, is exceedingly rare. Two parish churches at Willingale share the same churchyard. In plenty of places you will find two churches in the same yard—they are fairly common in Norfolk—but most often one is in ruins and the second is a replacement. Here, however, each serves a separate parish. The modern village which has this embarrassment of riches is very small; nevertheless, to its very great credit, each church is in good shape and both are in use. The buildings are nicely contrasted and make an exceedingly satisfactory scene. Willingale Spain, the older church, is typical Essex of the forest country; very plain, Norman—or could it be Saxon?—flint and re-used Roman brick, with a pretty wooden belfry. Willingale

Doe is large and showy with a great west tower. The architectural detail does not stand up to close examination, being largely of nineteenth-century restoration. The general impression is pleasing enough. Spain is very simple inside, Doe has a huge baroque monument. The view from the churchyard looking west over the Roding valley is as good as any in this part of Essex.

If you like absurd place-names or post-Reformation churches— and I collect both—you will not mind an extra mile or two off course to visit Shellow Bowells. The village is almost non-existent. The church stands on the entrance to Shellow Hall. It is simple as could be but quite delightful, a complete and unaltered Georgian building. The little cupola is comical but somehow entirely in keeping. The men who put up this church in 1754 were more accustomed to building formal and stately halls, but they did their best with an unfamiliar job and gave it just a touch of the newly fashionable Gothic style.

Here we have headed away from the Roding, though still in its catchment area for a tiny stream rises at Shellow to flow briefly (but in flood-time devastatingly) to the Roding near Miller's Green. To return, we go through Willingale again and then turn right to find the river at Fyfield. The view of the Roding at Passingford, further down stream, is more familiar, but to me the Roding is at its best here at Fyfield. The stream is artificially widened to serve a water-mill and trees twisted by the years into characteristic attitudes frame a watery scene of high excellence. Much of Fyfield sprawls along the main road, almost a suburb of Ongar, but the old village by the river is little spoiled. The hall, standing back from the road, is supported by admirable smaller houses and cottages. In the middle of this group stands quite the most extraordinary village church in Essex. I remember coming here as a boy and sketching it. I had not noticed quite how queer it looked until I saw it on paper. It looks as if it were the result of a whole string of afterthoughts, as in a sense it was. The successive builders of the central tower seemed unable to stop. But the absurdity is all outside. The interior is most impressive. Some of the rich detail in the nave may come from the church's early association with Bermondsey Abbey, but the splendid chancel was built after the manor had passed in the fourteenth century to the Scrope family. Here is a lavish set of three sedilia, the arches divided by elegant marble columns, and with elaborate label-stops. Three balls, symbol of the church's patron saint Nicholas, are carved above.

One of the lords of the manor was Lord Scrope of Masham, Shakespeare's

> *cruel,*
> *Ingrateful, savage and inhuman creature*

who was involved in that puzzling plot against Henry V which immediately preceded the Agincourt campaign. He was beheaded and according to tradition was brought back to Fyfield for burial in the chancel built by his ancestors a century earlier. If his tomb survives, it is quite hidden by the organ. Of all Fyfield's worthies it may seem strange to single out a traitor; in the tangled wilderness of Plantagenet dynastic policies one man's traitor was another's patriot, and Scrope's greatest fault, perhaps, was in being found out.

The high road from Chelmsford to Epping, which the Roding crosses near High Ongar, makes a stage in the progress of the river. Hereafter, although it still enjoys considerable immunity from the diseases of suburbia, it belongs to commuterland and there is a subtle change in the landscape. This is not to say that the scenery is any less pleasing; in fact between Ongar and Abridge, whatever the congestion of the main road, lies a countryside as lovely as it is remote.

Ongar—I prefer the full title, Chipping Ongar—is a curiosity, a town directly connected by railway with London and so highly popular with commuters, which retains almost intact its country-town atmosphere. The supermarkets have so far been kept at bay and residents make do—if that is the expression—with local shops. The town has considerable character and provides the normal approach to one of the major places of pilgrimage in these parts; it is moreover a centre for the exploration of much charming country. It makes no attempt whatever to capitalize on these potential assets.

Apart from the new developments on the northern edge and a little along the Greensted road, the town is largely one of a single street. A handsome inn, distinguished by a good sign, is evidence that in coaching days, at least, Ongar profited by its visitors. The high street is pleasantly irregular, but no house is of the first interest The corner of the lane leading to the church strikes the most memor able note. Here was the centre of the mediaeval, probably the earlier community. Beyond the church stood the castle which made this a place of major importance. Some defensive position might have been established before the Norman Conquest, and this per haps was strengthened by Eustace of Boulogne, one of William's principal knights, who made this his headquarters. It was further reinforced in the troubled reigns of Stephen and Henry II. It con sisted of a very large mound, 300 feet in diameter, linked with two —possibly more—baileys. The masonry of this complex fortress was pulled down in Elizabethan times when a new house, now vanished, was built on the site. Of all this only the earthworks re main, the motte conspicuous beyond an eighteenth-century house at the end of a private drive, the baileys obliterated or overgrown with trees.

Close to the castle, and possibly within one of the baileys, stands the parish church of St Martin (the patron saint can be seen on the weathervane). This is a humble building to serve a town which had some status even before the Conquest. It has a village-type wooden steeple and shows a lavish use of Roman brick in its structure. It is a hunting-ground for antiquarians who have not yet reconciled theories about the date. Is it a Saxon building? Or was it built by the great Richard de Lucy, Chief Justice to Henry II, when he acquired the castle in 1162? Whatever the facts, this is a building of great antiquity and equally great charm. Most visitors seek out the grave slab, in the chancel, of Jane Pallavicini, whom a hasty reading of the inscription would suggest was the daughter of Oliver Cromwell She belonged to another branch of the family, her father being another Huntingdonshire gentleman, Sir Oliver Cromwell. She died in 1637.

Jane Cromwell's name may remind us of another Jane who, with her sister, lived in Ongar and who made a very small but enduring mark on history. Jane and Ann Taylor came with their father from Colchester to live here in 1811. Isaac Taylor was a dissenting minis ter as well as a professional engraver and served as pastor here for 18 years, living first in Castle House under the shadow of the Norman motte. It was to this house that the Rev. Joseph Gilbert came 'to solicit the heart and hand' of Ann, an episode if not larger than

fe certainly stranger than fiction which might have served Charlotte
ßronté with material for an affecting chapter.

All the Taylors were enthusiastic writers, and *Original Poems for
nfant Minds* was a great success and continued popular throughout
he nineteenth century. This success has worked against the book in
hat parodies of poems like 'Twinkle twinkle little star' and 'My
Mother' are better remembered than the originals; but only popular
nd memorable poems provoke parody. In an age when literature
or children was almost invariably didactic and sententious and often
distressingly flat, the poems written by Jane and Ann Taylor had
ensibility and very considerable technical skill.

Beyond the car-park at the north end of Chipping Ongar's High
Street, a footpath leads across a little stream—not the Roding but a
ributary coming out of attractive country near the Lavers—into a
magnificent double avenue in the grand manner of landscape design.
This green way provides a fittingly noble approach to one of the
paramount 'sights' of Essex. One ought always to visit a holy place
on foot, and Greensted Church, whatever one's faith or lack of faith,
s holy ground.

Greensted has always held a specially firm grip on my heart. As
a boy living across the border in a northern suburb of London I had
heard about Greensted, the only wooden church in England to have
survived from the Saxons, and longed to see it for myself. For an
impoverished small boy Greensted, 20 miles away, seemed as inaccessible as Greenland. I hugged the thought of this place to myself
for years. At last—I suppose I was 13 or 14—I could bear it no
onger, and so walked to Greensted to make my personal pilgrimage
o this infinitely ancient shrine. As pilgrims should, I suffered, from
hirst and extreme fatigue; but I got to Greensted and returned home
again. Was it worth the 40-mile tramp? I believe so. I have been
o Greensted many times since, in comfort, and have never failed
o recapture the memory of dust and hot tar on gritty lanes and
the lifting of the heart which I felt at the fulfilment of my pilgrimage.

Visiting Greensted with the seeing eye and not the eye of memory,
we find a little building, associated in the Essex manner with hall
and farm. At the west end is a dumpy weather-board tower capped
with a slightly topheavy shingled spire. The east end is brick, of
Tudor red warmth. Between these extremities is a little log cabin, its

walls of split oak logs set upright with rounded sides outermost standing now in a modern brick sill. The roof over this venerable nave has dormer windows which give an effect at once absurd and homely.

It would be enough for lasting fame for this wooden church to have lasted for nine and a half centuries or more. What gives Greensted its great distinction is that it is associated with one of the greatest of Englishmen, Edmund, King and Martyr, who was until the regrettable importation of that Cappadocian foreigner St George, by Edward III, the patron saint of England. Edmund succeeded to the kingdom of the East Angles in 855. In 870 he met the army commanded by Halfden, Ingwar and Hubba, who were ravaging their way through England after killing the disreputable Northumbrian king Aella. Edmund was defeated at Hoxne in Suffolk; the Danes tied him to a tree, shot him full of arrows, and then hacked off his head. Survivors among his followers buried him where he died—in a nice story a wolf guarded his severed head until it could be recovered—and later his body was taken to London. In 1013 it was translated, with great ceremony, to a new shrine in the East Anglian capital, now Bury St Edmunds. The procession halted for the night on the way near Ongar and the body rested in a *lignea capella*. This, there seems no reason to doubt, was the wooden church of Greensted. It could not have been put up specially for this occasion and must therefore antedate 1013; scientific tests suggest that it may have been built before Edmund's reign, about the middle of the ninth century. This would make it not only the oldest by far of wooden buildings but among the oldest of surviving Saxon churches.

When the church was restored early in Victorian times—the work being done with, for those days, remarkable discretion—the occasion was taken to carve into the spandrels of the roof-beams some reminders of St Edmund. There are the three crowns of East Anglia and, charmingly portrayed, a docile and dog-like wolf protecting the saint's crowned head.

In the next few miles of this journey we come into a region of locked churches—three out of six. The guardians of these buildings which are at once local workshops of the spirit and national history treasures, are in a dilemma today. If, as surely every right instinct demands, they are to leave the church open through all the hours of the day, parishioners and pilgrims can enter them at will—and so can the shabby villains who steal the altar furnishings and the hangings which beautify them as well as the pitifully small contents of their collecting-box. So too can the lunatics who defile churches with phoney ceremonies of the Old Religion. So what happens? Are the harmless many to be denied spiritual and intellectual refreshment because of the evil and folly of the few? Here and there the answer, sadly, is Yes.

However, let us press on. Interesting things now lie on either side of the Roding, which is here a more formidable barrier, and we must look out for the comparatively few bridges. On the east bank there is a little less to distract us immediately. Stondon Massey has become a minor dormitory and its charms have faded a little in consequence. Only in the area of the church and hall does the village survive unimpaired. The views over the Roding valley from the churchyard are free of blemish. The church itself is small, Norman, and in a quite unnotable way, charming. Stondon Massey—the evocative name reminds us that this stony hill belonged to the Marci family who came from Normandy—is best remembered as the home of one of the greatest of English composers. William Byrd came here in 1593 and occupied Stondon Place, not the present house, as tenant of a Mistress Shelley, whose husband had been involved in one of the plots against Elizabeth. He spent the rest of his life here, in spite of Mistress Shelley's efforts to evict him. The complicated story is told in detail in Edmund Fellowes's biography of Byrd. What that book does not explain, because it is inexplicable, is the secret of Byrd's own survival, a Papist occupying an official post in the Chapel Royal, among the tangled intrigues of Elizabeth's Court. Byrd died at Stondon in 1623 and may have been buried in the church.

While we are on this side of the river, we might go by way of Kelvedon Hatch to Navestock, where the hall and church occupy a classic position on a wooded hill overlooking the Roding. A path past the church leads through the park to the delightful ornamental water near the river, a typical Georgian landscape now a little decayed. The church is seen most attractively from the road a few yards further on, from which point its spire emerges from a sea of trees. It is a remarkable tribute to the persistence and devotion of the priest in charge and his helpers, who restored the building after

wartime devastation. The essence of the story is contained in th
churchyard, where a sundial reads: 'An enemy landmine fell her
on 21st September 1940'. The dial stands in a depression made b
the explosion which has been transformed into a rose-garden. As th
mine exploded above ground—it was caught in a tree—the destruc
tion was very great, and some parishes would have written off th
church as a total loss. Visiting it today, one wonders at the skill o
the restoration and at the strength of the mediaeval structure whic
stood up to the blast of the explosion. The tower, one of the mos
impressive of the Essex 'pagodas', is a marvel of resourcefulnes
those thirteenth-century carpenter-engineers were Hitler's better
When the church was re-dedicated in 1955, exactly 15 years afte
the disaster, it was not just a patched-up ruin or a rebuilding but a
imaginative recreation, preserving what was worth keeping an
matching the old with good modern craftsmanship.

Among the details of this lovely building I most strongly remem
ber the beautiful and moving carving on the modern lectern, a finge
touching a pierced hand; the church's dedication is to St Thoma
the Apostle.

Beyond Navestock the road crosses the Roding and comes up t
the main Ongar road. Here if you turn—against all instinct—righ
and go towards Ongar again, passing a pretty rustic inn The Wood
man, you will come soon to a turning on the left to Stanford Rivers
The village is a scattered one, and the only readily identifiable par
is around the church. This is a characteristic Essex building wit
wooden belfry and spire and Norman walls. Hardly worth a specia
journey—particularly if it is locked—it offers the excuse for
drive through a tangle of narrow winding lanes, happily deserted
which lead at length to Stapleford Tawney. Half the pleasure o
these places is in the names. Reading Stapleford Tawney on a sign
post, a picture comes instantly to mind; and reality does not alto
gether dispel it, nor does the knowledge that the distinguishin
name recalls a (presumably) arrogant Norman knight de Tauny wh
lorded it over the Saxon serfs of Stapleford. That was long ago
Today there is a comfortable air about Stapleford Tawney. Its ha
and farm are clearly in good hands, and the church between them
even if it lost most of its antiquarian interest in the nineteenth
century restoration, is in good shape now. Its high spire on a woode
belfry is exceptionally tall and slim; the geometrical louvres piercin

ts sides are decoratively arranged. This is a characteristic and peace-
ul Essex scene, notwithstanding the planes from a nearby airfield.

If time allows it is rewarding to stay on this side of the Roding
n order to seek out the Theydons—at least Garnon and Mount;
Theydon Bois is further off and largely suburbanized. To take them
n the reverse order, which makes the better ride, Theydon Garnon
stands remote on a low hill, just a small group of hall, church and
a cottage or two. The church, in an unusually pretty churchyard, is
notable mainly for its majestic western tower, of brick. This, surpris-
ngly, is Elizabethan—the great Queen and her subjects were more
commonly engaged in secular occupations like making money. The
sponsor was one of the merchant princes who, under the leadership
of Gresham, were laying the foundations of London's mercantile
pre-eminence. He was Sir John Crosby (whose great house, crowded
out of Bishopsgate early in this century, was taken down and put
together again beside the Thames at Chelsea).

The Elizabethan age left its mark on Theydon Mount, too. Here
the inspiration came from Sir Thomas Smith, a scholar-politician.
This combination of occupations is an uncommon and an uneasy
one and, as readers of Mr F. G. Emmison's masterly *Tudor Secretary*
will know, Smith was by and large unhappy in his political life,
lacking the skill of Mr Emmison's hero, Petre, in the delicate adjust-
ment of conscience to the changing winds of state. Although he
occupied important posts in what we would now think of as the
Civil Service, including that of principal secretary to the Council,
he liked better the life of a retired scholar at Theydon, which had
come his way through a prudent marriage. He rebuilt the mansion,
Hill Hall, in the very newest classical fashion. It must have been
one of the earliest houses in England to reflect the mood of the
architectural Renaissance. Smith, a philosopher and a humanist,
might not have minded as much as some have done the modern
translation of Hill Hall as an open prison.

Is it the proximity of this necessary evil of our day that keeps
Theydon Mount church locked? It is a great pity, not only because
this is a rare example of a Jacobean parish church, one moreover
showing skill in reconciling Gothic tradition with the classical spirit
of the age, but also because it contains the famous monument where
Sir Thomas Smith lies, all the shifts and deceits of statecraft forgotten in the grave contemplation of death.

21 *Thaxted steeple*

Theydon Mount, as the name suggests, is on an appreciable hill—all of 250 feet—and looks over a scene of quiet beauty in which there are few discordant notes. Can this really be within 18 miles of Charing Cross? and the hills opposite in the London Borough of Havering? Descending the hill and turning left, then right, brings us back to the London road at its busiest as it crosses the Roding at Passingford Bridge. This is, or was, what is called a 'beauty spot' but in the peril of negotiating the bridge and the subsequent road junction no one has time to look at it: a pity, because the view downstream is closed most satisfyingly by the long white bulk of a watermill and riverside trees frame the scene.

The main London road follows the river fairly closely for two or three miles until a lane on the left leads away to Lambourne. This road has no outlet, but no diversion from the route could be more welcome than this. First there is Lambourne Place, halfway along the lane, which is a flawless example of the kind of house built for the leisured country gentleman of the mid-eighteenth century who, if he was not himself cultivated, knew enough to employ an architect who had perfect taste. At the end of the lane where it becomes a track offering further pleasures on foot, there is another lovely house and the church. In a journey consisting, as one of my critics has put it, 'of one damn church after another' there must be pressing reasons for giving one of these buildings special commendation. By any standard Lambourne church is of outstanding interest. First, and, to me, foremost, it has great visual appeal. The first glimpse delights the eye and closer study does nothing to contradict this impression. It has no grandeur but an abundance of that intimate charm which, in a country church, is so much more fitting. In the ground plan it is the Norman church of a small remote community, completely of one piece but with no pretensions to architecture. So it remained for 600 years, unchanged but for an extension of the chancel and the addition of the belfry, until a local worthy, Catlyn Thorogood, undertook major alterations in the 1720s. In the course of these the interior was transformed into that of a Georgian church. Outside, the windows and the west front, with its elegant doorway, prepare the visitor a little for the surprises within. Of these the kingpost in the nave is the most spectacular. This utilitarian structure has been disguised with decorative plaster until it looks for all the world like an upturned

Georgian table leg. Beyond this is the chancel arch, equally lavish in its ornament. Most people's eyes are conditioned to Gothic, but one's initial shock gives way quickly to enchantment. Hatchments and classical monuments and the Royal Arms of George II add to the effect of opulence, gentility and good taste. The whole work is a memorial to the age which built Lambourne Hall and turned this landscape into one great park.

During post-war repairs the mediaeval age made a come-back with the discovery of a wall-painting of St Christopher. This is a late example—perhaps early Tudor reworking of an earlier original—carried out with some spirit and with a vigorous use of colour.

Back to the main road and a mile to the left is Abridge, a small hamlet with Roman antecedents which has grown much since the war. Most of this development is away from the road and does not spoil the old centre which grew up around a kink in the road as it receives the lesser road from Theydon Bois. This has some effective buildings including a very handsome inn, with equally handsome sign, the Blue Boar. Connoisseurs of village design will notice how much Abridge gains by the sharp bend—less well appreciated by motorists in a hurry—which closes the view.

The lane on the left, passing new houses, goes to Lambourne End where there are the last sad fragments of Hainault Forest. These 300 acres or so might have gone the way of the rest but for the timely action of the Enclosure Commissioners in the mid-Victorian period. Hedged in as it is by crowded estates Hainault Forest has some of the shabby melancholy of the southern parts of Epping Forest, but like them serves as a most valuable lung for north-east London. The name of a railway station nearby is the only reminder of an historic forest tree, the Fairlop Oak.

The forest lies along the watershed which at the northern end rises to 300 feet. If you follow the road parallel with the forest through an urban area and then turn right, you come out into open country again and at length to the last undoubted village in Essex, Chigwell. Chigwell now has a large population but it has retained miraculously its village centre and much of its village spirit. In the course of this Roding journey we have seen many delightful places but few so satisfying as the group of buildings around the church and inn at Chigwell.

Chigwell has known many worthies, including John Rogers, an outspoken and uncompromising rector who translated the Bible into English and died at the first of Queen Mary's stakes, but the dominant figure in the village is that of Samuel Harsnett, Archbishop of York. Harsnett was born in Colchester, and was rector of Chigwell from 1597 to 1605. He seems to have been well equipped for preferment in the stormy Laudian age, being strongminded to the point of prejudice, quarrelsome and tactless. At any rate he rose by way of Chichester and Norwich to the Primacy in 1628, and but for an early death three years later might have exercised even greater power. Despite this rise to high office he retained, somewhat surprisingly, an affection for Chigwell, where he founded a grammar school in 1629 and where he was buried. His memorial in the church is of outstanding interest. It is one of the latest of all the great monumental brasses of England and shows Harsnett in all the splendour of archiepiscopal robes and mitre. So he struck his last blow at the Puritans who formed a large part of his flock. The brass has been taken from its original position in the chancel floor and now stands upright—and not far short of life-size—in the angle of the arch leading into the south chapel.

This is beyond question the greatest treasure of Chigwell church which is a small Norman building radically altered in the fifteenth century and about doubled in size in 1886 to the plans of Sir Arthur Blomfield. His work was the present nave and chancel, and the older church was downgraded to become the south aisle and Lady Chapel. The new work is on an ambitious scale but the effect is a little pedestrian. The building looks best from the road, where it seems the homely village church it once was. From this point too you may see its finest feature, a noble doorway, late Norman, which has come down from the original building.

Immediately opposite the church is what is still, despite large scale alterations, one of the finest inns in Essex. The King's Head is the coaching inn of the romantic imagination come true, richly black-and-white, with 'more gable ends than a lazy man would care to count on a sunny day'. Dickens, who describes the inn—as the Maypole—at length in the opening pages of *Barnaby Rudge*, exaggerates as usual, but it is the kind of building that inspires hyperbole. Just along the road, on the same side as the church, is the original building of Harsnett's Grammar School, very agreeable

in its Jacobean brick and with a most charming Georgian wing—
perhaps seventeenth century with a new face in the fashionable
mode—providing the headmaster's house. Later additions are in
keeping. In its long history Chigwell School has had its great days
but none greater, however little regarded at the time, than when
young William Penn walked over from his home in Wanstead to
slake his puritan thirst at this High Church source.

We have held the town at bay for a long time, but after Chigwell
it crowds in upon us. We cross the Roding again at Woodford Bridge,
where it is tempting to turn right through a solidly built-up area
to capture, on Woodford Green, a little of the atmosphere of an
earlier age. This was a fashionable place from the seventeenth century, and plenty of sound, prosperous, Georgian and Victorian houses
remain. There are memories too of greater men than the brewers
and bankers for whom these mansions were built. George Herbert
was here in 1628, staying in his brother's house to combat the first
onslaughts of the consumption that was so soon to kill him. Sydney
Smith uttered his first laugh and Coventry Patmore his first sigh
here, and William Morris was here in the formative period of his
life. It is not them however that Woodford remembers but Sir
Winston Churchill, whose constituency this was, and who stands
massively immovable in bronze on the Green.

Beyond Woodford lies one more oasis in the suburban desert of
north-east London. Wanstead was becoming fashionable among
London business-men at the end of the seventeenth century, as
witness a few surviving houses around the High Street and Nutter
Lane. One of these was Sir Josiah Child, who had chosen 'a barren
spot'—in Evelyn's phrase—for his seat. Evelyn visited the house
in 1683 to see how Child was landscaping the estate and did not
hide his contempt for 'these suddainly monied men'. Sir Josiah's
prodigious wealth came from the Indies through his management
of the affairs of the East India Company. He enclosed a large area
of Epping Forest and here, 16 years after his death, his son built
the first and most famous of English Palladian houses. Wanstead
House was designed by Colen Campbell on the most lavish scale and
around it was spread a magnificent landscape park which received
its final form almost a century later at the hands of Repton. By this
time the house was nearing the end of its life and in 1822, only 167
years after the building had been started, it was demolished. Only

the stables remain these days to provide a nineteenth hole for a famous golf club.

All this would matter little today but for the happy chance that the grounds of Wanstead House escaped development and have come down to us almost intact. Sir Josiah Child had stolen 200 acres or so from Epping Forest; by a satisfactory cycle of events this land is now administered for the public by the Commissioners of Epping Forest. The park is, I think, the best in Essex to which there is public access. Repton and the others had attempted to simulate nature, with such success that one might think the park a part of the forest, but for a certain conscious artistry about some of the ponds, the grotto which closes the vista at the foot of the most romantically beautiful of them, and an estate workshop designed as a Greek temple. The Central Electricity Board, with that sensitivity towards landscape for which they are justly famed, have run a string of pylons across the head of this charming valley.

If you approach the park by the west end of Overton Drive, where the pillars guarding the main gates still remain although the Drive is now a suburban road, you will pass the large formal waters of the hexagonal Basin in which the mansion was once mirrored, and beyond this is the parish church of St Mary. Built towards the end of the eighteenth century, to replace an older church standing within the estate, it was designed as part of the whole complex, the not unworthy chapel of a great house. It is a church of the highest excellence. The bravura of the Georgian high noon is here firmly controlled by good taste. The building is exquisite in proportion and in detail. The original has been altered little. Beautifully maintained, it glows with a golden light. Even the monstrous monument to Sir Josiah Child, brought in from the old church to fill completely the south wall of the chancel, is splendid of its kind and, anyway, illustrates the age's preoccupation with temporal wealth and grandeur. I have a sentimental preference for the Chantrey monument up in the gallery.

If you come here by chance, the odds are that the church will be protecting its treasures behind locked doors. It is wise to take steps beforehand, so that you are not denied a rich aesthetic experience. This lovely building, to which every detail—even the charmingly absurd palm trees which hold up the sounding-board over the pulpit—contributes, is not just the best Georgian church in Essex;

t is at once a building of national importance and a place which
nspires the most personal affection and admiration.

The Roding, which, with its feeders, supplies the delightful orna-
nental waters of Wanstead Park, goes on past suburban homes and
actories to find the Thames in Barking Reach. I am content to leave
he stream here at Wanstead, making its contribution to a masterpiece of landscape art.

CHAPTER FIVE

Chelmer

Thaxted—Tilty—Dunmow—Felsted—the Walthams—
Chelmsford—Ingatestone—Beeleigh Abbey—Maldon

If one includes the tributaries, which are slight but topographicall
of considerable importance, the Chelmer is the principal river o
Essex. It flows through the middle of the county, taking in much
that is important as history or as landscape, and it gives its name to
the county town. Below Chelmsford it becomes a 'navigation' and
in this artificial state is the most considerable of the non-tidal
waterways.

The Chelmer belongs to north-west Essex, where the boulder clay
lies on top of the chalk. It is a breezy, fertile upland country with
only a narrow watershed between the Chelmer and Blackwater
valleys. The actual source is on the edge of woodland near the very
pretty village of Debden, at about 350 feet. Our journey could star
here, for a footpath passes within striking distance of the source
but I should prefer to begin with a fine flourish at Thaxted.

If first impressions are important the way to enter Thaxted i
from the north, running in to the town uneventfully from Saffron
Walden. On either side are quite comfortable houses of the Esse
town kind. Then the road turns abruptly left, and—bang!—the
glory of Thaxted steeple bursts upon you without warning. Ther
is no more dramatic moment in this normally undemonstrativ
county.

After Finchingfield Thaxted is the principal tourist attraction
among the little towns (or large villages) of Essex. The reason fo
this appeal is clear enough. Thaxted has style. It is individual, as ar

for example Bradford-on-Avon and Ludlow. While living uncompromisingly in the twentieth century it refuses to adopt the protective coloration of most English towns and steadfastly looks like
itself. So, although it has no building of the first importance other
than the church, no stately home to visit, no picturesque ruins tidied
up by the Ministry, and it provides nothing much in the way of
tourist amenities, visitors continue to come to Thaxted in large
numbers for the comfort it affords to minds tired of grey conformity.

The Chelmer flows a little to the west of the town and makes no
contribution to the scene, although from early times the river produced the reeds which gave the town its name—the place where one
gathered thatch. It was a place of substance by the Norman Conquest, and by the end of the thirteenth century had begun to acquire
an urban character. The industry on which its prosperity was
founded was, surprisingly, cutlery. This boomed for about two
centuries, and out of it came the principal buildings of the town, the
church and the guildhall, as well, perhaps, as some of the older surviving houses. A string of houses out on the Debden road is called
Cutlers Green, possibly because it was a new settlement established
as an overflow of the town in the industry's heyday. When cutlery
failed in the middle of the sixteenth century, it was replaced in a
limited way by weaving. Immigrant craftsmen settled in the town
which during the century grew substantially to the north. Thaxted
achieved its first Charter under Queen Mary and held on to its
borough status until 1685. By that time its days of industrial greatness were nearly over, although there is ample evidence in the town
that Thaxted men of the eighteenth century could afford to give
their houses a fashionable new look. Little towns like this, if they do
not bounce into the modern world on a wave of some alien development, are apt to fade quietly. That Thaxted did neither is due largely
to one man, Conrad Noel.

Conrad Noel came to Thaxted in 1910 and from his church and
vicarage directed the spiritual, social and cultural renaissance of his
parish for the next 32 years. He made the town a more beautiful
place but, more important, he gave it a new spirit and a new direction. Under his inspiration the church became, as it had not been
for five centuries, the heart of the town, entering into every aspect
of life. Noel believed in Christianity, in social justice, in music and
drama and dancing, and, instead of keeping these things in separate

compartments, he mixed them up into one exhilarating whole. Like all radical reformers, he was misunderstood and reviled, but he left an indelible mark on Thaxted and in the hearts of countless people

I have made much of Noel's influence. He himself would have disliked this posthumous adulation, and would have preferred to switch attention on to other heroes, probably to John Ball, the Essex priest who inspired the Peasants' Revolt of 1381 and died hideously for his part in it. John Ball's words: 'Matters will not go well in England till all things are made common' might have been said by Noel, and he too would have approved the sturdiness of Ball's 'from [the King] we may obtain a favourable answer, and if not, we must ourselves seek to amend our condition'. The chapel in the room above Thaxted's glorious south porch, built 80 years after the failure of the Rebellion and almost within sight of the breakdown of the system against which he strove, is named in memory of the Blessed John Ball, a unique dedication.

There is a very fine bust of Conrad Noel, by Gertrude Hermes, in the crossing of Thaxted church. This great building is as much a memorial to him as to the fourteenth-century cutlers whose wealth was used to rebuild it. It is the earliest of the great Perpendicular churches of Essex and, next to Saffron Walden, the most splendid. Unlike Walden it is an open building. In his egalitarian zeal Noel swept away all the old pews and left the nave bare and uncluttered. From an antiquarian point of view this may not have been all gain, but aesthetically the change was probably sound, and the church was certainly better adapted for the music—for which Holst was responsible—the plays and the communal processions which were —and are—so much a part of Thaxted life.

Most Essex churches are more interesting for their detail than impressive in total effect. Thaxted is an exception. The fittings and monuments are for the most part irrelevant. It is the magnificence of the building, its scale and proportions, and the flood of light which streams through the clear windows and clerestories, which make so unforgettable a first impression. It is, I think, finer inside than out. The tower and spire certainly are noble, but the body of the building I find overfull of fascinating but distracting detail. Gargoyles leer from every corner. They are exuberantly carved and repay detailed study—one is a remarkable prophetic bust of Churchill—but because of them and of the general richness of decoration the purely architectural splendour of the exterior is somehow diminished.

This is a small and ungrateful criticism of a most lovely building. May its spire continue to dominate Thaxted for another 500 years, unthreatened by the airliners of Stansted.

Behind the church—where a pedestrian track links the two halves of the town—is an exceptionally charming scene, with the windmill framed between the two arms of a double row of almshouses. This is only one—but a very good one—of the many pictures into which the old town, its patterns dictated by former functionalism, so pleasingly falls. This aspect of the town is examined in detail in a survey sponsored by the County Council and published in 1966. It is just this kind of quality, the harmony produced by the conscious or fortuitous grouping of buildings of many periods and styles, which is so often squandered by modern developers. Here, in Thaxted, it is at this moment preserved, and the militant pride of the inhabitants provides some guarantee that it will not easily be destroyed.

There is hardly anything unworthy in the town between the Bullring (beside the church) to the far end of the wide Town Street. Beyond this, it tails off in a fashion common to most town fringes. Within this area there are admirable individual houses, mediaeval like the Recorder's House and Georgian like Clarence House opposite the church, but it is the subtle blending of buildings and their grouping that matters most. At the head of Town Street, where the road narrows and curves up around the church, stands the second accent in the Thaxted scene, the Guildhall of the Cutlers. This is worthy of its setting, a fine timbered building of the late fifteenth century, raised upon stilts and with a double gabled roof making an effect equally endearing and impressive.

Thaxted is so fine a town that it would be good to accept it without reservations. Like other towns, however, if less obviously than many others, it suffers from some of the diseases of our century. There is a spacious car-park harmlessly out of sight, but street parking disfigures the best of the town. The street furniture is as blatant as ever, and of course Thaxted is strangling in its own wires. These things we may note and deplore. There remain the many fine qualities which make this so inexhaustibly delightful a place.

Going south out of Thaxted, it is well to avoid the long stretch of main road by turning right immediately on to a secondary road.

Very soon this crosses the tiny trickle of the Chelmer, and then
minor road goes left to follow the river closely. This is landscape o
the unemphatic, deeply satisfying kind, which is one of the hal
marks of Essex. To the west, but not within sight, is Horham Hal
almost the finest of Essex houses of medium size. There is nothin
else which calls for comment, but everywhere a harmony of field
and trees and a few farm buildings. In two or three miles we ignor
a turning left (to Duton Hill) and shortly reach a right turn to Tilty

There is so little here today—barely a half-dozen houses—that i
is difficult to realize the former importance of Tilty, where ther
was a locally influential abbey. This was a Cistercian house. Th
Cistercians, as their abbeys of Tintern, Valle Crucis and Fountain
witness, had a genius for finding good sites. They were of cours
guided not by aesthetic impulses but by the need for solitude an
protection from the distraction of worldly vanities. They foun
these at Tilty on land which sloped gently to the Chelmer, thei
own requirements for water being supplied by a little stream whic
was later harnessed to drive a mill. The Abbey was founded in 115?
and during the next century a substantial group of buildings arose
presumably in the severe Cistercian manner which the Transitiona
and Early English styles so well suited. Like other Cistercians th
monks were corrupted by their own industry. They were efficien
sheep farmers and so became involved in the wool trade; prosperity
which was contrary to their rule, followed and they grew inevit
ably into habits of luxury. These had one result which was to prov
enduring. Towards the end, however, mismanagement brough
economic instability, and when Henry VIII's Commissioners looke
into the abbey's affairs they found that its value had fallen wel
below £200. So Tilty suffered the fate of the other minor house
and was suppressed in 1536.

Of the complex buildings needed for the administration of
mediaeval abbey hardly anything remains. There are in a field a fev
feet of almost featureless masonry. These mark part of the wester
range of the cloister, the walls of the building housing at groun
level the store-room with the lay-brothers' dormitory above. Aeria
photographs show with considerable clarity the outlines of muc
of the domestic and administrative quarters of the monks, less o
the abbey church.

These fragmentary remains are interesting to the antiquarian bu

ot evocative, and there would be nothing to justify the layman's
isit but for a chance survival. All Cistercian houses, in order to
eep themselves from contamination by the outside world, pro-
ided a chapel outside the gate. One of these we shall find later at
oggeshall. Another is here at Tilty. Somehow it was not destroyed
t the Dissolution and a good deal later it became the parish church.
he Cistercians built it in their familiar austere style, without orna-
ent and with plain lancet windows. Then, in the first half of the
ourteenth century, during the brief flowering of the English Decor-
ted style, they started to enlarge the chapel, building a chancel so
ut of scale that they must have intended to recast the whole build-
ng. The plan was never completed. Perhaps the sudden boom of the
vool-trade which had excited them into this extravagance was not
ustained, or the administrative incompetence which was so marked
ater was already showing itself. Whatever the reason we are left
with an extraordinary building, grotesque at first glance—the in-
ongruity accentuated by an absurd nineteenth-century belfry. From
he inside the abrupt transition from thirteenth to fourteenth
entury is less disturbing, and we can appreciate the splendour of
he later work. We shall find in Essex nothing finer of its style than
he east window with its exquisite tracery. Almost equally good
s the combined piscina and sedilia which have elaborate and unusual
racery in their heads. The detail of its work repays study. The
church has, as a bonus for antiquarians, three brasses of exceptional
quality. One is pre-Reformation, the others Elizabethan. In the nave
there is a brass memorial to an abbot of Tilty, Thomas of Takely,
from the fifteenth century, with a Latin epitaph in alternating
rhymes.

This, then, is Tilty, a little place but a memorable one. Apart
from the church with its associated cottages there is hardly anything, except the superb Grange on the hill to Broxted, which shows
the traditional Essex manner at its best. There are a few smaller villages, but none, I think, which I remember with more affection.

The lane southward continues to follow the Chelmer closely for
another mile and a half. Then a road left leads up to Great Easton.
The village grew up around a Norman castle of which the round
motte stands conspicuously beside the road in the grounds of the
hall. There is good unconscious planning, or conscious good taste, in
the alignment of this village. The church stands centrally, scenically

on a little island, with the road flowing around it on one side
and the churchyard path on the other. This closes the view eas
wards. Below the church the curving road is lined with houses of
many periods, one or two of them of good quality. On the triangula
green before the church there is a modern cross of good tradition
design. Altogether a handsome place; even if no individual feature
including the Norman church, is of the first interest, the village ha
a rare harmony. At the far eastern edge of the village, beyond th
main Dunmow road, Moat House opens its gardens from time t
time. The gardens themselves are perhaps over-picturesque, but
is well worth visiting them for the close view of the house, forma
Georgian brick with an exquisite porch.

At Great Easton the Chelmer begins to turn eastwards to cross th
main road. We might leave the river for a brief excursion to Littl
Easton, another very charming village. This is a 'Great House' vil
age, snuggled humbly at the gates of Easton Lodge. This was a hom
of the Maynards who left their mark in the pattern of the village, i
the fine landscaping of their park and the ornamental lake, and i
the monuments in the church. This building is, to my taste, over
ornate, but it has some extremely fine wall paintings, twelfth an
fifteenth century. The Bourchier or Maynard Chapel, on the south
provides a gallery of monumental sculpture. One of the oldest monu
ments is a large canopied chest between chapel and sanctuary
marking the tomb of Henry Bourchier, Earl of Essex and Treasure
of England, a great-grandson of King Edward III. He was marrie
to Isabel of York and played a moderating part in the dynastic War
of the Roses. They lie together in enamelled brass on the massiv
chest. Most of the other monuments are to Maynards; they exhibi
the range of sculpture from Jacobean (Sir Henry Maynard—wh
was Burleigh's secretary—in alabaster with mourning children
classical (Sir William Maynard complete with toga), Georgian (Lor
Maynard reclining against an urn with allegorical figures), an
Edwardian (Frances, Countess of Warwick—a good portrait bust

This is all most splendid. I must admit to a preference for th
group of houses just beside the church, and especially for a magnif
cent barn.

The lane through Little Easton comes to the main road precisel
at the point where the Chelmer passes under it. Here it is two mile
or so to the centre of Great Dunmow. The town has grown u

around the junction of Stane Street, the Roman road from Colchester, with the Chelmsford-Saffron Walden road. It is a bright busy town with plenty of shops and some good inns, probably older than they look. There is a purposeful air about the place which is pleasing, although it lacks the conventional tourist attractions. Dunmow was a market town and a borough with a charter dated 1555. The Town Hall, now offices, for the town was demoted during administrative reforms of the 1880s, is a half-timbered building with modern pargetting; Elizabethan originally, it has lost its antiquarian interest, but not its good looks, in successive restorations.

Although Dunmow has been a place of some standing since Roman times, it has one village characteristic—the Church End is far away from the town centre. To reach it you go back along the Thaxted road for a mile—passing the pond which has its place in history as the birthplace (as it were) of the first English lifeboat—to a turning right opposite a handsome gabled house with a clock tower. This is Tudor and so, no doubt, are the humbler cottages around the bend of the road up to the church. A fine corner house is later and more consciously designed. The whole group is most attractive, and would be more so but for an extravagant tangle of overhead wire. It is as if the providers of our essential modern services, faced with all this beauty, have been driven to an excess of zealous insensitivity.

The Chelmer passes under the road here, although one cannot see it well. It skirts the churchyard in which stands the large and splendid church. This is the typical parish church of a prosperous town built, apart from the Decorated chancel, about the middle of the fifteenth century. The tower is particularly fine, with a west front on the heroic scale. There is a fine display of Essex heraldry above the door. The most conspicuous feature of the interior is a gallery above the south door. This elaborate piece of early Tudor carpentry is in effect an extension of a guild chapel established in the porch-room. Much of the detail of the church belongs to the restoration of 1872 which was carried out, drastically but on the whole soundly, by G. E. Street.

For those with limited time a lane follows the Chelmer closely from Church End, Dunmow, to Stane Street. There is a rewarding alternative route north-east to Bran End—at Duck End, a mile further on, the disused forge is now a shop selling Essex wrought-iron work—and then south again along the valley of Stebbing Broo to the attractive village of Stebbing. The village has many goo houses and one half-timbered cottage of an almost excessiv picturesqueness which seems to lean all ways at once. The inr placed strategically on a bend just past the church, is an effectiv eye-catcher.

But it is the church that dominates Stebbing. If you look back o your way out of the village, just after crossing the brook, you wil see how well it is placed on a slight eminence. This is an importan building belonging to the first half of the fourteenth century. It ha the lushness of detail characteristic of the—in England—short-live Decorated style. Of this the piscina and sedilia are good example The best of the church, however, is the stone rood-screen. Its onl parallel in this country is just over the hill at Great Bardfield, and i seems reasonable to suppose that both came, if not from the sam hand, at least from the same inspiration. Three slim arches leap u to fill the span of the chancel arch, the outermost filled with elegan tracery, the central one left open at the top to contain the rood. modern cross has been provided in place of this, but the bases pu up to take the figures of Mary and John are unoccupied. The scree is adorned with grotesque carving, notably some head-downwar ladies. These are comical enough but they somehow fail to detrac at all from the grave seriousness of this noble work.

Coming from the church, and admiring a lovely house opposite we turn right to drop down to Stane Street, right along this for a fe yards and then left into Little Dunmow. Here we are back in th Chelmer valley again with the river over beyond the railway. public-house sign in the village street is a reminder, if one wer needed, of this small place's large claim to fame. The Dunmov Flitch is known in most parts of the world, even if the knowledg is confused and inaccurate. The origin of the custom is obscure, a though it may perhaps be hidden in the early history of the prior founded here probably in 1104. It is first mentioned in *Piers Plowma* late in the fourteenth century :

> *Thei don hem to Donemowe*
> *To folwen for the flicche*

and there is the more famous comment made by Chaucer's Wif of Bath about

22   *The chapel at the gate, Tilty Abbe*

Chelmer

The Bacoun . . .
That some men han in Essex at Dunmowe.

hat two poets, one a west-midlander, the other a court poet from
ondon, should refer to a local custom is some indication of its
opularity; this although, as Mr F. W. Steer shows in his scholarly
History of the Dunmow Flitch Ceremony (1951) the known awards
f the Flitch in mediaeval times are very few.

The essence of the custom of the Flitch is that 'he which repents
im not of his marriage, either sleeping or waking, in a year and a
ay, may lawfully go to Dunmow and fetch a gammon of bacon'.
he mediaeval practice by which the Prior examined a male claim-
nt became, after the Dissolution, a more elaborate 'trial' of man
nd wife by the Lord of the Manor. The last of these trials was held
n 1751. Thereafter the custom, like many others, faded in the grim
ight of the Industrial Revolution. It might have been remembered
nly as a part of the picturesque past of 'Merrie Englande' but for
he zeal and the showmanship of William Harrison Ainsworth. This
naster of pseudo-historical romance was a colourful figure in the
nid-Victorian scene. He took up the cause—today we might use
he word gimmick—of the Flitch and presented the first of the new-
tyle 'trials'. These have continued intermittently to the present
ay. Little Dunmow is not equipped for a show on this scale, and
ince Ainsworth the trials have always been held at Great Dunmow.
hey have run through a long phase of vulgarity and farce and now
rovide a stage for a comedy in which wit and eloquence have a
lace.

So much for the Flitch. The priory from which the custom sprang
vas a house of Augustinian canons first established by the Lady
uga Baynard, whose husband had fought at Hastings. Her son
Geoffrey confirmed the gift, and the priory was further enriched in
Henry I's reign by Robert FitzRichard and his wife Maud. Their
lescendants were the great FitzWalter family who played a part in
he mediaeval history of Essex. By the reign of Henry VIII the priory
vas in decline and it was suppressed in 1536. The buildings were
lestroyed, except for a small part of the church and possibly the
;uesthouse. The south aisle of the priory became the parish church.
t looks very strange as you approach by driving into a small
ouncil-house estate. The gaunt, imperfect state is not helped by a

ridiculous belfry, not charmingly incongruous like those at Tilty
and Finchingfield but grotesquely inadequate. The church shows it
blank north side to the village, for where the priory nave stood are
only the arcades blocked with masonry. On the south, however
there are five very lovely windows, all but one from the end of the
Decorated period and representing the last fine flowering of this
style. These look even better from the inside, and here too there is
some charming carving of animals. An anonymous tomb, perhaps
that of the founder, lies here, and so do Walter and Matilda Fitz
Walter, whose effigies are magnificent examples of fifteenth-century
sculpture; they illustrate in detail the armour and costume of this
age.

Halfway between Little Dunmow and Felsted is a huge factory
building, not bad in design but overpowering in this modest land
scape. One cannot escape its insistence.

In Felsted itself the Norman tower of the church fights for pre
eminence with a miscellaneous collection of school buildings, some
in public-school Gothic, some—a good deal more pleasingly—in
neo-Tudor. These belong to the great school which has grown out
of the Elizabethan Free School of Richard Lord Rich. This was
originally housed in the long two-storeyed building which also en
closes the lichgate. This, like a very similar building at Finchingfield
was a mediaeval guildhall. It certainly makes a most effective
picture, especially when viewed from the road to Hartford End
This is the prettiest corner of an attractive little town. Opposite the
old grammar school is George Boote's House (dated 1596) whose
upper storey is supported by a curious creature, female with goats
hooves, wearing what appear to be harness or possibly a topless
swim-suit.

The School was a foundation of Richard Rich who was a general
benefactor to the town. His almshouses, pleasantly rebuilt in brick
in mid-Victorian times, are near the school. Felsted has public-school
status and a high reputation, scholastic and sporting. It has, no doubt
built into its traditions some discreet whitewashing of the illustri
ous founder, whose huge monument half-fills the south chapel of
the parish church. Richard Rich was one of the outstandingly evil
people of history. He betrayed Bishop Fisher of Rochester, Sir
Thomas More, Thomas Cromwell, Thomas Wriothesley, Lord
Seymour, the Protector Somerset, the Duke of Northumberland

nd Lady Jane Grey. He took part in that hideously bizarre episode
1 the Tower of London when Wriothesley and Rich racked Anne
skew with their own hands, and he was active in the burning of
Marian heretics. One might compare Rich with Judas, except that
udas had the grace to hang himself, while Rich saw his patrons
xecuted one by one and then went on with the important business
f amassing a vast fortune. He became Lord Chancellor in 1548
nd survived the perilous changes of Edward VI, Mary and Elizabeth
y a policy of acting consistently in his own interests, being influ-
nced neither by conscience nor honour. He died in 1568, a peer
nd a man of immense wealth and unchallenged respectability.
Vhen I look at his effigy, on the monument erected more than 50
ears after his death, am I deceived in seeing some hint of torment
1 those large open eyes? It is a masterly monument in the extrava-
ant Jacobean manner—attributed to Evesham—with a great deal
f symbolic sculpture in addition to the usual heraldic magnificence.
ich's son kneels alongside. (His chief claim to fame is that he
narried Lady Penelope Devereux, who was Sir Philip Sidney's
tella.)

Rich has taken up space here, as he does in the church, which
night have been spent on pleasanter subjects, but he has the fascina-
on of the unrelievedly wicked. If you can tear yourself away from
is corner, look at the rest of this large church, with its Transitional
ave. The best of it is the tower; a massive late Norman structure,
nuch like that at Finchingfield and with a similar little belfry.

Once again the direct route, by way of Hartford End and Howe
treet, is less attractive than a more devious journey past Felsted
Mill. Here the Chelmer passes a tall brick mill just by the roadside
nd follows the road closely for half a mile. Just beyond the bridge
; North End—North of what, one wonders? The nearest place
outh, Pleshey, is a long way off—with several attractive cottages
nd one, timber-framed, which is quite exceptionally fine, arousing
ich-like feelings of covetousness in the passer-by! If you wish to
tretch your legs, there is a chance of a walk here, by bridleway and
ane, to the tiny village of Barnston with its Norman church, hall
nd dovecote. Our route joins the main road from Dunmow just
eside Black Chapel, which is a surprising building to find, even in
nis county of surprises. It is a chapel of about fifteenth-century date,
ntirely half-timbered and with an attached cottage, for the priest,

of the same date. Appropriately, the chapel has a homely air, with its
dormer windows and its primitive wooden tracery. It contains fit
tings which are precisely right for so rustic a building, which has
been little changed and not at all spoilt in the last century and
more.

There seems no reasonable alternative here to a few miles of main
road through Ford End and Howe Street to Great Waltham. This
journey is fairly uneventful. There are the usual pleasant houses
and a cottage with good modern pargetting on the corner where the
Felsted main road comes in. At Howe Street, where the Chelmer
is very near, the road swings round the large park of Langleys and
we follow the wall of this all the way to Great Waltham.

Langleys, which you can glimpse from time to time from the
road, is not open to the public. Occasionally the grounds are opened
in some good cause and it is well worth looking out for these rare
events partly because of the excellence of the gardens, partly for the
opportunity of a close view of an outstandingly splendid mansion
It is well to enter the park by the South Lodge, which gives in
miniature an introduction to the architectural glories to follow. From
the outside Langleys seems typical of the more opulent Queen Anne
country house. (In fact it dates from 1719 but in style belongs to the
earlier reign.) Samuel Tufnell, who came here in that year, was a
London business-man of wealth and refined taste. He allowed his fine
new house to encase an earlier one and so preserved some of the
most extravagant Jacobean baroque in this country. The present
façades are much more subdued. As to the gardens, they have some
degree of formality, as befits the house. There are some excellent
figures and other garden ornaments, and a memorable long vista
from the back of the house, the geometrically correct avenue merg
ing at length with the open farmland of the Chelmer valley. Even
more to modern taste is the wild garden with woodland paths beside
and above the river giving enchanting views across the stream into
a landscape of quite exceptional harmony.

Mr J. J. Tufnell, the present owner of Langleys, has been respons
ible for much admirable restoration of houses on the estate. One of
these stands at the eastern end of the churchyard, the so-called
Guildhall, an immaculate timber-framed house with, it seems, the
tallest chimney-stacks in the world! This was until recently a shop
and in the conversion the finest modern craftsmanship has matched

the old. This is the best house in the village exceptionally rich in minor domestic architecture.

The church is of a scale appropriate to so prosperous a village. Originally Norman and very big for that period, it has been filled out and updated to obliterate all but a few traces of Norman work, so that it now seems a typical large building of the fifteenth century. To the same period belong the carved pews and the noble hammer-beam roof with its soaring angels. Memorials and hatchments bear witness to the influence of Langleys on the life of the parish. In the north aisle there is a most lavish alabaster monument to Sir Richard Everard of Langleys and his wife Anne. This was erected in 1611, while Sir Richard was still alive. Husband and wife recline on their right elbows on marble shelves. Below them, on the floor, are three little coffins on which rest naked babies, one Richard and two 'Anonymus'. There was no male heir, only a daughter who married Sir William Maynard of Little Easton. The deep round-arched monument is lit from behind by two windows with original glass. The colouring of this quite magnificent work has recently been renewed; it must be among the finest of its period in the country.

We might make Great Waltham the starting-point of a substantial diversion to take in the villages of the Can valley. The river Can itself, which rises just to the east of the ridge at High Roding and joins the Chelmer in Chelmsford, is inconsiderable enough, but it drains some very attractive country. A lane immediately south of Great Waltham church winds down towards the Can valley and eventually reaches Chignall Smealy. Some of the apparently old houses here are 'mock' Tudor, but very well done, and the village is highly picturesque. It has the most completely brick church in this or, I suspect, in any other county. Even the font is in brick, and so are the pillars. It is a pretty building, early Tudor, with skilful use of blue brick for ornament. On the edge of the village is the home of the foremost English exponent of miniature gardening, and examples of her work can be seen.

Chignall St James is further south, and perhaps not worth a special journey, although the tiny church has some good modern woodcarving and a peaceful atmosphere. Mashbury too has a very small church, plain Norman work, but seems to be kept locked. There are many fine farmhouses in this parish, two of them, Gatehouse and Baileys, in the best Essex manner.

Beyond Mashbury a lane leads to Good Easter, a village which has a seasonal interest for photographic journalists. The church here promises well, with its very tall slim spire, but it has been left rather clinically tidy after restoration. There are some nice details, especially the elegant Early English piscina and the curious arcading by the sedilia. Opposite the church there is a fine barn.

The best of this country however is at High Easter, the tall tower of whose church is a landmark for miles. Although 'High' here refers to status rather than altitude the village stands fairly high (around 250 feet) and has an attractive clean breeziness about it. As you ascend the hill there is a handsome farm on the left and a lovely garden as foreground in the view of the church. Then, at the crossroads, the road widens to form almost a little square with the inn, half-timbered and attractive, on one side and on the other a pair of ancient houses framing the entrance to the churchyard.

Even those who normally resist the charms of village churches might try this one. Leaving the architectural history to others— there is an excellent guidebook on sale—they should concentrate on just a few things. First the tower, very tall, boldly ornamented in checkerboard flint and stone, noble west door, battlemented parapet with figures of a winged lion and what I take to be a Green Man with club—he is badly worn and might as well be St Michael! Next —a fine brick porch. Then, inside, after a few minutes in enjoying the noble proportions, a careful look at the roof, as good a piece of craftsmanship of the forest country as Essex can show. Next, the font, fifteenth century, octagonal with alternating shields and symbols of the Evangelists on its faces. And lastly, as a reminder that no single century has the monopoly of craftsmanship, there is the rood, an exquisite modern cross of plaited straw which hangs, in traditional manner, within the chancel arch.

The return to Great Waltham may be made by way of Pleshey. This historic village does not show its best face to the casual visitor. Pleshey means 'enclosure', a good descriptive name for the whole of the original village is encircled by a great earthwork. Opinion is divided as to the age of this. It may be an extra-large bailey, or perhaps a pre-Conquest fortification taken over and strengthened by the Normans. In one corner of the great ring is the 50-foot motte with its smaller inner bailey. To this in due course were added masonry walls and a keep to make one of the largest of Essex castles.

It belonged to the Mandevilles and passed from them to the Bohuns and so through marriage to Thomas of Woodstock, Duke of Gloucester, the youngest son of King Edward III. At this point Pleshey came into national history as the scene of one act in an ugly tragedy of the middle ages. Gloucester was at odds with his nephew Richard II, whom he had schooled during his minority and who broke violently away from his tutelage on assuming power. In the autumn of 1397 the king went out hunting from the royal palace of Havering. He rode across to Pleshey where he was entertained by his aunt and uncle. When the time came to leave, the king asked Gloucester to travel to London with him to discuss business of state. When the party reached Stratford the Duke was seized in an ambush, taken to France and imprisoned. By the time that formal charges had been prepared against him he was dead, presumably murdered. Gloucester had been no saint. Most of his career had been dictated by self-interest and he had been ruthless in manipulating Parliament to destroy his enemies. His murder was however so blatant a crime that it marked the beginning of the collapse of Richard's power. Gloucester's body was brought back to Pleshey for burial—it was later transferred to Westminster Abbey—and the castle was abandoned. Shakespeare paints a picture of

> . . . *empty lodgings, and unfurnished walls,*
> *Unpeopled offices, untrodden stones.*

The castle gradually fell into ruin and was dismantled for the sake of its stone. The only masonry still surviving is a bridge lining the motte with the inner bailey. The earthworks are opened to visitors during the summer; their scale is impressive, but it needs a strong historical imagination to recreate the castle in its heyday. It is an interesting exercise to trace the line of the outer ramparts which enclose the northern half of the village and the site of the original church.

The ill-fated Duke of Gloucester founded a college of priests in Pleshey and built a new parish church to house it. The college was suppressed in 1546 and thereafter the church fell into decay, to be rebuilt early in the eighteenth century and again, on a lavish scale, in mid-Victorian times. This large cruciform building encloses part of the original central tower and its crossing arches. It contains two exuberant Georgian monuments, one to the Samuel Tufnell whose rebuilt Langleys we saw at Great Waltham.

At Pleshey we are on the way back to Great Waltham and to our route along the Chelmer. Two main roads come together at Little Waltham and the village street is noisy with traffic. Here is a rarity even in this county of craftsmen, a wood-carver's workshop. You may escape a few miles of main road by going past the church—nicely patched tower with comical turret, Norman nave and later, much restored, capitals—and then along a byway which follows the river. A road right crosses the Chelmer at a mill and joins the main road at Broomfield. The hand of Chelmsford lies heavy here, but there is a pretty village group around the green with an ancient round-towered church behind. From here it is houses, houses all the way into the centre of Chelmsford, and only a little respite can be gained by staying on the east bank of the river, so entering the county town through Springfield.

I find it difficult to become enthusiastic about Chelmsford, which lacks the style one expects of a county town and the atmosphere appropriate to a cathedral city. Its status is due to geographical position, for it is placed centrally and roads radiate from it to all parts of the county. This apart, it is much less a county town than Colchester. The visitor determined to do the town justice should prepare himself by reading Lynton Lamb's *County Town* (1950). Mr Lamb is providing here not so much a portrait of Chelmsford as a composite picture of county-towndom, but his illustrations—he is one of the most accomplished of living draughtsmen—were all done here. Through his artist's eyes we can see the humanity and the latent beauty of these drab streets.

Chelmsford is essentially a modern town, despite its long history. It is commonly identified with the Roman post of Caesaromagus and Roman remains have been found. It was from early times a favourite seat of the Bishops of London, and a Norman bishop built the first bridge and so brought trade and wealth to the town. It grew steadily thereafter, acquiring a market in King John's reign. The Black Friars arrived shortly afterwards, usually a sign of prosperity. Within the same century Chelmsford had achieved its status as the administrative centre of the shire. The town had grown up on the peninsula made by the Chelmer and the Can, and here the chief interest remains. It is not easy to evaluate the buildings because of the extreme congestion which the town suffers almost without respite. The principal eye-catcher is the Shire Hall which occupies an effective position at the head of the High Street. This is a good example of late Georgian public architecture, from the designs of the locally famous John Johnson. The proportions are pleasing and the decorative reliefs spirited. Just behind this, and facing the cathedral, there is a quiet street where momentarily the right atmosphere is caught. Perhaps in a smaller, or a more richly endowed, town we should hardly notice these grave and dignified façades; here they are doubly welcome because of the clamour just around the corner.

Since 1914 Chelmsford has been the centre of the see of Essex. It took a long time for so large a county to gain its own cathedral. The capital of the Saxon kingdom had been London and Essex remained in the diocese of London until the nineteenth century. Then, after some fumbling—it was attached for a time to Rochester—Essex passed to St Albans for nearly 40 years. It was separated in 1914, and the parish church of Chelmsford became the cathedral. The choice was inevitable, although in scale and dignity St Mary's, Chelmsford, was surpassed by at least two other Essex churches. It was, and still is, a town church of some distinction but lacking in some of the essential qualities of a cathedral.

Architecturally, much the best of the cathedral is the south porch, which is in the East Anglian manner. The decorative flint-and-stone work is highly effective. The tower too is good of its kind and even the homely spire and lantern are endearing if not impressive. Much of the external detail is new; the heraldry and the symbolism illustrate the history of see and town. St Peter, to whom, with St Cedd, the dedication has been extended, sits on a corner in his sea boots, clutching an outsized Yale key. The church built at the height of Chelmsford's fifteenth-century boom has been substantially modified twice, first as a result of a disastrous collapse of the nave in 1800, then from the need to provide for the ceremonial and administration of a cathedral. The changes are not all loss. John Johnson's nineteenth-century repairs are stylish essays in the fashionable Gothic of his day, and Sir Charles Nicholson's new sanctuary is in the best traditional manner. There is much opulent modern detail, some quite excellent, a little of it rather overpowering.

The cathedral has retained much of its parish-church atmosphere and its memorials to local worthies. The finest of these is to Thomas Mildmay, a knight of Henry VIII's reign, and a member of a family prominent in Chelmsford affairs during several centuries. The monument is dated 1571, and shows the 15 'pledges of their prosperous love'. This, although exceedingly handsome, can be matched elsewhere. A much rarer possession of Chelmsford is the pair of banner lockers built into the projecting internal buttresses of the tower; these are a treasure indeed for ecclesiologists and a reminder of the pageantry which was a part of life in a wealthy mediaeval town.

The growth of Chelmsford (30,000 in 1936, 40,000 in 1956, 53,000 in 1966) has come partly from the increasing complexity of county town and city administration and largely from a great increase in industry. Large industrial estates are a feature of the view from the by-pass roads, and some of these are of considerable architectural quality, in contrast to the almost unrelieved mediocrity of the new domestic building. The town has often been a pioneer. It was the first town to adopt street lighting by electricity, and much of the early experiment in radio telegraphy was carried out here. It may therefore be appropriate that the most memorable of Chelmsford buildings is not the cathedral or County Hall or even the county gaol but Marconi's factory.

The Chelmer flows through Chelmsford just east of the town centre and is joined by the Can just as the by-pass road crosses it. Here the Can is a substantial stream, augmented by a larger tributary, the Wid. At the risk of wearying the traveller I think we must look, however briefly, at this stream which drains a most attractive and historic part of Essex.

The Wid joins the Can near the agricultural college in Writtle and from here it is a short mile to the green of this attractive town. Before the Bishop's bridge was built Writtle was a more important place than Chelmsford and although the county town has all but swallowed it up now it still bears the marks of a distinguished past. It has for example beyond question the best green in Essex, large, surrounded by fine houses and, alas, hideously cluttered with traffic. Seldom does one curse the ubiquitous motor-car so vigorously as here. If you can come here early enough in the morning, the exquisite taste which found harmony in houses of half a dozen centuries may be enjoyed, despite the litter and the wires which are our century's contribution to this civilized scene.

Writtle was a royal manor and a favourite haunt of King John, the site of whose 'palace', a hunting-lodge in the forest, has been discovered. Through royal patronage it acquired a market but lost the rights later. While Chelmsford grew, Writtle stayed much the same size until in recent years it has begun to show distressing signs of turning into a suburb.

I think that the essential quality of Writtle lies in its houses. Perhaps none of these is of outstanding quality, but there is hardly a jarring note in the vicinity of the green. A feature of this scene is the squat, pinnacled tower of the church which peers over the roofs of two picturesque houses. The tower in fact is the least satisfactory feature of a large and imposing building. It was built in 1802 to replace an older tower which had collapsed, and this in turn was tarted-up in 1924. The church itself, particularly the interior, is splendid. It illustrates the steady increase in prosperity of the town through the centuries of the middle ages, each adding its contribution without quite obliterating what had gone before. All this is described in an exceptionally good church handbook. Much of the old detail is destroyed or falsified in later restorations. Much the most interesting part of the church is the chantry chapel of William Carpenter. Carpenter, the parish priest, died in 1526, and his chapel consequently had a very short life for the chantry was dissolved in 1548. It is a delightful piece of late Gothic in miniature, with old benches—probably not in their original position—carved with animals. The finest of the monuments is an elaborate allegorical composition (by Nicholas Stone) in memory of Sir Edward Pinchon and his wife. The agricultural imagery is spirited, if rather over-lavish.

The Wid passes under the road a little to the east of Writtle Green and skirts the large estate of Hylands. There is a gaunt early Georgian mansion in the park, of which the principal feature—a great portico—was added a century later. The estate was recently acquired by the Corporation of Chelmsford and the park is now opened freely. There are pleasant walks, and these will be even better when the gardens are back in condition. The house faces the main London road, where a long brick park wall is familiar to all motorists; public access is now by way of Writtle.

Widford, where the London road crosses the Wid, is now in Chelmsford and offers no special attraction. I suggest keeping on

by a by-road from Writtle to Margaretting. This cuts out a lon
stretch of main road. If you travel this way on the right Sunday i
summer, you may be able to visit Park Lodge, a small house ju
off the lane on the right, which is famous for an excellent collectio
of wildfowl and still more for flights of budgerigars which fly freel
in their hundreds in the garden. They make a most charming pictur

In another mile the lane comes to the main road in Margarettin
village. This is largely spoilt by heavy traffic, but there is a have
a mile along where the hall and church stand well back from th
road, trapped between the railway and the river. Margaretting h
many of the typical features of the Essex parish church. The belfr
tower is one of those masterpieces of rural craftsmanship whic
belong to this formerly forest country. It is engaging from the ou
side; inside, the magnitude of this engineering feat is overwhelmin
Much of the church is of one period, the fifteenth century, supe
imposed on an older structure of probably Norman origin. Th
north porch is of wood and in a more modest way is as fine as th
tower. The east window is also contemporary. The fine coloure
glass, gravely formal, portrays the tree of Jesse. The font is of th
same period, too; it is octagonal and elegantly carved on each fac
Only one important fitting is not of the fifteenth century. That is th
lectern, a notable piece of modern work with a quite beautiful
composed Pelican in her Piety on the face.

The lane up to the church goes no further, although a bridle pat
continues across the meadows of the Wid towards higher groun
at Stock. With a car you must return to the London road, leaving i
again quickly at the Ingatestone By-pass. In half a mile the over
grown 'commuter' village of Ingatestone will engulf you. Thi
place must have until recently been charming, but the demand
of a suddenly enlarged population have not been met withou
sacrifice of visual amenities and personality. There are still som
good houses, Victorian as well as Georgian, and the almshouse
rebuilt in 1840 make a pretty picture. Early in the High Street come
the church, which is just a little too crowded by neighbours to loo
its best. The tower, when one can get back far enough to appreciat
it, is probably the best brickwork in the county. (Only its neighbou
at Fryerning is a serious rival.) The proportions are perfect. Nea
the south door there is a large chunk of puddingstone which ma
be the 'stone' of the village name.

The village has a long history, but its importance grew at the Dissolution when Sir William (then Doctor) Petre made his home here. The manor had belonged to Barking Abbey. Petre was appointed one of the commissioners charged with the investigation of the monasteries, and Ingatestone formed part of his reward. He is the subject of one of the finest of modern biographies (*Tudor Secretary* by F. G. Emmison, 1961). Mr Emmison, the County Archivist, paints a convincing picture not only of the age but also of his difficult unheroic hero, who held high office under Henry VIII, Edward VI, Mary and Elizabeth. Clearly a master of the art of survival, Petre, bending almost imperceptibly to the changing winds of policy, ought to be despicable. He was politic, certainly, pliable and infinitely discreet, yet out of the tangled jungle of Tudor statecraft his integrity shines clear.

As we are at the church, we must see the end of Petre's story first. He lies on the south side of the chancel, with his second wife beside him. This is one of the best of Tudor monuments in Essex. The figures are in alabaster, coloured, and the altar-tomb and the iron heraldic canopy are finely done. The old statesman—civil servant would perhaps be a better title—lies quietly, discreet still in death. His brother Robert is nearby, and in the opposite chapel there is a lavish and extravagant memorial to his son John, the first Lord Petre, who built the enormous family mansion at West Horndon.

Lord Petre, I suppose, found his father's house at Ingatestone insufficient for his state. The thousands of visitors who come yearly to Ingatestone Hall are unlikely to agree with him. The brick house built by William Petre on the land of the Barking nuns is, despite many additions and demolitions, still one of the loveliest of Essex houses. It is still a home of the Petre's, but for some years one wing has been let to the County Council as a stage for exhibitions arranged by the Archives Office. Each year a different selection of treasures, documents, estate maps and the like, supported by modern photographic and other material, illustrates a theme or a period in Essex history. The material and the presentation are admirable, but it is the setting which makes these exhibitions so memorable. Visitors see not only the exhibition rooms but also a garden chamber with original furniture and the superb Long Gallery which is lined with family portraits. Here Sir William, who built the house and founded the fortune—with more scruples than most of his contemporaries employed—looks gravely at the work of his hands and finds it good. So, I think, do most of those who come here today.

If you want to enjoy this valley of the Wid to the full, you must take the lane in Ingatestone which runs east past the church. This will bring you in a mile to the river and shortly after to the little church of Buttsbury—there is no village—which stands just above the stream. The view across the valley is most appealing. Then there are long narrow lanes and a watersplash on the way to Mountnessing Hall and church, far from the village on the main road. There is a delightful view here, too, and the church, framed in trees and mirrored in a pond, has as good a setting as one could ask. From here it is a good three miles to the main cross-roads in Mountnessing. From Ingatestone Hall the journey can be halved by cutting out the two churches.

The best of Mountnessing is the mill which stands on a little mound close to the road. It is one of several restored and preserved by the County Council, and probably the finest surviving post-mill in the county. Post-mills, by their nature, lack the grace of tower-mills. They are necessarily squat and dumpy; but this one is well proportioned. Here, as in the towers of Thames Haven, beauty is a by-product. The millwright of Mountnessing was concerned not with aesthetics but with making a good working job; by concentrating on function he achieved the clean unfussy forms which we accept as beautiful.

We follow the lane running past the mill through country which as yet holds Brentwood at bay. Across on the right, in wooded country, there was once a priory of Augustinian canons. It was never large and was one of those suppressed in 1525 by Wolsey to supply funds for his abortive educational schemes. The Wid is over on the left, now so small a stream as hardly to be seen. After six miles or so we are at the source in the village of Blackmore, and across park land on the left we see the best known, and the best, of the great timber belfries of Essex.

The waters of the Wid form a large mediaeval moat at Blackmore, enclosing the site of yet another Augustinian priory. It may seem strange that there should be so many houses of Austin Canons in the county, but they were all small—Blackmore had only 12 canons —and they performed a practical function in providing priests to sing mass in the numerous tiny villages scattered about the forest.

,ike Thoby, Blackmore Priory was dissolved by Cardinal Wolsey and after his fall it passed to the Crown and then to Waltham Abbey. Before long Waltham in its turn was suppressed, and Blackmore was granted to John Smyth. His son Thomas resolved to pull the priory church down, but the villagers protested and claimed parish rights over the nave. They were successful, and so the existing church was saved. The church is not what one usually thinks of as a priory; it is a modest building, seeming more homely by reason of its dormer windows. The only claim to magnificence lies in the Norman west front and this is now masked by the fifteenth-century tower. There is some elaboration in the south-east, which was the nave-aisle of the original church, giving access to the cloister by a doorway, now blocked, which displays a curious mythical beast, perhaps a salamander, above it. In this chapel is the battered, but fine, monument to Sir Thomas Smyth, the reluctant saviour of the church, with his wife. The detail of costume is interesting, and there is some hint of portraiture in the face of the arrogant old magnate.

The glory of Blackmore however is its tower. This is in three stages, arranged pagoda-like in diminishing scale and with a tall shingled spire capping all. The effect is both homely and stimulating. Seen across the fields from all sides of the village, it is distinctive and lovely. Inside—for unlike most villages Blackmore allows its visitors access to the lower stage of the tower—it is a massive engineering feat. The enormous weight of the tower and the five bells is borne on a complex structure of oak piers and beams crossing one another in purposeful geometry.

Next to the church is a large brick house called Jericho. A nice story, of doubtful authenticity, is that Henry VIII liked to visit here incognito. His bastard son Henry Fitzroy—how much simpler history might have been had he been able to beget legitimate sons!— was born here; and when the king slipped away courtiers said with a wink that he had 'gone to Jericho'. The phrase lived on.

The best of Blackmore village is Church Street, where there is a very fine inn and several old houses in good repair. Elsewhere there is overmuch new building of an undistinguished kind and the village has lost its original proportions. There is attractive country round, much of it wooded. We may see some of this in returning from this long diversion to Chelmsford. The shorter route is by

Highwood and Oxney Green, the longer and more enjoyable by way of Fryerning and Mill Green.

In 1795 the Chelmer was made navigable to Chelmsford. The Chelmer and Blackwater Navigation from Chelmsford to Maldon was the most ambitious, but not the longest, of those undertaken in Essex during the great canal craze. Before very long the canal became largely obsolete through the development of railways, but this stretch of the river is still a major contribution to landscape. The towpath offers one of the best walks in the county, through country which is always unemphatic but deeply satisfying. There is much wild life in the river and the marshes around. Apart from an occasional lock-house and Ulting church there are few buildings on the riverside and, except on Sundays during the fishing season, the walker will have the world very much to himself.

Anyone wishing to get to know this characteristic countryside should walk at least part of the way to Maldon. For those tied to a car there is a choice of ways out of Chelmsford. One might go north through Springfield, past a huge weatherboard mill and brick miller's house, and so to the busy main road to Boreham and down to the river at Little Baddow. This has comparatively little attraction. There is an excess of traffic, and one has no time even to glimpse the distant brick towers of New Hall, Henry VIII's beloved Beaulieu. The church, off the main road, has some good Elizabethan monuments to the Radcliffs of New Hall. An alternative route is east through Great Baddow, where there are some interesting factory buildings, a church with spectacular brick clerestory, and a lot of modest Georgian houses, to Sandon. There is a pretty green, with the church on one side and the inn on the other in classic rivalry. The church has a really fine brick tower, patterned with great crosses in blue. There is just a hint of suburbanism here still, but going north by a by-road towards Little Baddow the town drops behind as we run towards the river through breezy open country. On the right are the wooded heights crowned with the spire of Danbury church, some of the most popular commons in Essex and largely protected by the National Trust. Our way, however, is on lower ground where stunted willows mark a crossing of the Chelmer and the tower of Little Baddow church stands above the valley. Here on a fine spring day, one may have a satisfying short walk to the next lock downstream, passing a nature reserve beside the towpath.

Some superb elms compete with the church tower for first place in the view.

Little Baddow is a large scattered village with no clearly identifiable centre. As usual the church and hall stand apart, the hall half-timbered and comely, the church large and varied. Though not of exceptional architectural quality, this is a most satisfactory building for its detail and contents and above all for its atmosphere. It is quiet, very light, and self-contained. As you enter a large wall painting of St Christopher and the Christ Child faces you. At one time almost every church had such a picture to hearten the traveller, but few perhaps portrayed with such tenderness and strength. The huge crude font has been newly set on the grindstone of some vanished mill. Behind this, and occupying much of the wall of the south aisle, are two elaborately canopied recesses, treated as a single architectural feature with the piscina. Behind ornamental iron rails lie two oak figures, life size. These are masterly in technique, and the two faces, man and woman, are rendered with a rare individuality. Here, we feel, are real portraits, or if not portraits generalizations which capture fundamental human qualities. These sculptures, from the fourteenth century, make a sharp contrast to the great monument to Sir Henry Mildmay, a Jacobean worthy, who lies with his two wives kneeling below right beside the high altar. Sir Henry puts God firmly in His place, while the anonymous pair in the nave lie modestly in their narrow graves. Arrogance apart, the Mildmay piece is handsome and finely conceived.

Sir Henry Mildmay lived at Great Graces, on a road which meanders off south and comes out eventually at Danbury, passing two other fine houses, New and Old Riffhams. The woods and commons nearby are National Trust property, and there is much to enjoy, especially on foot. A road runs off across the river to Ulting where a plain little church stands right on the river bank. It needed only a little more architectural distinction to make this a really pretty scene.

Half a mile west of Ulting Church there is another tributary from the north, the Ter. This is from first to last a very small stream which passes through good country. A diversion here would take you more than halfway back to the source of the Chelmer—making of this journey a glorified game of Snakes and Ladders—because the Ter rises near Stebbing. You might keep the stream for a later exploration, a rewarding one. There are two highlights in this valley of the Ter. Leez Priory, where the stream feeds a large decorative pond, was the home of the unspeakable Richard Rich, who built himself a palace on the site and partly from the materials of a small Augustinian priory. Much of this has now gone and the whole property is private, but the brick walls and the great gatehouse can be seen from the road. They are among the best Tudor brickwork extant. The roadside scene is highly picturesque. The other treasure beside the Ter is Great Leighs church, which has the finest of the Essex round towers and some exquisite stonework of the fourteenth century in the chancel, an Easter Sepulchre on the north and a matching set of piscina and sedilia opposite. Other villages on the Ter are Little Leighs (small Norman church—locked), Terling, and Hatfield Peverel (where the parish church was the nave of a Benedictine priory). Terling has a tower-mill and a fourteenth-century church. I remember it best for its watersplash, the widest and deepest I have met. If you too venture in, and stick, and conscript a wife into pushing, do not attempt—successfully—to restart the engine just as she is giving her hardest shove.

This is by way of interlude. We are now not far from the tidal waters where the river Blackwater takes over. South of the river is Woodham Walter, once a hamlet in the forest, now suffering a little from new development. There are three Woodhams, each distinguished by a family name. At Woodham Walter there is an exceptionally fine inn, the Bell, with a top-heavy gable. This is roughly contemporary with the nearby church, which is of unusual interest for its date. It was built at the beginning of Elizabeth's reign by Thomas, Earl of Essex. This was the reign when churches fell into ruin; very few were built. This church, moreover, was built surely with deliberate intent, in an archaic mode. It is pure late Gothic, with no hint of the Renaissance motifs which found their way into almost all buildings of the age. Only the stepped gables, charming in themselves, are out of style.

The road going south-east past the church soon joins another heading for Maldon. A mile outside the town, a side road descends towards the Chelmer, coming in a mile to Beeleigh Abbey. This gracious house will make a fitting conclusion to this long journey.

Beeleigh was the only house in Essex of the Premonstratensian Order, the White Canons. They resembled in many ways the Cister-

an Order, in much of their rule and in their preference for solitude.
they chose remote places, away from worldly temptation. In
enry II's reign, when they came to Beeleigh, this must have been
lonely a place as they could wish; it had, too, another essential
communal life, a good water supply. In the centuries Beeleigh
as, in common with most other abbeys, acquired a quality of
hich the Norman canons took no account: it is very beautiful.

The Abbey had its great moments, of which the most notable
as the visit of Edward I and Queen Eleanor in 1289. It was in de-
ine by the time Cromwell's Commissioners made their investiga-
on, and it was dissolved with the other minor houses in 1536. The
tate passed through several owners in a few years, and it is not
ear which of them destroyed the abbey church and built the
esent pleasant timber-framed house among the conventual build-
gs.

The abbey house came at length into the possession of Mr W. A.
oyle who restored and enriched it and instituted the practice,
hich continues, of opening the older parts of the building to the
ablic. These parts include the undercroft of the canons' dormitory,
e dormitory itself, and the chapter house. The first of these was
e calefactory, the one place where a fire might be enjoyed by the
rethren. The fireplace is large and elaborate, with a carved row
angel musicians. This, according to tradition, was originally part
the tomb of Henry Bourchier and his wife Isabel of York. He is
id to have been buried at 'Bylegh', which does not explain the
tar tomb at Little Easton church which we saw earlier in this
urney. Was this a cenotaph? The chapter house, like the under-
oft, is vaulted. It is now in use as a private chapel and is suitably
rnished with, *inter alia*, one of Handel's many organs! For some
sitors, the best part of the abbey is the dormitory, a long room
ith a splendid trussed roof. This was Mr Foyle's library and its
alls are completely covered with books, magnificently bound.

At Beeleigh we find that comparative rarity of the twentieth
entury, an ancient and historic building which has become a satis-
actory and functional modern house with no sacrifice of its archi-
ectural integrity; one moreover whose treasures are shared
enerously with the public. It is a delightful place, not in the least
mposing but quietly welcoming and sitting in its gently lovely set-
ng beside the Chelmer as if it grew there.

135

CHAPTER SIX

Blackwater

Wimbish—Hempstead—the Sampfords—the Bardfields—
Finchingfield—Bocking—Coggeshall—Witham—
the Notleys—Cressing Temple—Maldon—Bradwell

On the map the indentation of the Blackwater estuary is the mo
conspicuous break in the jagged coastline of Essex. From the s
to Maldon it is a great waterway, although a treacherous o
by reason of shoals and capricious tides. It is over two mil
wide at Sales Point and on the landward side of this promonto
its average width is not much short of this. Above Maldon ho
ever the river is so inconsiderable that it may be missed altogeth
Dr Cox, who wrote the *Little Guide to Essex* in the early yea
of this century, seemed blind to its existence, and spoke of the Blac
water estuary as having 'for its feeder from the north th
Podsbrook'. (Pod's Brook, the old name for the Brain, enters th
Blackwater at Witham, well above the tidal waters.) If the lan
ward river is slight, it is an agreeable feature in the scene and
leads to much charming country, to the prettiest village in Esse
and to its most famous small house.

In its upper reaches the stream is now known as the Pant, whic
was the original name for the whole river. Bede used it to descri
the tidal estuary at Bradwell. The Pant is a chalk stream. It rises
the chalk hills to the east of Saffron Walden, not far from Sewar
End and like all chalk streams is clear and clean throughout i
length.

As this is going to be a long journey, we may as well extend
right at the start and set off on the Cambridgeshire border at Ba

low. The village itself is in Cambridgeshire, but the Bartlow Hills are across the boundary, in the parish of Ashdon. They are a group of large round barrows, seven in all, and now rather overgrown; they are the most notable antiquities of their kind in the county. Tradition made them the graves of heroes killed in battle between Canute and Edmund Ironside, presumably by a confusion between Ashdon and Ashingdon in the Crouch valley. They are in fact the burial mounds of Romano-British worthies. Other archaeological discoveries in the area suggest that this was a place of some religious or civic significance in prehistoric times, and perhaps because of this was chosen for what was clearly a most important necropolis.

The road through Ashdon picks up the Pant valley at Seward's End. A footpath here goes past Tiptofts, a hall house dating from the middle of the fourteenth century, but its great historical interest is not apparent from outside. A mile further on, near Cole End, Mr Richard Church once had a house, and the essays written there, published in 1939 as *Calling for a Spade*, making a fitting introduction to this countryside. Mr Church saw this scene with a poet's eye, but his impressions are laced with humour and with a realistic acceptance of the limitations of country life.

Cole End is in Wimbish parish, and down by the church and hall we pick up the river. The church has a strangely unfinished look. The tower was demolished in the nineteenth century and the west end still has a raw look. A late Norman building was here redeveloped a century later, with fifteenth-century additions and the usual Victorian embellishments. The roof of the aisle is good timber-work. There is a most delicate small brass from the high noon of this art just before the Black Death.

Wimbish, even if one includes Wimbish Green and Upper Green, is a very small village. Radwinter is a good deal bigger and a place of some substance at a junction of roads. There are some good houses here, and an inn whose sign is a real plough. The church dominates the village with its flint tower and slim spire. It is an astonishing building. The original mediaeval church was transformed around 1870 under the inspiration of the Rector, J. F. W. Bullock, and at his expense. The architect was Eden Nesfield. The old work was rebuilt or overladen with lavish, highly decorated detail. This process has been continued until now the building seems rather a museum of late Victorian art and taste than a modest village church.

You may not like it, but, my goodness, you can't disregard it. Among things to look out for are the Stations of the Cross, the Font which is engulfed in its carved wooden case, and the magpie south porch. The most magnificent feature of the interior is the reredos, which would not look out of place in a cathedral. This is early Renaissance Flemish work, with wings of matching modern sculpture. The whole fantastic structure illustrates episodes in the life of the Virgin, to whom the church is dedicated.

The people of Radwinter had a distinguished Rector in Elizabeth's reign, William Harrison, who was a fine scholar and antiquarian. He was the author of that remarkable book *A Description of England* which is a major source of information about the social life of Shakespeare's England.

The Pant passes very near Radwinter church and then turns south-east, flowing not far from the road to Great Sampford. We could go that way too, but I should like to make a short diversion due east to Hempstead, to pay my respects to a very great man and to a naval hero and to acknowledge with no respect at all the birthplace of an Essex rascal. To dispose of the rascal first, at Hempstead, Dick Turpin was born, the son of the innkeeper. Legend and romance turned Dick Turpin into a hero who robbed with style and courtesy and made an epic ride to York. As well might one glorify the present-day exploits of wage-snatchers and sub-post office thieves. Turpin was a seedy rogue who died appropriately at Tyburn after a life of small-scale crime. The two great men of Hempstead are both of the Harvey family. William Harvey came of Kentish stock and was born at Folkestone. His younger brother Eliab had property in Essex at Chigwell and at some time during the Civil War had acquired a fine house (now vanished) in Hempstead called Winslow, which he made the principal family seat. It is not clear that William ever lived there, but after his death in Roehampton Eliab brought the body for burial in the newly built family chapel in the north transept of Hempstead church. The Fellows of the College of Physicians, of which Harvey had been a founder-member, made the long journey from London in procession. He is commemorated by a contemporary wall-monument with a noble and convincing portrait bust by the foremost monumental sculptor of the day, Edward Marshall. In 1883 his body was transferred from the vault to the colossal and to my mind unlovely marble sarcophagus which now lutters up the Harvey chapel. William Harvey, whose discovery f the circulation of the blood crowned a life fully dedicated to cience, was by any recognizable standard a very great man, and a ıan of character too, strong, clear thinking and positive.

The family continued to use the Harvey chapel for another 200 ears and to put up monuments in the fashion of their day. Here is ıdeed a gallery of monumental sculptures, including one admirable lassical column dedicated to a minor Harvey, Sir William, who died n 1719. On the west wall is one in typical 'Gothick' style to another Liab, with a long commemorative inscription. This again brings us lose to history, for in the vault below lies a man who moved in ıne with Nelson on 21st October 1805 off Cape Trafalgar and read he immortal signal which flew from Victory. Eliab Harvey, great-randson of Doctor Harvey's brother, was a politician and a man ıf fashion who took to the sea and commanded the Fighting Teme-aire at Trafalgar and after. A choleric man (as, on the authority ıf that old gossip Aubrey, all the Harveys were) he fell foul of uthority, and although he rose to vice-admiral his active service vas curtailed and he never recaptured the glory of his one great lay. No matter; for most mortals, it was enough to have served vith Nelson.

The church at Hempstead was a building of the fourteenth century vith a tall tower. This later collapsed in 1882 and largely wrecked he church, and what remains today, apart from the Harvey chapel, »elongs mainly to the rebuilding of 1888. The work was completed ıagnificently in 1962 by the erection of a new tower, in traditional tyle, which constitutes another and a most noble Harvey memorial.

The lane past the church, narrow and wandering and consequently o be negotiated with care, eventually regains the main road and he Pant at Great Sampford. There is not much of interest here apart rom the church. This however is a quite exceptionally fine one. It »elonged to Battle Abbey and to this owes the richness of its detail, ıotably external niches—now empty—in the buttresses and beneath he great east window, and in the chancel a quite extraordinary louble arcade of canopied seats, one for each of the parishes in the ural deanery. The whole building is on a grand scale. One small letail is especially endearing. An arch into the south chapel has :nriched capitals of foliage out of which peep faces of men and ıonsters and amongst them sits the most charming owl.

The main road continues on the north bank of the Pant, but pays to take the Thaxted road out of Great Sampford for a whil and then leave it by a minor road on the left. A mile along this farm road on the right leads to Tewes.

Tewes is the smallest manor house in Essex to be opened regularl to the public. It seems to me to be quite the most delightful. It be longs to the last days of the Middle Ages. Originally moated, it wa nevertheless built for comfort more than for safety. The principa room is a hall of the characteristic mediaeval kind flanked at eithe end by solar and buttery. The house is timber-framed and plastered The interior beams are richly carved. In its modest way it is a architectural masterpiece. Many of the visitors who take Tewe to their hearts will feel that it is much more than that. Coming to on a sunny day in early Spring you feel the warmth of its welcome The creamy white walls glow. Inside, the wood is warm and colou ful. The owner is obviously pleased to see you. As you walk withou restriction through the rooms and corridors you know, as you s seldom do in a show-house, that this is a home, and that you ar privileged to share it briefly. The furniture is there for use; th furnishings—dolls' house, snuff boxes, corner cupboard—are pr served because they are good and because their owner loves then little touches such as the agreeably unprofessional murals in th bedrooms reflect the personalities of the occupants. And when last you reluctantly leave the house there is an unobtrusively ex cellent small garden, and the moat behind the house is full c athletic and humorous ducks.

The countryside around Tewes is, apart from the usual intrusiv festoons of wire, particularly delightful. Here is Wells' 'real En land'. The lane goes on to Little Sampford village with a handsomel ornate church above the road. The Hall has gone now, but the lorc and their ladies are here, flamboyant in alabaster and marble.

The main road is not far away, inviting us to enjoy the redoub able charms of Finchingfield. If we can postpone this pleasure, w stay on the by-road a little longer, passing a lane leading down na rowly to a ford over the Pant at a tempting picnic spot, and so t Little Bardfield. The Hall here, now an hotel, has spectacular parge ting. The church tower alongside is spectacular too. Its massive rud masonry is surely Saxon rather than Norman; it seems to posse: some of that uninhibited vigour which gave place to technical con petence at the Conquest. The church, as like as not, will be locked, and so we may not be able to see the famous organ, its elaborate casing as dignified and stilted as the periwigged gentry who worshipped here when its sweet tone was first heard.

Back now to the Pant, and to Great Bardfield. This is no longer quite the favoured home of artists that it was between the wars. Some of the houses in its fine streets are a little less than perfectly maintained. It is still a place of enormous charm. There is a town-like complexity about its little system of streets—indeed it once had its own market—and some of the best of the houses are essentially town-houses. Flights of steps, guarded with elegant iron rails, lead to porticoed front doors. The mannered simplicity of the formal façades has been borrowed from the city, or at least from the copybooks of fashionable architects. But it is the charm of such towns that they are never all of one piece. Georgian whitewash and symmetry stand beside rustic half-timbering, wattle and daub, without offence or incongruity. There is matter here for an agreeable hour's stroll before heading away from the centre to Great Bardfield's showpiece, the parish church.

This has obvious affiliations with that at Stebbing, just a few miles away across the hill. Both belong to the early fourteenth century. Stebbing, it seems to me, is a shade the finer building, but there is not much to choose between their stone rood-screens, which are both superb and without parallel elsewhere in England. There is a good early Tudor monumental brass. The church is richly decorated and very well maintained, and is clearly in high regard in its community. Among modern details I greatly like the Virgin and Child which fill the niche designed in mediaeval times for a similar group above the arch of the south porch.

Just outside Great Bardfield, on the Saling road, is a most characteristic Essex view. This is not extensive, but the quiet rolling country, fully cultivated but with enough trees to break the monotony of plough or grain, gives an impression of large scale. The sky plays a paramount part in the scene, and it is good to be here in unsettled weather when towering castles of cloud march across the blue.

Here we are rather more than two miles from the most famous village in Essex, and it is now time to cross the Pant and go up to Finchingfield. I call it 'village' but like Bardfield this has a complex

pattern which gives it just a little of the character of a town. It is
the only place in Essex which has been adopted by the tourists. The
scene across the pond to the steep main street with the church beyond has been photographed and painted times beyond numbering.
(No one can photograph it satisfactorily now, except perhaps at
dawn or in mid-winter, because of the cars which clog its streets
and litter the banks of the pond.) It is as delightful as its popular
image, more interesting, and as yet admirably resistant to exploita-
tion.

This clearance in the forest made by Finc's folk in Saxon times
was a natural choice for a settlement. The hill, a steep one by local
standards, has defensive possibilities, and the stream which flows
via the village pond down to the Pant guarantees a water-supply.
Certainly since the Norman Conquest, and probably before, the hill
has been crowned by a church and the houses have gathered around
beneath its shadow.

On the slope of the hill and straddled across the entrance to the
churchyard is a very long overhanging timber-framed building which
was until the Reformation the hall of a religious and charitable Guild
of the Holy Trinity. Opposite are almshouses endowed by Sir Robert
Kempe of Spains Hall, whose family chapel is in the church. The
church is approached through the Guildhall arch, from which its
massive Norman tower can be best seen. This is capped, not by the
original tall spire which fell during the great gale of 1658 but by
a little bell-turret surmounted by an elaborate weathervane. The
effect is pleasantly absurd, like a bank manager paper-hatted at a
children's party. This however is the only touch of low comedy in
a most handsome and interesting building. It is very large and is the
result of centuries of restorations and additions, but is basically of
the late fourteenth century enriched and lightened by a fifteenth-
century clerestory. Many details are worth studying: the original
south door with carved decorations, the octagonal font held up, in
the Essex manner, by flying angels, the roofs of nave and choir,
respectively Elizabethan and Jacobean, resting on vigorously carved
corbels, the carved screens of nave and south aisle. Among monuments the most interesting, but not the best looking, is that of a
Jacobean Kempe, William, who 'did by a voluntary constancy, hold
his peace for seven years'. This self-imposed penance of silence,
which he undertook after discovering that he had unjustly accused

is wife of infidelity, had disastrous consequences for himself, the family fortune, and the village. He died in 1628. Another monument, to a later owner of Spains, commemorates Sir Evelyn Ruggles-Brise who devised the system of Borstal training for young offenders.

After a walk through the village, enjoying the fine and varied houses with their delightful small gardens and the impression of style and good living, it is worth going briefly north-west by a by-road through Duck End, where there is a post-mill, to Spains Hall. The gardens are opened to the public from time to time for good causes, but the house can in any case be fairly well seen from the road. Spains is perhaps the finest of Essex houses built before the influence of the Renaissance reached the county; that is, it makes no attempt at symmetry but delights by reason of an almost perverse informality. Of warmest Tudor brick, it has tall chimneys of decorative brick and curved gables of the kind we think of as Dutch, all put together in the most haphazard way. The Kempes who built this house in Elizabeth's reign and had lived in an earlier one on the site, continued to add to it through the next two centuries until the line died out in the eighteenth century. Spains was then bought by Samuel Ruggles, and his family, later the Ruggles-Brises, have held the house ever since.

Anything is likely to be anti-climax after Finchingfield, and the next few miles are not of the best. The road runs well above the river—at one point not far short of 300 feet—and comes in about three miles to Wethersfield. Compared with Finchingfield this is a workaday village. The cottages are varied but not all too well kept. Somehow the place lacks spirit. Even the church, pitched high above the village, its copper spire a landmark in the countryside around, does not add up to much. The interior is very gloomy and it is difficult to do justice to the detail. Much the best of Wethersfield is the view from the churchyard.

Below Wethersfield there is on the right a small house salmon-washed with excellent pargetting, one of those houses, unassuming enough, which come suddenly to delight the traveller on a dull road. A mile further along, the road crosses the Pant and comes into the long straggling village of Shalford. There is a handsome inn here and some good cottages. The church and hall are opposite the inn and near the banks of the river. Of the old hall only a richly red curtain wall remains. Across the yard from this is a gauntly dignified

church of fourteenth-century date, with tall tower and batter
south porch. There are some good things here, including some scra
of old glass, the rood-screen and sedilia. What catches the eye i
mediately are three most elaborate canopied sepulchral recesses, o
in each aisle of the nave and one in the chancel. Tantalizingly,
evidence survives as to which local notables great enough to quali
for such splendid memorials lived here in the troubled years of t
Black Death.

After Shalford the road follows the west bank of the Pan
approaching it closely where the highway makes a sharp be
around the park of Abbot's Hall. If the river is not high after ra
it can be crossed here by a ford and followed on the other bank
a quieter and pretty lane. Ahead looms the bulk of Courtaulds' fa
tory, quite dwarfing the fifteenth-century tower of Bocki
church. All at once we are out of the country and in an industri
town.

Courtaulds dominates Bocking today and has done so now f
more than a century, ever since Samuel Courtauld the elder set
his silk-mill here in 1816. The Courtaulds were Huguenots, one
the families who came to England to escape the renewal of persec
tion which followed the revocation of the Edict of Nantes. The
craft at that time was silver-smithing, but towards the end of t
eighteenth century they turned to silk, first at Pebmarsh in norther
Essex and then at Bocking. The family home was Bocking Place. T
Courtaulds had long been minor patrons of art, and this intere
reached its height in the career of the younger Samuel, who direct
the activities of the firm towards rayon and turned it from a mode
family concern into a major international industry, and out of t
profits of this enormous enterprise founded the Courtauld Institu
of Art. His work was of national importance, but the family ha
left their mark also in many parts of Essex.

One thinks of an industrial town as inevitably ugly. Certainl
not many people are going to see much beauty in the factory buil
ings themselves which have spread out over the river in shapele
fashion. Bocking itself remains surprisingly attractive. It is not t
difficult to recreate in imagination the old village with its wate
mill and with a cluster of houses at the gates of the hall and t
church. It is no longer a favoured place to live in and some of t
houses are now past their best, but plenty of good fronts can

seen. The row of almshouses opposite the church, with elegant gable and wooden finial, is attractive.

The church is large and imposing and enclosed with an ancient battlemented churchyard wall. It is administratively unusual, being a 'Peculiar' directly responsible to the Archbishop of Canterbury. The parish priest has the title of 'Dean'. Local benefactions, by the Courtaulds and others, have not always been beneficial. The large modern rood is impressive, but some of the furnishings are oppressively 'splendid'. Recent attempts at recapturing the mediaeval colourings of carvings have had unfortunate results. The very fine south door is so much the worse for the 'tarting up' of the king and queen label-stops. The best features of the building, including some nicely grotesque gargoyles and a huge Tudor-style window dating from an early twentieth-century restoration, can be seen from outside, which is as well because the church is habitually kept locked.

If the delights of the town are calling, Braintree is barely two miles away. I should prefer to keep to the country at present and therefore take Church Street out of Bocking, passing the post-mill, and so head across the Halstead road towards Stisted. The late Tudor Lyons Hall is close to the road along here and the lane is pleasantly wooded.

Stisted itself is very close to the river (now called the Blackwater) which skirts the park of Stisted Hall. It is worth taking a short walk by a footpath beside the church to enjoy the mild pleasures of this highly civilized scene, English parkland and pasture and the little stream, still clear and bright, flowing serenely between high clay banks. From the bridge there is a glimpse of the Hall, a classical building of George IV's reign, and an excellent view of the church, its tower and spire so much a part of the landscape that it comes as a surprise to realize that they are not much more than a hundred years old. Stisted village is attractive, with many high-chimneyed houses of the traditional kind, not all as old as they appear. The church seems a bit of an architectural oddity, but as it seems to be kept permanently locked it is not easy to read its history correctly.

The road going south through the village crosses the Blackwater in about a mile and then comes to the busy Colchester road. If you follow this eastwards, relief comes quickly and you escape on the right through the village of Bradwell—Bradwell-juxta-Coggeshall to distinguish it from its more famous namesake at the mouth of the river. There is not much in the village, but a mile further on the hall and church stand together close to the banks of the stream, here accessible by a footpath which offers a welcome short stroll. The hall is now just a farmhouse, but the church looks very attractive and is of considerable interest. It seems, and is, humble enough with its stumpy broach spire, the typical Norman church of a small remote parish. It has, thanks no doubt to that very remoteness, escaped the worst attentions of the restorer. A richer parish might have touched up the wall paintings which give the building its greatest distinction; they would have been easier to identify, but they might well have lost their essentially mediaeval quality. A restorer too might have been tempted to shift the Maxey monument which occupies, to modern tastes, a totally inappropriate position behind the high altar. Worshippers at Bradwell have for their reredos not scenes from the life of Christ or the Virgin but the figures of Anthony Maxey and his wife and their son and his wife, each pair kneeling face to face at a prie-dieu, and the whole framed most elegantly in alabaster. So the Elizabethans emphasized their belief in the superiority of secular over spiritual values.

The lane outside winds uneventfully but most pleasingly on for three miles or so till it reaches a main road just short of Coggeshall. Places like Great Bardfield and Finchingfield have had something of town character about them, but here is undeniably a town. It has managed to avoid too rapid growth in recent years and is still in its ground plan the town of a prosperous cloth-working community which it became in the fifteenth century. The profits of this industry paid for the great parish church and for some of the surviving houses in the town, and continuing prosperity enriched it further in the next two and a half centuries. The inevitable decline came later, to be followed in recent years by recovery; a few signs in the town, decaying old buildings and unworthy new ones, suggest that Coggeshall has not quite come to terms with the twentieth century. It is nevertheless a place of considerable charm and interest. It has a church which has risen miraculously out of disaster. It has the finest small town-house in Essex.

Before we look at these, however, we should visit an older site, one which stood outside the bounds of the original town. Coming in from the south at Coggeshall Hamlet there is a narrow rough lane on the right, just opposite a farm with a great half-ruined barn. The

ne leads in a quarter-mile to all that remains of Coggeshall Abbey,
 house of Cistercian monks founded originally by King Stephen.
y tradition the Cistercians preferred a lonely site, near water and
way from houses, and here, as so often, they chose a setting which
10dern taste regards as highly attractive. If you go to the extreme
nd of the lane, past a lovely Tudor house built within the abbey
te, and partly out of its materials, you come to the river and to a
ondescript collection of farm buildings, some of which show marks
f their original function as domestic buildings of the abbey. The
bbey church has vanished completely and it is extremely difficult
) visualize the original layout. An aerial photograph is reproduced
1 David Knowles and J. K. St Joseph's *Monastic Sites from the Air*
(1952) and this helps a little to unravel the mystery. What gives great
nterest to the scanty remains is their material. Mixed in with the
int and rubble is a good deal of brick, not re-used Roman brick
vhich you find so often in Essex but native mediaeval brick of early
hirteenth-century date about the earliest examples known in
ngland.

Before the end of the lane there is a small brick and rubble chapel
n the left, with an excellent restored south doorway. As at Tilty, on
he Chelmer, the only part of the abbey to survive intact is the
hapel at the gate. It became a barn after the Reformation but was
uccessfully restored by Bodley in 1897 and now serves a parochial
purpose. The whole group: chapel, house, barns and mill, has very
reat charm and fully rewards a visit.

The centre of Coggeshall, where five roads meet, is an attractive
lace. The weatherboard clock-tower is mildly comical but there
re several admirable houses especially in Market Street running up
owards Tilkey. The great parish church is some way along the Earls
Colne road, next to the Woolpack, a handsome timber-framed inn.
3efore the War this was one of the finest churches in Essex, next
nly after Thaxted, Walden and Dedham. During the War it was
xtensively damaged and the tower was destroyed. Heroic efforts
ave now been rewarded and the building, if not as good as new,
s again among the great buildings of the county. The new work
as been entirely traditional, but the church has gained in lightness
nd freedom from clutter by the destruction. It seems a monument
o the wealth and the civic aspirations of fifteenth-century Cogges-
all; in fact it is equally a memorial to the present-day spirit which

has put the building together again after its great fall. As much as possible of the older details have been salvaged, but many visitors while admiring these, will like equally some of the new work, more especially the noble altar frontal depicting the miraculous draught of fishes.

To complete a circuit of the town, the road past the church may be followed as far as the first turning right, and this leads to the main Colchester road back to the town centre, passing a house with excellent modern (1902) pargetting. A little beyond the centre in West Street is the most celebrated building in Coggeshall, Paycockes. Paycockes must surely be one of the most splendid of all wedding presents. John Paycocke, a butcher, seems to have built the house for his son Thomas on his marriage to Margaret Horrold, and the craftsmen who enriched its timbers carved their initials TP and M among the elegant decorations of the joists in the great chamber. John confirmed his gift in his will at his death in 1505. Thomas was a cloth-maker and his merchant's mark appears several times among the decorations. The house, which is unusually long, has a timber-framed frontage to the street, filled in with modern brick. The timbers are richly carved and the doors have linenfold panels. Inside there is the same opulence and liveliness. Beams and fireplaces are embellished with charming and amusing detail. The house passed from the Paycockes to a related family, the Buxtons, and later into alien hands. Happily in 1904 it was bought back by the Rt. Hon. Noel Edward Buxton, who restored it and 20 years later gave it to the National Trust. It is now open to the public with generous frequency, and visitors can enjoy the unique charm of a lovely house and garden.

In the low country—mostly around the hundred-foot contour—between Coggeshall and Kelvedon the Blackwater goes through a series of contortions, travelling two miles for every one gained towards the sea. The simplest route for the motorist is by a winding secondary road, but I prefer the minor road on the east bank because this provides the excuse for a visit to Feering, one of my favourite villages. It is difficult to say just what makes this place so attractive. There is nothing here of the very highest quality, only a happy grouping of modestly attractive buildings at a junction of minor roads. The one building calling for individual comment is the church, which has some of the best Tudor brickwork even Essex has to how. Masterly craftsmanship gives variety to what can be a very dull medium; the pinnacles and stepped gable of the porch and its little canopied niche, the battlements and tracery of the nave, and a cunning use of blue brick to break the monotony of the red, all these exploit brilliantly the potential of the material. The glowing red is set against the grey of an older flint tower. Inside there is one undoubted treasure and several precious things. The treasure is, believe it or not, a Constable, almost his only sacred canvas, painted for the church at Manningtree and transferred later to Feering. It hangs above the altar in the north (Lady) chapel. In quite uncharacteristic style it shows a large figure rising from the ground, presumably symbolizing the Ascension. Much as I love Constable, at least in his East Anglian manner, I would readily swap this for the figure of the Madonna just beside it. Even in its restored state I am tempted to call this the best mediaeval carving in Essex. It was found broken in ground near the site of Colne Priory at Earls Colne and must have stood in the Priory Church before the Dissolution. Both Virgin and Child were headless, and new heads have been provided with great success by a local craftsman. It was a happy idea to make the Altar in this little chapel out of fragments of stone from four destroyed monasteries. The furnishings on this altar are fittingly beautiful.

Kelvedon, now by-passed by the busy Colchester road, is barely a mile away. Some travellers, of whom I am one, may not even be able to complete this short distance without being side-tracked to Inworth (on the Maldon road) where there is a church with a very early Norman chancel arch and astonishing contemporary wall-paintings. Kelvedon itself is a small town showing signs of the days when it was a stage on the coach-journey from London to Colchester, Harwich and Ipswich. It has some style but suffers from comparison with nearby Witham. As usual the church is away from the main street. It is a very handsome and unusual building, of which perhaps the best feature is the massive nave roof with fifteenth-century citizens playing rather stolidly on a variety of musical instruments.

At the end of Church Street, where the High Street bends sharply, it is possible to escape the traffic by taking a lane south over the river—there is a watermill here set in a scene of placid charm—and following this roughly parallel with the by-pass towards Great Braxted. It is not too easy to find Great Braxted village itself and possibly not worth the search, but the short journey off the road up to the church is justified not so much by this building, which is grossly over-restored—there is one curiosity, the Royal Arms of Queen Elizabeth II—as by the setting. The church stands in a corner of Braxted Park and from the churchyard you can look across a large and exceedingly beautiful lake.

Almost opposite the church drive a lane goes off south and this, in four twisting miles, makes the crow's-flight mile trip to Little Braxted, a tiny village beside the Blackwater. A mill spans the stream here with the miller's house alongside. Next to this is the Tudor hall, and the group is completed by a minute church, Norman and almost untouched until the 1880s. This was the church of a celebrated Gothic-Revival vicar, Ernest Geldart, who left his mark here and in many other parts of the county. Here he filled his church with rather more decoration than it can carry, and the result, though interesting enough, is very oppressive. It is a relief to come out from these dim splendours into the sunlight of the churchyard.

Across the river and under the by-pass, you are quickly in Witham, which is entered from the industrial end. Most of the factories are very recent, and on the whole they have been done admirably. The best of them stops just short of being architecturally exciting, but they have the style that comes from good clean lines and no fuss. Moreover, they are concentrated, and one leaves them behind before entering Witham's handsome High Street. Before the coming of the by-pass this was the main road and had been so from Roman times. Not many of the houses, at least on the outside, are earlier than the beginning of the eighteenth century. They are sufficiently varied, but the general impression is of symmetry and good solid prosperity. Recent developments in Witham have brought new life to the town without quite spoiling its character, and there is no sign of shabbiness in these parts. The rash of supermarketry in the centre is inevitable but a pity, and the new housing towards Chippinghill lacks the style of the industrial district at the other extreme of Witham.

Chippinghill is the old church-end of the town, and has the oldest surviving houses. This must at one time have been a most delightful spot. There is a little triangular green framed with ancient houses and with the massive church beyond. Some of these houses are still in good shape but not all and there is just a hint that all is not well at this end of the town. The church looks splendid, but seems to be kept locked. Those cut off from the treasures within must make do with the grotesques on tower and porch which are the best gargoyles in these parts. There is a nice earthiness about their fantasy.

Chippinghill in Witham is the starting point of a rewarding diversion up the valley of the River Brain. This little tributary of the Blackwater is insignificant enough now, although in its great days it provided power for a string of mills. During its course it links a number of villages quite attractive enough to justify this deviation from the route.

The first of these villages above Witham is Faulkbourne. Here is a straggle of cottages by the roadside and a park, just inside which stands the little church. This is a pretty building, Norman in general plan with a Tudor porch and a characteristic wooden spire. The monuments provide a potted history of the parish and its great families.

One of these, the Bullocks, lived at Faulkbourne Hall, at the end of the private drive which passes the church. This is not shown to the public; it can however be reasonably well seen through a clearing in the trees. It is a highly romantic building of brick, of many periods from early fifteenth century to Victorian, and good of each, a complex and exceptionally fine example of the kind of house in which this country abounds.

Beyond Faulkbourne the road follows the stream through most agreeable open country to White Notley. Here a lane goes down to the river at one of the few places where it can easily be seen. Just beyond there is a charming white cottage with elaborately carved porch. There is not much else of interest here apart from the church, and this is stronger in atmosphere than in antiquarian or architectural quality. The slim broach spire, on a little white weatherboard turret, dominates the village in a satisfactory fashion, and the steep nave roof with its dormer window is a homely touch. Inside, the best feature is the font which is octagonal with a quatrefoil in each panel. One of these frames a nicely grotesque head complete with peaked dome and Cyrano-like nose. A tiny pane of mediaeval glass, in a vestry window, is worth seeing.

The road beyond White Notley begins to show ominous signs of the nearness of Braintree and most of the next village—Black Notley —is distressingly suburban. There is a big hospital here. The church-end, off the main road, alone preserves a rural air. This is the classic grouping of church and hall, splendidly set among great trees. The former is at first sight identical with its neighbour at White Notley, except for its black turret. A second glance reveals the Norman origin of the little building. It is indeed in ground plan a characteristic early Norman church for a small remote community, founded by that formidable co-warrior of the Conqueror Geoffrey de Mandeville. The interior holds no surprises, if one excepts the double piscina and the High-Church atmosphere.

A monument in the churchyard is of outstanding interest, for it introduces Black Notley's most famous son and one of the outstanding men of his age.[1] John Ray was born in the village in 1627, the son of the local blacksmith. At a time when scientific enquiry was slowly ousting superstition he was distinguished above almost all of his contemporaries for his combination of precise observation and broad interpretation. In spite of his humble origin—although it has to be remembered that the blacksmith was a man of substance and a craftsman vital to rural economy—Ray went from the little grammar school at Braintree to Cambridge, where he had a brilliant scholastic career, staying on after graduation as a lecturer, first in Greek, later in mathematics and humanities and occupying a number of college offices. Before he was 30 he had begun the series of scientific expeditions which was to fill much of his life and from which came a succession of major scientific works, first in botany, then extending to zoology, from which was to grow the philosophical interpretation of nature contained in his masterpiece *The Wisdom of God manifested in the Works of the Creation*.

So much briefly for the work. As for the man, John Ray emerges from history as a person of character and integrity. In an age of growing cynicism he refused offers of clerical advancement which would have given him a comfortable living and social status, and by rejecting Charles II's Act of Uniformity he forfeited his Fellowship at Cambridge and his academic career. He was demonstrably an admirable son who, after his father's death, set his mother up in a new house in Black Notley and was frequently there during his Cambridge and travelling years. When his mother died in 1679 he returned to his home village for good. Although he could write to John Aubrey: 'This country wherein I live is barren of wits' there is no reason to doubt that he loved Essex, where he had first learnt

---

[1] The definitive biography is Charles Raven's *John Ray Naturalist*, Cambridge U.P., 1942.

to observe accurately the anatomy of nature. He died in his house called Dewlands—it was destroyed at the beginning of this century —and was buried not far from the porch in Black Notley church-yard. A great man, and a good one: we may well echo White of Sel-borne in calling him 'the excellent Ray'.

At Black Notley we are very near to Braintree and the normal course, following the stream, would be to go straight there. Those who prefer to postpone the ordeal might take the lane beyond the church which leads towards Great Leighs, passing one very fine small house shortly before reaching the main Chelmsford road. Over this another lane goes across to Stane Street at the village of Rayne. The Brain has here reverted to its earlier, and more evocative, name of Pod's Brook. There are some notable old houses by the highway here, although those who stop to admire them run the risk of being mown down by cars hurtling towards Dunmow. The discreet and cowardly will take refuge in the old village, just off this road. Suburbia is breaking out here like a rather refined rash, but the genuine village-green atmosphere has not yet been quite banished. But for the ubiquitous overhead wires this would be a most attrac-tive scene. The war-memorial, in style like a wayside Calvary, stands on a green which is only a little too trim with formal flower-beds. Beyond this, meadows lead the eye to the Hall, which despite restora-tion is still good sixteenth-century work. It was the home of the Capels who held the earldom of Essex in Tudor times. Their monu-ments are in the neighbouring church. This looks magnificent from this distance. A closer view shows that it had been rebuilt when the Gothic revival was at a low ebb around 1840. This sorry structure replaced a Norman building to which a brick tower had been added by a Capel in Henry VII's reign. This latter remains. It is a truly noble brick tower, well up to the highest Essex standard, attractively checkered in black and having a curiously pleasing stair-turret with a knobbly cap, one of the homely touches in which Essex craftsmen so often succeed against all probability. Visitors, even if they are not morbidly attracted to bad early-Victorian churches, should walk up the church path for a closer sight of this tower, for a glimpse of the crumbling but still fine walls surrounding the Hall, and for the gentle meadows beyond the church which slope to our brook.

Above Rayne Pod's Brook meanders just short of the watershed which on the other side descends almost imperceptibly to the Pant.

This is quiet country, except where the commuters have found the village of Great Saling. Lanes wander with no strong concern for direction, and off them are tracks and green lanes which are far more purposeful. From Saling to Stebbing by road is about five miles, by track barely three.

In the middle of this largely inaccessible tract Pod's Brook has its inconspicuous source. We need not persist as far as this, unless time allows for the pure pleasures of walking. No one however, even if pressed for time, ought to miss Little Saling, for which I prefer the variant name of Bardfield Saling. (Great Bardfield is just over the hill ahead.) This is a straggly village with some poor modern houses and a fine old one opposite the church. The church itself has one of the Essex round towers, a late one whose crumbling stucco gives it an unexpectedly attractive texture. This mild quiet building is among my best favourites of village churches. It is beautifully set among trees and ought to appeal irresistibly to artists. Those sensitive to atmosphere will react to the interior. This, thanks to a lot of clear glass, is light but by no means devoid of mystery. Antiquarians will puzzle over the enigmatic east end, rather like a flattened apse, and will ask why so archaic a plan should have been adopted two centuries after the Conquest. Good floral decorations soften the finely austere lines of an uncluttered building.

Here we are, halfway back to the source of the Pant again. To return to the confluence of the Brain and Blackwater at Witham there is an alternative route on the other bank of the Brain. This leads inevitably to Braintree. I rarely like towns and this is no exception. Braintree, astride the Roman road between Colonia and Verulamium, is of historical importance. There was a lake-village here, built in a mere formed by the silted Brain before the Romans came. In later centuries the town has enjoyed industrial prosperity. Today it is one of the key towns of mid-Essex. It seems to me unattractive beyond the average and lacking in style. There is a small flourish near the mediaeval church, where a modern fountain, nicely designed, plays in that half-apologetic fashion common to most provincial civic piazzas.

However, Braintree relinquishes its hold on the countryside around Cressing and in the next mile the road leads to one of the great architectural sights of Essex, the barns of Cressing Temple.

The historical imagination reacts sharply to the name Temple, wherever it is to be met in these islands. Here, we remember, was a manor of those arrogant, greedy and heroic warrior monks who were dedicated to the defence of Jerusalem. Their great wealth, which came perhaps from malpractices but possibly also as a result of efficient organization and strict discipline, attracted envious attention, and the Order was suppressed early in the fourteenth century. The Knights were accused of blasphemy and various immoral activities, and many of them suffered a hideous fate. There may have been something in the charges; certainly the Order was sufficiently prosperous to justify the 'framing' of false accusations by enemies whose avarice was stronger than their scruples.

The possessions of the Templars went to the rival order of Knights Hospitallers, among them Cressing Temple. The Templars' house is long vanished, but the barns survive as indisputable evidence of their wealth. The Barley Barn is 120 feet long and 42 wide. The Wheat Barn is a shade narrower but goes to 160 feet in length. It was long assumed that they belonged to the end of the mediaeval period, perhaps built after the commandery was sacked in the Peasants' Revolt of 1381; recent scientific tests however suggest that these utilitarian structures are 800 years old. It is no exaggeration to say that these superb buildings, privately owned and not accessible but well enough seen from the road, are among the wonders of England. They represent a peak of achievement in rural craftsmanship, and in their setting of trees and fields they are surpassingly beautiful.

The road past Cressing Temple follows the Brain straight and uneventfully to Witham, and so if time presses may the visitor. A minor extension of the journey may be undertaken by way of Silver End, a modern industrial estate among the cornfields serving the Crittall factory, to Rivenhall. Short of the latter village the road skirts a rather sad reminder of past glories, Rivenhall Place. The house, glimpsed in the trees, belonged to a patron of the last great exponent of the English art of landscape design, Humphry Repton, Repton, who lived in Essex, worked here for Charles Callis Western around 1794. The disposition of the now-overgrown trees was no doubt his work, and so certainly was the lake which is today so attractive to the passing eye and to the angler.

Rivenhall village itself is of minor interest, and one might pass with only a glance the neo-Gothic church with its slightly absurd white tower. A Victorian parson brought back some mediaeval glass from France and set it in the east window. The setting may be quite incongruous, but the glass is the finest in the county. There are three lights, of which the central shows fine medallions exquisite in design and jewel-like in colour.

The road comes out at the industrial end of Witham, whence our main route is some two miles distant.

I must admit to finding the country south of Witham, whether viewed from the main road or the tangle of lanes around Wickham Bishops, just a little dull. Whichever route is taken comes in time to Langford. Here are some notable houses, including one, the hall, which might be taken as the type of the country gentleman's residence of Queen Anne's day. This is well seen from the churchyard. As to the church, this may be dismissed at a glance as late Victorian Gothic at its least exciting. A second look may show that something is very odd here, for the church has an apse, what is more an apse at the wrong end. Here at Langford is the only survival in England of a western apse. This was a feature of pre-Norman churches in western Europe and may have been common enough in this country too. What a pity that the eastern apse, which doubtless completed the design, has been lost. Even without it Langford church is of unique interest to the collector of village churches; it is also surprisingly satisfying to the eye.

After Langford there is unrelieved main-road to Heybridge and then across the canal and up a steep little hill to the centre of Maldon.

It is doubtful whether Maldon is cherished more by the historian than the sportsman. It is, next to Burnham, the principal yachting centre in Essex and the base for the sailing barges which, after long service to commerce, now provide the finest spectacle in these waters when they go out for their annual races. The historian knows Maldon as the main Essex port in mediaeval times, as the scene of a battle which had its part in the forging of England, and as the oldest borough in Essex.

Of all this former greatness not much meets the casual visitor's eye. Apart from the churches little remains of mediaeval Maldon. The Moot Hall in the High Street was built by Robert D'Arcy in the mid-fifteenth century; it is a brick tower with later additions. Most of the old houses in the town were rebuilt or given a new look in the

Georgian age. Many of them deserve a second look, especially two substantial inns.

There are, or were, three parish churches. The middle one of these, St Peter's at the corner of High Street and Market Hill, became ruinous during the seventeenth century, and an enterprising cleric, Dr Plume, Archdeacon of Rochester, demolished all but the tower and put up on the site a handsome building to house his library. This he presented to the town and it survives today, the ground floor providing a home for the County Library, the upper left in all its Queen Anne dignity. Down by the river, and on the edge of an area of playing fields and pleasure grounds, is St Mary's, whose brick tower and spike are a landmark for yachtsmen coming up the Blackwater. It is the oldest of these churches in origin and still shows some Norman work. All Saints, in the High Street, is a most distinguished building, spoilt by some inept restoration but still a worthy civic church for an historic town. The most conspicuous feature, but not the most notable, is the very strange triangular tower, which has not, I believe, its like in England. Presumably it was designed thus to fit an awkwardly crowded town site.

For the sake of completeness, and because such remains are rare in Essex, one should go along Spital Street for about half a mile to see the ruins of St Giles Hospital. This was a leper hospital—were there really all those lepers in mediaeval England?—founded in the reign of Henry II and, if archaeological evidence is interpreted aright, built on the site of an older foundation. Part of the chapel, belonging to the turn of the twelfth century, remains in a little garden. The ruins are not without a certain visual appeal.

Maldon's 'finest hour' belonged to an earlier age. The Anglo-Saxon Chronicle says tersely under the year 991: 'This year . . . was Alderman Brithnoth slain at Maldron.' There our knowledge would have rested but for the chance survival of a manuscript description of the battle. *The Battle of Maldon* is among the most remarkable of all Old English poems which have come down to us. It is not an epic, which is a narrative pondered and matured and given a universal interpretation, but a partisan narrative; if not an eyewitness account, at least one—like the best kind of modern journalism—which is written out of the experiences of eye-witnesses.

To visit the scene, you must go out on the Burnham road for a mile or so till a rough road goes left towards the estuary. A marshy island, Northey, is joined to the mainland here by a causeway which goes under water at high tide. Here the Danish horde was encamped when the East Anglian Alderman Byrhtnoth arrived on the shore with an army. There was an exchange of abuse and challenges, but the two forces could not get at one another because of the tide. When the water went down the Saxon leader rashly, or chivalrously, allowed the Danes to land and give battle. Byrhtnoth was killed, and one by one the Saxon warriors, each one called by name in the poem, fell. The English defeat was total, but the poet finds in their desperate defiance a kind of triumph.

> *Will shall be tougher, courage keener,*
> *Spirit grow great as our strength lessens*

says old Byrhtwold, words which have been remembered and echoed with profit at other times of national disaster.

Within view of Northey and the mud wastes of the Blackwater estuary, we are on the last stage of this long journey. Our road runs steadily away from the river, and tempting byways on the left all peter out in the marsh or at the sea-wall. At Latchingdon the main road goes south and we leave it in favour of a lesser one which goes off to Mayland, Steeple and St Lawrence, attractive names but villages with little enough to offer.

This long tortuous road, if persisted in to the end, leads to the waterfront of the estuary almost under the substantial shadow of the nuclear power station. A mile short of this, however, a couple of lanes go off right to the town-like centre of Bradwell. Bradwell-on-Sea it calls itself now. The old name—Bradwell-juxta-Mare—was less misleading, as the nearest sea, distinct from river estuary, is three miles or so away and even then between shore and tide lies a wide belt of salting. Never mind. The charms of Bradwell depend in no wise on the sea.

Happily, Bradwell has relatively little through-traffic, for even the secondary road coming up from Burnham by-passes it. The village has had the chance to develop some personality of its own, and this the visitor senses, just as he senses that he is in some way an intruder. There is an agreeable self-absorbment about the cottages, most of them pleasant if none are distinguished, which cluster around the church. Nearby is one large house, Bradwell Lodge, memorable for the kind of look-out cupola with which it is capped and which softens its severe symmetry. Visitors are welcomed here throughout the summer. Immediately adjoining the churchyard, and making an amusing full-stop to a terrace of cottages, the line of whose billowing tiled roofs is broken by dormers, is the diminutive lock-up. One hopes that Bradwell was never much troubled by crime, for even two prisoners would be at least one too many here.

The church stands in a commanding position at the junction of roads. It is mostly an eighteenth-century remodelling of the mediaeval church, pleasing enough visually but with no great antiquarian interest. The font shows a carved face which despite, or perhaps because of, its shattered nose is surprisingly Churchillian. The gallery at the rear of the church is dominated by a restored and gaily gaudy Royal Arms.

The road past the church, discouragingly faint on the map, continues for about two miles to a farm where cars may be left. The track continues, straight as befits its Roman origin, towards the distant sea. Trees lining the roadside and a small barn-like building at the end of the track alone relieve the dead flatness of the scene. Nowadays this country is no longer inaccessible and there are usually people about. Somehow it still seems remote and quiet as if where the track drops over the low cliffs to the saltings is a land's-end.

So it is, but it is also a beginning, for here is the opening of a major chapter—some might say the greatest—in Essex history. Within the crumbling walls of a Roman fortress the Christian mission to the East Saxons was launched here in the year 653.

This story should begin even further back in the third century and have for hero a vigorous and unconventional warrior named Carausius. Bede said that Carausius was 'of very mean birth, but an expert and able soldier'. He was certainly an ambitious one who manipulated the disorders of Diocletian's reign to put himself in power in both Gaul and Britain. During the brief years of his 'reign', when he had coins struck with his own bearded and bibulous head on them, Carausius prepared for the inevitable counter-attack from Rome by setting up a series of strongpoints around the coast from the Wash to Southampton Water. These were admirably suited as bases for naval operations of which he was a master. In the event Carausius was defeated by treachery on his own staff. His coastal fortresses came into their own during the next century and a hal as Forts of the Saxon Shore, used for operations against the Saxo pirates whose raids were now being intensified into invasion.

One of these forts was Othona, which is usually identified with this tip of the Essex coast. Certainly there was a Roman fort here for excavations a hundred years ago revealed enough of the wall to show that it was originally roughly rectangular, with 12-foo thick walls. Like all the surviving Saxon Shore forts except Port chester only about half remains and the rest has now fallen into the sea. In the time of the Saxon raids Othona was manned by auxiliarie from North Africa, supplemented later no doubt by local force who were left in control when the legions were finally recalled fo. the defence of Rome. No evidence or tradition remains to show whether the fortress fell easily to the invading hordes or whethe it was carried, like Anderida, in a desperately heroic last action.

When Augustine arrived for the conversion of the English in 59; he made his peaceful bridgehead in the principal Saxon Shore for at Richborough. Seven years later he commissioned Mellitus to carry out the conversion of the East Saxons as Bishop of London. Mellitu made some progress in this task under the patronage of the Eas Saxon King Sabert, a vassal of the Kentish King Ethelbert. Mellitus' mission came to an abrupt end when Sabert died in 616 and his son. reverted to an uncompromising paganism. Essex remained in thi state until 653, when the Northumbrian King Oswy persuade Sigebert of the East Saxons to receive another mission, this time le by Cedd. Cedd was one of Aidan's graduates from Lindisfarne, traine in one of the most advanced and active centres in Europe. He wa of a most remarkable family; there were four brothers, all of whom became priests, and two, Cedd and Chad, became bishops—'a rar thing to be met with', is Bede's comment.

Like Augustine, Cedd made his landfall at a Saxon Shore fort Othona, which the Saxons called Ithancester, was a natural choice However decayed the Roman buildings, they offered some shelte on an inhospitable marshy coast, and what remained of the Roma road led inland along a low ridge which provided the only dry rout to what was to become Cedd's diocese.

There seems no reason to doubt that the tiny chapel which stil remains on the shore at Bradwell was built by Cedd as the base fo his mission, to be in effect his cathedral. By a happy chance, or mor

kely by calculated choice, the building was erected on the founda-
ions of the Roman wall and gateway so that it had the support of
oman engineering and cement. This, together with the remote
ituation and the early abandonment of Ithancester in favour of the
iore sheltered settlement of Bradwell inland, explains how such a
uilding should survive for 1,300 years. It was strongly based, and
: was worth no one's while to destroy or change it.

Go inside and be still. The peace and the silence of this place
ivades you. Here, if anywhere in these islands, one gets a sense of
ime and of timelessness. Here is a building as plain as could well be,
xternally a rectangle relieved only by flat buttresses in the familiar
axon manner at the west end (for no trace remains of the original
astern apse and *portici*), internally severe and unadorned except
or the modern rood. What impresses the visitor most, after the still-
iess, is the scale. This is a strikingly tall building, even before taking
ccount of the normal rise of the ground level over these centuries.
he early Saxons built boldly, here and elsewhere, raising high slim
valls of Roman brick, rubble and other debris from the decaying
ort and bonding them with strong cement.

It may seem absurd to speak of so plain a building, which served
vithout incongruity for at least two centuries as a barn, as beauti-
ul, and yet no other word is acceptable.

Aesthetics cannot here be separated from history and sentiment.
he chapel of St Peter's on the Wall is old almost beyond imagining.
t is directly associated with a vital period of history, a time when the
irst shafts of light were breaking into the Dark Ages. It has sim-
licity and fine proportions. A visit here, on foot as all such pilgrim-
ges should be, is an unforgettable experience.[1]

The impression left by St Peter's is accentuated by the loneliness
if the site. There is only one cottage nearby and that is hidden be-
ind the swell of the Roman wall, a short stretch of which is exposed
iere. The only blemish in the scene is a modern timber vestry built,
vith striking lack of discretion, beside the entrance to the chapel.
Beyond is the sea-wall, on one side the bird-infested acres of salt
nud, on the others a wide view of fertile flats, at their most lovely
n early spring when the newly ploughed land glows pale gold in
he thin sunlight. In the distance, against the blue of the estuary, is

---

[1] The official guide: *The Fort of Othona and the Chapel of St Peter-on-the-Wall*,
y H. Malcolm Carter, is a model of its kind.

the vast block of Bradwell Power Station. How one hated the ide
of a monument to twentieth-century materialism within sight of th
cradle of East Saxon Christianity; it was a proposal insensitive eve
by the standards of the Central Electricity Board. In fact it ha
turned out remarkably well. Those massive cubes, their bulk scale
down by distance, make a satisfactory point of interest in the wid
largely featureless view.

CHAPTER SEVEN

Colne

Birdbrook—Castle Hedingham—the Maplesteads—
Halstead—the Colnes—Colchester—Mersea—
Wivenhoe—Brightlingsea—St Osyth

he River Colne gives its name to the oldest and most important
wn in Essex. Or does it? It is a common river name, as Colne in
ertfordshire and Coln in Gloucestershire witness, as well as the
etathesized form Clun in Shropshire. The word, like so many river
ames, is Celtic. Despite this evidence, I find it difficult to ignore
e conflicting fact that the Roman name for Colchester was *Colonia*
he Colony). It is not unknown for a river to derive its name by this
ind of back-formation from a principal town on its banks; the
run in Sussex was originally the Tarrant.

The river crosses the county from very near the Suffolk border
the estuary beyond Colchester. There is a narrow watershed at
ther more than 300 feet a few miles south of Haverhill. The
orthern face drains to the Stour barely two miles away. On the
uth a tiny trickle comes out of Moyns Park, a large estate with
art of an Elizabethan manor-house. This is private, but a public
ath crosses the park and comes out along a fine avenue to the
eginning of Birdbrook village.

It is an auspicious start to our journey. There are fewer lovelier
illages than Birdbrook, and a happy chance has kept it unspoilt and
ncrowded. There is nothing more than a single street, and no
ouse in it qualifies for mention by Dr Pevsner. Lucky place so to
reserve its anonymity? One would not wish one house away or
hanged. Every typical Essex style and material is represented here,

brick, timber, parge-work, thatch, all without ostentation and wit
rare craftsmanship.

These are the qualities found too in the church. One feels th
immediately. There is nothing exciting about the architecture, bu
discreet good taste has been set to work in the churchyard to pr
duce a little garden. Inside the building the same spirit has bee
active. There are treasures here, some imported, some of goo
modern—and one suspects local—craftsmanship. The furnishing
of the sanctuary are particularly good. Money has been spent gene
ously, but quiet perfection of this quality needs more than wealt
to achieve.

There is an amusing tablet on the west wall of the tower, com
memorating the achievements of Martha Blewitt who was 'th
wife of nine husbands successively, buried 8 of them, but last of al
the woman dyed allso, was buried May 7, 1681', as well as a late
Robert Hogan, much married also. Such Herculean matrimoni
labours make it easier to appreciate the monument to a Harvey a
Hempstead who is described deprecatingly as having an 'only wife

Just beyond Birdbrook church a lane wanders away in a roughl
easterly direction through exceptionally pleasing country. Th
distinguishing feature of this landscape, as it is of the very differen
Thameside country, is the wayside elm and there are some nobl
specimens. The road follows for a time the track of a disuse
railway. Here wild flowers grow in colourful wastefulness an
rabbits abound. In two miles the road turns to cross the track an
comes to Ridgewell.

Ridgewell is on the main Halstead road. It is a large village, b
the standards of this quiet country, and a mixture of styles an
qualities. The central green is pretty, and there are a few fine co
tages facing it. There is, however, some dilapidation of a kind on
does not expect in so favoured an area. The church stands well bac
beyond the green with a background of meadows. It is a larg
fifteenth-century building with a tall tower, fine in a slightly gaun
and austere fashion. The best of it is the nave roof, where fores
craftsmen were at work, as they were also on the rood-screen.

A pond behind the church is the source of a small tributary of th
Colne, joining it at Great Yeldham. Our direct route is along th
main road, but, as always, I prefer a more circuitous journey (whic
involves a brief return along our approach road) by way of Stam

ourne and Toppesfield. Neither place is of outstanding interest, but
hey are characteristic villages of the north Essex country, and the
ourney is by quiet lanes. Much of the new development at Stam-
ourne is towards the green, and we shall avoid this by turning left
ast the church and inn. The latter (the *Lion*) is worth a close look.
t is early Tudor and has a heavy carved beam supporting the over-
ang. The church, immediately opposite, is best remembered—not
lways with admiration—for its massive and disproportionately
vide tower. It is a little like Finchingfield and of the same Norman
ate, but the mass lacks any relief. It would be a pity to dwell on
his, for there are good things to be seen here. The body of the
hurch was rebuilt, probably in the late fifteenth and early sixteenth
enturies, under the patronage of the Macwilliam family. The new
vindows were provided with elaborately canopied niches to con-
ain now-vanished statues. On the arch between chancel and north
hapel was carved the achievement of Henry Macwilliam, a remark-
ble piece of heraldic sculpture, formally correct but adapted effect-
vely to its setting. The same concern for heraldry is seen in the east
vindow with its contemporary glass. So, in this remote parish, the
ge of chivalry died with a fine flourish.

The rood-screen belongs probably to the same period. It is plain
vork, made interesting by the survival of one side of four painted
panels. These are debased work of the kind familiar at its best in
he great Norfolk screens like Ranworth and Barton Turf. The figures
epresented are historical (or mythical), not Biblical: St Denis, head
n hands, St George, St Edmund holding one of the arrows that slew
im, and an unidentified king—the antelope suggests that it is
Henry VI.

Stambourne had a part in the upbringing of that most celebrated
of dissenting preachers of the Victorian age, Charles Spurgeon. He
vas born at Kelvedon, in central Essex, of an old nonconformist
amily. In childhood he came to Stambourne to live with his grand-
ather at the manse. Here he made his first acquaintance with the
iches of the Puritan heritage. It was in Essex too that he experienced
is personal enlightenment in the improbable setting of a Primitive
Methodist chapel in Colchester, and this was to set him on the road
o London and to outstanding fame.

Toppesfield, a few miles further on, has rather more intrusive
modern building. It is within commuting distance of Haverhill and

7 *Pargetting at Earls Colne*

Halstead as well as the factories of Hedingham. It is a more closely integrated village than most, with the church at its centre. This is much the best thing here. The building is of brick, early Tudor with the exception of a handsome tower. This, in a most interesting in scription, is dated 1699; it has unusual and elaborate pinnacles and other decorations. There are a number of monuments, notable a lavish baroque memorial to Dorcas Smyth with symbolic devices A less ostentatious tablet, to Sarah Howlett, has a touching epitaph :

> Enriched with uncommon extent and variety of attainment, of which she was so far from making an ostentatious display that she seemed unconscious that she possessed them. Nay, the degrading conception she unhappily formed of her own virtues, moral and intellectual, were probably the cause of unsupportable suffering

Had poor Sarah lived today, she might have derived comfort from psychiatric treatment and enjoyed a tranquil girlhood. She died in 1793 at 18.

The lanes around Toppesfield invite independent exploration The countryside is full of charm—and surprises. Near here I found a peacock in a muck-cart. Our present course must be to Great Yeld ham, a village which suffers by being stretched out on the rack of a main road. It is at its best at the cross-roads, where lanes go off north and east into some of my favourite country, to the Belchamps which we shall visit on the next journey and Tilbury—Tilbury juxta-Clare to distinguish it from its namesake on Thameside. A beautifully situated brick church here. Great Yeldham has one famous possession, an oak. It stands on a small green at the cross roads, immensely ancient and immeasurably scarred and battered by the years. If, as seems likely, it has now entered its last century, there is promise of continuity in the nearby tree which was planted in 1865 to commemorate the wedding of Edward, Prince of Wales, to Princess Alexandra.

Great Yeldham church stands on the main road a little to the north of the great oak. It is a handsome early fifteenth-century building with a very tall and elaborate tower. This has the stepped battlements and pinnacles so characteristic of Essex towers and decorative double buttresses at each angle. The south porch is a curiosity. Was it, as Dr Pevsner suggests, a first false start on a south-west tower? Clearly the third stage with its brick gable is an after-thought, a slightly unworthy one but not without a little charm. The rood-screen remains, pleasantly adorned with little animals as well as more conventional heraldic ornament. The lower panels on one side are painted, in just the same style as those which we saw a few miles back at Stambourne. They must surely be from the same hand, not a very skilled one; but can it be only coincidental that two half-sets of panels together make one whole? The helpful rector's wife who showed me this church had an ingenious explanation based on mediaeval dishonesty—or resourcefulness.

The main road runs very close to the Colne all the way to Heding-ham. At Nunnery Bridge we turn off left with the grey towers of the castle ahead showing above the trees.

Castle Hedingham is a small town which grew up under the shadow of one of the two great fortresses of mediaeval Essex. It was the principal home of the powerful family of De Vere. Aubrey de Vere fought at Hastings and was richly rewarded by the Conqueror. His son, another Aubrey (or Alberic), built a castle to control his Essex estates. This was in the period of anarchy that followed William's death, and the purpose of the castle was protective rather than strategic. It represented probably the last word in military architecture of its day. The walls were immensely thick—12 feet at the base—and they were faced with some of the best building stone in the country, limestone brought from Barnack in Northamptonshire. The site was a hilltop, artificially strengthened with a moat and steep banks, on the crown of which was a wide flat bailey. The keep rose from the centre of this platform to a height of more than a hundred feet, and there was a surrounding wall as well as other buildings.

Of all this the earthworks and the keep remain. The latter is the finest of its period still extant. It still looks formidable after more than 800 years. Its nearest parallel in England is at Rochester, but while Rochester is an empty shell Hedingham has retained its great hall and many other architectural features. There have been losses: two of the four corner turrets have gone and the survivors are battered, and of the forebuilding only the base remains; but these are small casualties to compare with the splendour that can still be seen. The entrance is at first-floor level, into a gaunt open hall surrounded by numerous small chambers—latrines and store rooms—

in the thickness of the walls. The floor above is the Hall itself, the principal place of state and of business for one of the leaders of feudal society. There is an astonishing sight here, a huge Norman arch which spans the full width of the room, more than 30 feet. There is nothing comparable in England, probably in the world. It can be best seen from the gallery which runs right around the hall halfway up its height. There is much enrichment of detail in the windows and doors. There is a further floor above this, with sleeping quarters.

The de Veres, later Earls of Oxford and hereditary Lord Great Chamberlains of England, held Hedingham for 550 years. Although the Earls were deeply involved in the violent politics of the middle ages the castles stood siege only twice, both times in King John's reign. Robert de Vere was on the barons' side against the king, and John took Hedingham and left a garrison to hold it against the French invaders. In 1216 the Dauphin's forces besieged the castle successfully. At other times the de Veres carried out their king-making elsewhere. They were on the Lancastrian side in the Wars of the Roses, and John, the thirteenth Earl, led Richmond's victorious forces at Bosworth. For these services he was rewarded by Henry VII with many honours. When the King visited Hedingham in 1498 the Earl put on a magnificent show for him but quickly regretted it Henry never let personal affection or loyalty deflect him from the letter of the law or an opportunity to strengthen the Exchequer he pointed out that de Vere had broken the newly revived Statute of Liveries and fined him 15,000 marks.

The castle is still privately owned, but is often open to the public Entrance is past a gracious Queen Anne house where the owners now live and across a fine brick bridge, probably the work of Earl John in the years of peace following Bosworth Field.

Castle Hedingham, which was granted a market in the thirteenth century, is an exceptionally delightful little town. It is compactly planned and singularly rich in good buildings around the area of St James Street and Falcon Square. The former was the old market place. The older buildings grew up under the patronage of the castle. Later ones, like Sheepcote, reflect the success of local wool trading. The town has seen several industries come and go, wool straw-plaiting, hope and pottery. Hedingham ware still has its collectors.

Of the nunnery founded by the first Earl of Oxford, of which his wife Lucy was the first prioress, nothing remains. The hospital of St James founded in 1250 is remembered only in the town's principal street. The parish church of St Nicholas remains, and this is among the finest in the county. In general it belongs to the very end of the Norman period. The heavy arcades of the long nave represent the last fine flourish of this style, which in the chancel arch moves towards Early English. The work, for so late a date, is austere and not the worse for it. The great wheel window is a more extravagant exercise and an extraordinary one. These things are very fine, but above them is a finer. Castle Hedingham has the most magnificent double-hammerbeam roof in Essex and one of the best anywhere. It is Tudor work, like the clerestory windows which illuminate it. The detail is excellent but subordinated to the general effect; here is the beauty which comes from strict observance of the rules, pure craftsmanship.

One enters the chancel through a fine screen, rich but not heavy. This is fifteenth-century work, considerably restored. Beyond this is the dimly lit choir. The choir-stalls are mediaeval, with the original misericords—much the better of the only two sets in Essex. The subjects are familiar: Reynard carrying off an ape in the guise of a priest, and again spinning a distaff, and a beautifully designed Pelican in her Piety. It may seem strange that there is only one de Vere buried in his home-town, John, who was Earl of Oxford in Henry VIII's reign. As we shall see later the earlier Earls chose to lie in their priory in Earls Colne. The Norman detail in the chancel is richer than that in the nave. Some of this, especially the sedilia which are much too good to be true, may be the result of exuberant Victorian restoration. Even if this is so, the building is nevertheless of quite outstanding quality. In architectural terms we shall see nothing better along the course of the Colne.

The unsightly manifestations of twentieth-century prosperity, held at bay in Castle Hedingham, break out violently along the main road at Sible Hedingham. ('Sible' commemorates the mother-in-law of the Alberic de Vere who came over with the Conqueror.) There is nothing to be said, at least nothing printable, about this. A few fine houses struggle for breath among the modern mass. Behind the main road however lies a charming corner near the church, where there is a very handsome inn, the White Horse, and the elegant rectory. The church is well placed on a steep knoll and looks best as one approaches the village from the west. Much of the building belongs to the fourteenth century, good plain work of which the chancel arch is typical. The tower is later but some of the detail belongs to an earlier structure. On the tower you will notice twice the device of a hawk, and there is another in oak in the lovely modern altar furnishings of the south chapel. These are all references to Sible Hedingham's most famous son, Sir John Hawkwood.

Readers of Hubert Cole's powerful historical romance *Hawkwood* published in 1967, must have admired the author's imaginative resources. How, one wondered, could he invent so wild and convincing a tall story? The story was, in broad outline, true. John Hawkwood was born in the village. (Hawkwoods is the name of a Queen Anne house in the main road; this may be the successor of a house belonging to a family, or perhaps merely be named after the local hero.) Tradition, never to be despised as evidence, says that he came from mean stock and that his father was a tanner. It would have been natural for a young man of Hedingham, especially if he were a lad of spirit, to be recruited into the Earl of Oxford's forces. What is more surprising is that, without benefit of family, he won promotion and was knighted by the Black Prince after the battle of Poitiers. In the intervals of peace which, for the professional soldier, inconveniently interrupted the business of war, Hawkwood went marauding as captain of one of the free companies which ravaged Europe more effectively than the regular armies. His was the White Company, whose fame gave Conan Doyle the title for a once-famous novel. It seems to have been a first-rate fighting troop for, during the next 30 years, the Company sold their services to the city states of Italy. Their last contract was with Florence. Hawkwood died there in 1394 and was buried in the Duomo with a superb fresco by Uccello as memorial. He had kept contact with Hedingham during this time and had given instructions for a tomb in his village church. This, it may be presumed, is the very fine monument in the south aisle, which is surmounted by an elegant arch. The decoration is lavish, and among the figures are a boar, a pelican and a hawk. Whether Hawkwood was in fact buried here or in Florence seems in doubt. It would however not be without precedent for a distinguished man to be represented in his home town by a cenotaph.

The thousands in France and Italy who had suffered at the hands of the White Company might not have thought of Hawkwood with any sensation less than horror. He was a soldier of fortune pursuing his career with ruthless brutality. So, on a higher social and political plane, was the Black Prince. What distinguished Hawkwood from most of his contemporaries was his efficiency. He took 3,000 of the toughest warriors in Europe and turned them into a disciplined fighting machine. It seems that he had one other rare quality; he had his own kind of loyalty to the states which employed him. No doubt he deserved to win, in true storybook fashion, the Duke of Milan's daughter and to be painted in full panoply by the greatest artist of the age. Nor should we grudge him the splendid monument in the church where he had worshipped as a poor boy.

The road from Hedingham to Halstead has no special claim to attention, and I am inclined to go wandering away from our route in search of the Maplesteads. This is very good country, undulating and wooded. Great Maplestead village is a little disappointing and Little Maplestead hardly exists at all. Scenery apart, the outstanding interest of these places is in their churches.

Great Maplestead stands on a peninsula formed by two arms of a tiny stream dropping down to the Colne. The church stands high and looks particularly well from the south-east, across the valley from Lucking Street. Beginners in the fine art of church visiting will find this a good one to practise on. It is sufficiently varied and fairly easy to read. The site is obviously an ancient one, and the present building may well be at least the third here. The basis of it is early Norman, nave, choir and apsidal sanctuary. A low, massive tower was added at the west end later in the same century; this bears obvious signs of repairs carried out in James I's reign after severe damage by lightning. Early in the thirteenth century a start was made on a rebuilding of the church in the new pointed style, but apparently funds ran out after the chancel had been remodelled. More than a century later a transept was built to the south, probably to form a Lady Chapel. A Jacobean family, the Deanes, extended this early in the seventeenth century to make room for the family monuments. Finally the Victorians built a dull north aisle and tidied the whole building to conform to their standards. Miraculously they left the perfect Norman apse alone.

The font, tall octagonal fifteenth-century work, is tantalizing. When it was cleaned, during the present century, traces of the original decoration were found, and these remain, just enough to hint at their former beauty. Each of the panels seems to have been painted with an emblem of the Passion. The most fascinating contents of the church are however the Deane monuments. On the east side of the transept chapel lies Sir John Deane, who died in 1625. He is in formal armour, lying rather uncomfortably on one elbow with his family—in unconventional position—above him kneeling along a narrow shelf. On the opposite wall is his widow's memorial. Lady Deane died in 1633, and her son provided her with a memorial a year later. He put himself into it, choosing to lie with his head on a pillow while his mother rises ghost-like behind him in her shroud. It ought to seem, to irreverent modern eyes, comic, but somehow it is strangely disturbing. The work is very fine, with masterly treatment of costume. The canopy is adorned with angels. All these motifs were conventions of an age much occupied with thoughts of mortality, but the interpretation is highly individual.

For every person who has heard of Great Maplestead a dozen know about Little Maplestead. This has a distinction shared with only three other places; it has a round church. The manor was given in about 1185 to the Order of the Knights of St John of Jerusalem the Knights Hospitallers. This militant order had been founded in Jerusalem nearly a hundred years earlier to provide a hospital for pilgrims in the Holy Land and to protect them on their journey. The order was older than the rival order of Knights Templars and followed a less rigid rule, that of St Augustine. The Hospitallers set up a preceptory in Little Maplestead with the principal object of finding recruits for the order. The Knights built a group of buildings for their members and servants and a round church in which they might worship. This presumably was late Norman in style.

Then, about 150 years later the church was rebuilt. Why this was done is not clear, although by that time the Hospitallers had benefited from the forcible suppression of the Knights Templars, and a new and enriched church might have been an expression of their enhanced prosperity. Whatever the reason, they chose to adhere to the old traditional ground-plan which had by now become long out of fashion. The round nave and apsidal sanctuary were a deliberate archaism, a most unusual phenomenon in mediaeval England where confidence in the present led invariably to a sense of patronage towards the past. On the old plan therefore, which had been adopted

by both Templars and Hospitallers in imitation of the Church of the Holy Sepulchre in Jerusalem, the Hospitallers built their new church, designing it however in the elaborate style in vogue in 1335. This church survived the suppression of the Order in 1540, when the conventual buildings were destroyed, and its later use as the chapel of a brotherhood of dissenters, and even the ravages of a full-scale Victorian restoration. This last removed all trace of the peculiar internal divisions dictated by Hospitaller ritual, but otherwise did less harm here than in most churches. So far as ornamental detail was concerned, the restorers were content to patch and renew rather than to recreate in their own image. The exquisite corbels on which the arches of the circular nave rest are Victorian but almost certainly careful copies of the worn carvings they replaced. The west door, newly protected by an ugly porch, was patched up but not altered.

I must admit to a very personal affection for Little Maplestead church. The round nave is topped with a very odd hexagonal crown and the cone rising to this is broken with tiny dormers. This work is modern, but presumably reproduces the original design. It is homely rather than impressive, and the same is true of the rest of the exterior, excepting the west door. Inside, it is quite another matter. The 'round' frames a six-sided nave consisting of a continuous arcade with elegant clustered pillars and graceful arches. In the time of the Knights this was cut off from the choir by a stone screen. This has gone, and the central eastern arch of the arcade opens into a very small chancel terminated by a windowless apse. The effect, if historically incorrect, is very pleasing. The building, restoration apart, is all of one period except for the font which is early Norman and belonged to a church preceding the first chapel of the Hospitallers.

We are here some way from the Colne, although this country still drains to the river, and we may be tempted to cut across country and pick up the river in the valley of the Colne villages. Gluttons for punishment, and those who are interested in industrial history, should go south to Halstead. This is a large town, now much involved in the Courtauld enterprises. The history of the town is much older than this. It was one of the principal towns of the cloth trade, particularly when the declining industry was rejuvenated by refugees from religious persecution in the sixteenth century. When this trade in turn began to decay the silk trade established originally at

Pebmarsh by the Courtauld family came here and has so far proved a more viable and adaptable industry.

Of early days only the church is a witness, and this has lost much of its interest in drastic restoration. The Bourchier chapel alone evokes memories of the past. Some houses recall a prosperous community of the eighteenth century, but Halstead is essentially a modern town. Visitors concerned with the history of the Gothic revival will want to see two examples of the work of George Gilbert Scott at Holy Trinity and St James's.

Below Halstead we enter the country to which the term Colne Valley is more precisely given. This consists of the four Colne villages—Engaine, Earls, White and Wakes—and the tiny hamlet of Chappel. It is attractive country, even if Earls Colne shows signs of excessive growth. The river, still narrow and insignificant, used to provide power for a string of mills and makes necessary a most spectacular railway viaduct.

The most pleasant route is north of the river, through byways which lead to the cross-roads at Colne Engaine. There is a steep hill here and fine views across the valley. The church is not far short of the highest point and its brick battlements make a landmark. In fact we might prefer the church and its views to the church itself, which is of minor interest. The best of it is the handsome stepped porch, excellent brickwork in the traditional Essex manner.

I should be inclined to resist the temptation of a direct route to Earls Colne, and instead to stay north of the river for a further two miles, passing the fine landscaped grounds of Colne Park, surviving after the demolition of most of the Georgian mansion. From here there is one of the best distant views of the magnificent tower of Earls Colne church, dwarfing the rest of the little town.

The 'Earls' of Earls Colne were the de Veres of Castle Hedingham, Earls of Oxford. Aubrey de Vere founded a Benedictine priory here about the year 1100. The parent house was Abingdon Abbey in Berkshire. The Earls favoured this above the parish church at Hedingham, and they were buried in the priory up to the time of the Suppression. The priory occupied land very near to the river south-west of the point where the main road crosses it. The buildings were completely destroyed after Dissolution, and a picturesque 'Gothick' house in red brick stands partly on the site. The monuments of the de Veres were kept here for a long time, but have now been transferred to a church in Suffolk. The only considerable memorial to this great foundation to survive in Essex is the lovely Virgin and Child now in the church at Feering.

There are some good houses in the wide main street, together with a great many inferior ones. In fact the town, which is of ancient foundation and has an old grammar school, is a good deal less attractive than one expects. The best of it is a house with very good pargetting at Pounds Green, well away from the centre.

The church is large and for the most part dull. Before the Reformation the de Veres devoted themselves to the priory to the exclusion of the church. In 1534, when the priory was still in being but doomed, the sixteenth Earl, John de Vere, built a new and sumptuous west tower. This is among the best in the county. The battlements display exuberant flushwork, with the de Vere Arms and the Mullet (star) badge which they won in the Crusades. The stair-turret, partly in brick, is topped with the Earl's coronet in wrought-iron, a pleasing flourish but presumably not original.

By approaching Earls Colne from the north we have missed an important tributary. This is the Bourne Brook—a tautological name: one might as well call the Colne the River River—which rises on the edge of Wethersfield airfield and enters the Colne just south-west of Colne Engaine. We need not concern ourselves with much of this but it would be regrettable if we missed Gosfield where, thanks to the whim of an eighteenth-century politician and social climber, the stream opens out to form a most attractive lake. Until recently Gosfield Park must have been one of the best examples in Essex of the fine art of landscape design. During the present century, however, the Hall has passed through many hands, including the Army's, and the grounds are reduced and not in the best condition. The lake has a camping site on its banks and speed-boats on its waters.

Gosfield Hall is a house of outstanding interest. It was built in Henry VIII's reign by Sir John Wentworth, of warm Tudor brick. Sir John clearly had no great confidence in the powers of the law, because he made his house resistant to anything short of siege. There was a substantial gatehouse, and no windows were provided at ground level. Some of this building remains, including a fine long gallery—called the Queen's Gallery after Elizabeth who visited the house twice—more than 100 feet long and lined with magnificent key panelling. The Hall was reconstructed towards the end of the

seventeenth century under the inspiration of Sir Thomas Millington
a distinguished scientist and physician. His principal contribution to
the house was the Grand Salon. Major alterations were also carried
out in the early Georgian period by another owner, John Knight
and his widow, later Lady Nugent. Nugent himself, a man of some
notoriety in political life, was responsible for the layout of the park
and for further modernizing of the Hall. Under him the house perhaps reached its peak. It is now occupied by members of the Mutual
Households' Association, and some of the best rooms are shown to
the public regularly.

Gosfield church stands in a corner of the park not far from the
lake. In foundation it is much older than the Hall, but shows clearly
the signs of the dominance of the great family. The present building
dates from 1435, the tower from the end of that century, and the
chancel and Wentworth chapel are roughly contemporary with the
Hall. Additions were made to the chapel to make room for the huge
monument to John Knight. Here then is a most interesting and
varied building, containing moreover some unusual details. The
monumental brass to Sir Thomas Rolfe, who rebuilt the church, is
one of the best of its date in the country. The choir fittings are
attractive, particularly the fine Tudor panelling of the choir stalls.
The extravagant Knight monument, by Rysbrack, is in its way
admirable, and the chapel built to receive it illustrates nicely
the relationship between church and hall in the eighteenth
century.

Let us now return to the Colne, going north of the river again to
visit White Colne. The little church stands high and in a very pretty
setting. Apart from this, and an elaborate Jacobean pulpit, this
hardly merits a special journey. The road past it meets the main
road at Wakes Colne. Here a very attractive early Victorian hall
with Doric portico, stands well back from the road. This is now a
centre for valiant work with spastic sufferers and some of the pro-
ducts are sold at a little shop by the roadside. Further along the road
is the church, typical Essex in its simplicity, its antiquity—the
massive walls are surely very early Norman work—and the charm
of its wooden belfry. Beyond this again is the most memorable thing
in Wakes Colne, the great viaduct which carries the railway across
the Colne valley on 30 tall brick arches. This is a more characteristic
expression of the Victorian spirit than the porch of Wakes Hall.

ow admirable the touch of drama which it gives to this mild
andscape.

Just over the river there is a pretty scene with an old watermill
eside the Colne and, next to it, the small fourteenth-century parish
hurch of Chappel.

The last miles to Colchester offer no great attractions. The villages
ie north and south of the main road, which passes only nondescript
hamlets and new developments and, at Fordstreet where the Colne
passes north of the road, some houses of quality. None of the villages
eems to justify a diversion. At Fordham the tall fifteenth-century
church is hemmed in with new developments, and West Bergholt has
a pretty locked church in a poor state of repair, strikingly in con-
rast with the immaculate hall nearby which stands up arrogantly
among these gentle hills. Aldham, south of the road and river, is
another place of recent growth. The church, which used to stand
near Church House Farm, more than a mile from the village, was
aken down and reassembled on its present site in 1855. The work
was done with unusual integrity, only the new spire striking a
slightly false note.

Aldham is to be best remembered as the home of Philip Morant
who was rector and died here in 1770. Morant was outstanding
among the scholar-parsons of the eighteenth century who devoted
hemselves equally to their flock and to local studies. His *History of
Essex*, published in 1768, was the foundation on which all later
work was based. A great man, 'abounding in every kind of erudition',
as his epitaph states, and moreover 'benevolent to all'.

So to Colchester. The river winds to the north of the main road
and the new by-pass and so avoids—but we cannot—the westward
sprawl of the town. It passes outside the ancient walls and finally
enters the built-up area past the Siege House at the foot of East Hill.

As with Kent and Canterbury, Lancashire and Lancaster, the
ancient capital of Essex is not the modern administrative centre.
Colchester is the oldest town in Essex—and probably, as it claims,
he oldest of which historical records exist in the country. It is the
argest town today apart from those on the London fringe, and it is
much the most interesting in history and architecture. A town moreover of vigorous modern activity with a lively theatre and other
manifestations of cultural awareness. It is also, to my mind, grossly
overgrown, and has much that is unworthy of the best. Like most

garrison towns, it has paid dearly for the liveliness introduced by th
military in the sacrifice of a large central area to army buildings o
a striking dreariness. A great deal of urban squalor survives; an
recent attempts to meet the demands of the modern world, inclu
ing the introduction of a traffic system of baffling complexity, hav
not had uniformly happy results. There remains however enough t
make this a major objective for any antiquarian and archaeologic
outing in Essex.

Not only is Colchester the oldest of English towns; it has th
longest continuous history. Once the town comes into prominenc
it stays there. The tribal capital of the Trinobantes who were i
control of Essex in the first century BC was Camulodunum, whic
lay a little to the west of the present town-centre. The town's nam
came from the Celtic war-god Camulos; it was appropriate for th
inhabitants were warlike and their city strongly defended. It wa
indeed a naturally good site, lying along a gravel ridge between th
Colne and the Roman River, both of which were then far mor
formidable waterways than one could guess from their present size
On the landward side of this peninsula artificial boundaries wer
created. Of these considerable stretches of Grim's Dyke and Lexde
Dyke still remain visible, and there may have been—but this
disputed—a forward line of defence north of the Colne at Pitchbur
Ramparts in West Bergholt. This was the city ruled by Cunobelin—
whom we know better as Shakespeare's Cymbeline—whose grave
treasure it may have been which was discovered within the grea
barrow in Lexden Park. Cunobelin was the leading prince of Belgi
Britain in the first century AD and inevitably his capital was th
objective of Claudius in the Roman invasion of AD 43. It was a
earlier dynastic dispute which had given Julius Caesar an excuse fo
the first Roman invasion, and the treaties then agreed gave Claudiu
his flimsy legal justification nearly a century later. The Roman force
took Camulodunum in AD 44 and established on a neighbouring sit
a colony of retired legionaries. This Colonia was to be a mode
Roman community, and at its centre was built a huge monumen
to the might of Rome, the temple of the God Claudius. Poor stam
mering scholarly Claudius was the least godlike of the Caesars, bu
he served as a symbol of his Empire. Building the Temple was
costly operation, and the local tribes had to pay for it. No wonde
that when Boadicea's army swept into Colonia and massacred th

habitants they took pains to destroy this emblem of conquest. But he Romans were soon back. The town became an important centre f trade and administration, although some of its style was lost for ood in Boadicea's raid. The walls put up to defend the town were made largely of septaria—that chunky limestone embedded in the ondon clay which makes a useful substitute for more conventional uilding stone—with strips of thin brick, the whole bonded with ndestructible Roman mortar. This wall survived the centuries of Roman rule, the centuries of Saxon neglect, their re-use in the mediaeval town, and even the pressures of modern times. Colchester is not as picturesque a walled town as York or Canterbury, but none hows so nearly complete a range of what is still essentially Roman work.

The wall is a recurrent theme in any walk around Colchester. Assuming that time is limited—and it must be said that nothing less han several lifetimes of study is likely to do justice to the town— we will take a leisurely stroll, or as leisurely as the hazards which ll the busy streets will allow.

Parking a car on the western edge of the town centre—perhaps in Maldon Road—we will start off up Balkerne Lane, opposite. Very oon the ancient masonry of the wall will appear on the right. There is a good view of the wall where it is broken at St Mary's Steps. This marks the site of a postern gate: the church tower, high above and with a charming cottage in front, makes a pretty picture, but the mediaeval church was badly damaged by artillery fire during the iege of 1648 and mostly rebuilt twice thereafter. Just up the lane rom here is one of the great sights of Colchester, the Balkerne Gate. This is what is left of the western gate of the Roman city, the prinipal entrance from London. What you see is an arched entrance or pedestrians. Part of the adjacent carriageway is exposed under he garden of a public-house built on top of the wall; this was once he King's Head but is now more appropriately the Hole in the Wall.

Behind the Balkerne Gate, and copying its rounded arch groesquely, is an extraordinary structure known with a mixture of ffection and derision as Jumbo. This is a water tower built in 1882. he Victorians did not lack confidence. Jumbo dominates the town, utclassing the Town Hall, the castle and all the churches. I must dmit that I like its blatant ugliness. A path skirts Jumbo, with on he other side a glimpse of a charming Victorian square built in a conservative classical manner. The path comes out at the top of North Hill, with the projecting clock of St Peter's church opposite. The brick tower—seventeenth century—makes an effective foreground in the view down the hill, but otherwise should not delay us. Opposite is the entrance to High Street, where the first building is the Fire Office, originally the Corn Exchange, built in 1820. The Doric colonnade is handsome. After this comes the Town Hall. Colchester has had a charter since 1189. The present Town Hall belongs to the beginning of the present century and looks like it. Not that it is bad of its kind. The tall tower is generously provided with allegorical statuary, and on top stands the patron-saint of Colchester Helena, holding the True Cross which she discovered on Calvary. St Helena, in history the mother of the Emperor Constantine the Great, was in legend the daughter of King Cole—who had fiddlers three—and was born here, being taken to Rome by the Roman general whom she married. On the face of the Town Hall are statues —rather well done—of worthies famous in the Colchester story from Boadicea—who hardly deserves this honour—to Archbishop Harsnett.

It is pleasant to escape from all this civic splendour to the quiet of the so-called Dutch Quarter, narrow lanes dropping down towards the river which were old when the Flemish weavers moved here in Elizabeth's reign to put new life into the cloth trade. There are some delightful houses in West and East Stockwell Lanes, a few just a little dilapidated but most of them in appreciative hands. At the corner of St Helen's Lane is an old chapel, now used for storage by the Castle Museum. Between two nice houses across the road is a path leading into the Castle grounds.

By this approach we may notice the steep ramparts of earth which provide outer defences for the keep. These, we may guess, are the remains of the earthworks thrown up hurriedly after the Conquest pending the construction of a stone fortress. The latter followed very quickly. This may well have been, next to the Tower of London, the first permanent castle in Norman England. It was also one of the largest. All the outer works, which extended as far as the Roman wall to the north, have vanished and the last surviving building, the keep, is sadly mutilated, but it is still the greatest Norman keep extant.

It was built on the foundations of Claudius's temple, still sound after a thousand years. The building followed the conventional Norman pattern, with one semi-circular corner containing the chapel. It rose four storeys high probably with higher turrets at the angles. This formidable fortress was in the hands of William's most trusted baron, Eudo the Dapifer, the Royal Steward. It remained nominally a royal castle, but with growing national stability in the later middle ages it degenerated into a prison. The most famous prisoner to suffer here was Sir Thomas Malory who, while serving sentence for a number of most unchivalrous crimes, wrote that most sublime elegy for the passing of the spirit of Chivalry, the *Morte d'Arthur*. Some of the Marian martyrs passed their last hours here before dying in hideous agony in the yard outside; and a pioneer Quaker, James Parnell, starved himself to death in a castle cell out of, it is tempting to say, sheer perversity. After the Restoration the castle was sold to a local dealer who undermined the foundations in a vain search for treasure and then demolished the upper storeys for the sake of their materials. The dilapidated building came at length to a local antiquary, Charles Gray, who restored it. Eventually Lord Cowdray presented the castle to the Corporation of Colchester, and it now houses one of the finest museums in the country.

As with all Norman keeps, access was at first-floor level through a forebuilding. This has been destroyed and we cross its ruins by a wooden bridge. There is little architectural interest inside the keep, which is not much more than a huge shell. This is just what the museum needs. There is ample room for the display of even the largest exhibits. The timber-framed frontage of a house formerly in Culver Street is not in the least constricted. There are a few large bygones on this floor, but it is the archaeological exhibits which give the Castle Museum its distinction. There is a wide range of prehistoric finds; the richest collection however is appropriately enough from the Roman period. Two of the finest treasures are monuments, one to a centurion—Marcus Favonius—of the XXth Legion, the other to Longinus, an officer of the Thracian cavalry. Both are impressive work, the centurion's stone formal and austere, the cavalryman's flamboyant. Both were found on the site of a Roman cemetery in Beverley Road. The so-called Colchester Sphinx has a sombre beauty: it shows the sphinx, winged, with a dead face framed between its paws; this seems to have formed part of a large funerary monument. Much the finest work in the collection, however, is very small, a quite exquisite votive figure of Mercury in bronze.

The Castle Museum also includes exhibits from the middle ages. Later periods are illustrated in the Holly Trees Museum, in a house beside the modern gates to the Castle Park. Holly Trees is well worth examining for its own sake, for it is an admirable Georgian town house. The central frontage of five bays with a singularly perfect porch is extremely satisfying. This was the home of Charles Gray, who saved the castle from destruction. The collections displayed here include examples of Colchester cloth, costume, dolls' houses and toys and, most impressive, a magnificent collection of tea-ladles.

While we are in the mood for museums, we should cross the road and go into All Saints Church. It is a dilemma shared by all towns which were prosperous in the middle ages that they have far more ancient parish churches than they can use. A remedy, applied elsewhere in Colchester, is to demolish the unwanted ones. Happily a less drastic solution was found for the disposal of All Saints, which is a building of modest architectural and historical pretensions but a valuable feature in the Colchester scene at this important point in the town. The church, no longer parochial, became a museum of natural history. The work of displaying a collection to illustrate the geology, the flora and the fauna of the district is still in progress. What has been done shows an imaginative approach. In one particular the museum is a pioneer: many of the exhibits are living.

The wide main road drops steeply down East Hill towards the river. There are good houses on either side: Gate House, a stylish plaster frontage—now the Education Office—Grey Friars, a very large brick Georgian house on the site of the Franciscan friary, and, opposite, the Minories, late Georgian and now an art gallery. St James Church, the biggest of the mediaeval parish churches and a handsome town church largely of the fifteenth century, stands just inside the city wall. You may wish to go beyond this, passing more fine houses, to cross the Colne and see the big half-timbered Siege House with its bullet holes carefully preserved. Otherwise, turn right past St James's into Priory Street where one of the best lengths of the wall is exposed. The bastions which give distinction to the blank wall are mediaeval. Like other ancient towns, Colchester finds its ancient wall ideal for car-parking.

Priory Street leads to the ruins of the Priory Church of St Botolph. We are accustomed to ruined monasteries, and, according to mood, praise their romantic dilapidation or curse the greed and stupidity of Henry VIII's minions which caused this destruction. St Botolph's is not romantic and the blame for its ruin lies elsewhere. It was a house of Augustinian canons founded in 1095, the first of its Order in England and nominally having the primacy of all others. It did not prosper, being outclassed by the neighbouring Abbey of St John, and it was suppressed in 1536. The nave of the priory church was spared as it served a parochial function, and it became after the Reformation the civic church of Colchester. It was left to the Parliamentary forces to knock the church to bits with their artillery during the siege of 1648. There remain parts of the arcades of the nave, with their ponderous round piers, and the lower stages of a west front which, when intact with its twin flanking towers, must have been one of the finest examples of Norman work in the country. Ingenious use was made of the Roman brick so plentiful in the area.

A new parish church of St Botolph was built right alongside this masterpiece in 1837, when the architect, with spectacular obtuseness, used what he imagined to be 'Norman' motifs in white brick.

We are not far from the site of St John's Abbey. This was a foundation of Eudo Dapifer, the builder of the castle, a Benedictine abbey whose abbot held high rank among the peers spiritual of England. At the Dissolution, the last abbot, John Beche, refused to surrender his house, and he was briskly tried for treason and as briskly executed. The buildings passed to the town clerk of Colchester, John Lucas. His descendant, Sir Charles, fortified the house which had been built within the abbey site during the Siege. It was destroyed by Parliamentary fire, and Sir Charles, as one of the leading defenders, was shot after the surrender. Of the abbey, one of the richest in Essex, only the fifteenth-century gatehouse, in typical East Anglian decorative flintwork, still survives, and this only in a much patched-up state.

From St Botolph's a very narrow lane—Eld Lane—and its continuation Sir Isaac's Walk run along the top of the town wall. Half-way along, a mediaeval gate surmounted by a house, called Scheregate, gives access by a flight of steps to the foot of the wall. The passageway is flanked with old houses, now shops. Just beyond Scheregate, Trinity Street goes right past the oldest of Colchester's churches, Holy Trinity. At least, the tower is pre-Conquest but attached to a mediaeval church of no great merit. The tower is

characteristic late Saxon work, tall, slim and unbuttressed. The west
doorway has a triangular head and is so narrow as to evoke specula
tion about the dimensions of our ancestors. Holy Trinity is at
present in a deplorable state of disrepair; perhaps some appropriate
secular use will be found to keep it from complete ruin. There are
two outstandingly interesting monuments. One—modern—com
memorates John Wilbye, the Elizabethan composer, one of the
sweetest madrigal writers of the golden age, who lived in the lovely
house just opposite the church as music master to Lady Rivers. The
other is a contemporary memorial to William Gilberd who lived
just along the street in a house called Tymperleys.

It is curious how many of the worthies of Essex were scientists.
William Gilberd, who was born in Colchester, the son of the Re
corder, was a doctor by profession and Physician to Queen Elizabeth
I and James I. By inclination he was a research scientist. He dis
covered the principles of electro-magnetism and so laid the founda
tions of the science of electricity. His book *De Magnete* which was
published in 1600, the year in which he was elected President o
the College of Physicians, was the first important study of physic
in England. Dryden, writing more than half a century later, was no
exaggerating when he said:

> *Gilberd shall live till loadstones cease*
> *to draw.*

Gilberd died in 1603 and was buried in Holy Trinity.

Trinity Street leads into Culver Street, where we turn left, seeing
a few good houses and much of what one hopes is temporary mess
At Head Street, turn left and cross the road for a glimpse, up an
alleyway, of the old King's Head, now offices. In its day this was
the principal coaching inn of Colchester. It became the headquarter
of the Parliamentary forces after the Siege, and here Fairfax decided
the fate of Sir Charles Lucas and Sir George Lisle. It is customary to
deplore the fate of the Royalist leaders. Certainly their execution had
barely a colour of legality, but they had held the town against the
will of a majority of its citizens; it is not difficult to understand
either Fairfax's anger or Colchester's distress at having to pay twice
over for the destruction of their town and their trade.

The King's Head is only a short step from the beginning of ou
tour. This has merely skimmed the surface of the town, and sensible

visitors will wish to look more closely at some of the back streets and to go beyond the old town to study the ancient earthworks. Then there is the Hythe, the old port of Colchester, which has atmosphere. Another profitable short journey is to Bourne Mill (National Trust). The mill of St John's Abbey was rebuilt after the destruction of the Abbey and became a fishing lodge. Later it again became a mill, engaged in the cloth-trade. The mainly Elizabethan building has great charm. Its stepped gables are decorated with elegant stone pinnacles of a distinctive design.

The last bridge over the Colne is at the Hythe. The conclusion of this journey consequently presents problems. Each shore of the estuary demands our attention vigorously. At the risk of making the journey intolerably long, I must have a hasty look at the western side before going back through Colchester to see the last of the Colne from its eastern shore.

A few miles out of Colchester, just where the town relinquishes its grasp at Rowhedge, there is a major tributary. The Roman River looks insignificant enough. Right up to its confluence with the Colne it is a narrow stream. In prehistoric times it was a formidable barrier and played an important part in determining the boundaries of the tribal capital at Camulodunum. Today it offers an attractive minor journey, bringing a generous reward to those with time to spare. The stream rises near Great Tey, where the church has a massive early Norman central tower, reminiscent of St Alban's Abbey, and a nave of ludicrously inadequate proportions. South of this is a tiny Norman church at Little Tey, and then the Roman River passes just north at Marks Tey. Most people know this only as the scene of exasperating delays at the notorious road-junction, but resourceful motorists will slip round to the church which has one rare treasure, a wooden font. This is early Tudor, panelled and showing the remains of fine decoration. The river crosses the London Road at Stanway, and then passes very close to the remote and lovely church of Copford. This is one of the wonders of Essex, an almost perfect late Norman building which has retained its original wall-paintings. At Heckfordbridge the stream skirts the grounds of Stanway Hall, which has recently made an attractive setting for an admirably laid-out zoo. South of this is the huge Abberton Reservoir, almost an inland sea and the home of a large bird population. There is no finer place in the county at which to watch wildfowl which are found

in astronomical numbers. A feature in the wide view is the bulk
of Layer Marney Tower, far to the west.

The last village on the Roman River is Fingringhoe. This is a pretty
village with an inn, a picturesque mill-pond and an extremely hand
some church. Over the door of the south porch, decorated with
flintwork, St Michael and the Dragon are poised perpetually on the
brink of strife. The lane past the church ends beside the Colne where
a ferry once plied to Wivenhoe. This is a riverside scene not less
delightful for its familiarity, for it has been painted and photographed numberless times.

The mouth of the Colne can best be seen from the tip of Mersea
Island, a genuine island although it is joined to the mainland at low
water by an ancient causeway, the Strood. Mersea has lost its former
remoteness and is now a popular holiday island with a rash of
beach-huts along the low shore. It still has a great deal of charm
West Mersea has that fine air of purposeful inactivity common to
sailing communities, and the church at East Mersea stands splendidly
on its low hillock. The island will repay further visiting, preferably
—and suitably muffled against the North Sea winds—out of season.

Now back to Colchester to see the eastern shore of the estuary.
The immediate scene is dominated by the towers of the University
of Essex, rising above the trees of Wivenhoe Park. It is perhaps un-
fair to pass any kind of judgement on the architecture, as the master-
plan—by Kenneth Capon—will not be fully realized for many
years. At present it is the towers, which house the students' living
quarters, which overrule everything else. They are vast, black and
uncompromisingly imposed on the landscape. If not immediately
pleasing the architecture is challenging and insistent, an appropriate
symbol of an unusual university concept. In its first years the University of Essex has established a reputation for originality—the
idea of related studies is likely to produce the 'full man' if not the
'exact man'—for permissiveness and for 'protest'.

A minor road skirts Wivenhoe Park and comes down to the quay
at Wivenhoe. Like so many towns which live by the river this is a
place of character. There is an attractive messiness about the waterfront, where an ordered tangle of ropes traps the uninitiated and
persistent smells—of tar and oil—remind us that this is a place only
half—if as much as that—dedicated to dry land. There is a pretty
cottage or two on the quay and, behind, the Garrison House with

uperb seventeenth-century pargetting. The church looks at its best
rom across the river. It is of no great architectural interest, but it
ias three of the finest monumental brasses in the county. These are
ill early Tudor. The best, to William, Lord Beaumont and Bardolfe,
s damaged but was originally in the most lavish style of the day
vith an intricate canopy and full armorial detail. Lord Beaumont
vas a friend and protégé of John, Earl of Oxford—whom we met
it Hedingham—and after his death his widow—whose brass, only
i little less splendid, lies beside his—married the Earl.

Behind Wivenhoe a lane, now much built upon, winds away
hrough Alresford to the Clacton road. Those with a fancy for wild
lesolation might, outside the sailing season, go down a side road
o Alresford Creek where at half tide herons fish the muddy chan-
iels. The creek can be followed to within sight of Brightlingsea
:hurch, on a hill well away from the parent town. Brightlingsea
tself is something of a disappointment, especially after Wivenhoe.
[t has lost much of its maritime atmosphere without discernible
:ompensatory gain. There is little to remind us that this was a
member, the only one north of the Thames, of the powerful Brother-
iood of the Cinque Ports which, in return for privileges commercial
ind ceremonial, provided ships for the King's fleet during the stormy
:enturies of the middle ages. For reasons which are not clear it was
i 'limb' of the Kentish port of Sandwich.

If the town is disappointing, Brightlingsea church is not. A
smaller building, Norman and later, was brought up to date in the
ifteenth century when trade was booming. To this time the tower
belongs. It is a spectacular structure in flint, decorated with flushwork. The massive buttresses have niches, now alas empty. The work
is much like that at Dedham and certainly not less splendid. The
monuments reflect civic and mercantile pride in the fifteenth and
sixteenth centuries. Much the largest, however, and good of its
ostentatious kind, belongs to a later age. This is to Nicholas Magens,
an insurance man who died in 1764. Some of the symbolism is conventional enough, with winged angels and cherubs, but Magens'
to the sea is discharged by a display of ships and a huge anchor.
The cornucopia spews not only fruit but coins. All this, I suppose,
is very vulgar, but there is a hearty exuberance about it which
appeals.

A wide seawater creek which reaches inland for several miles contributed to Brightlingsea's former success as a port. One arm of the creek goes a little south of east to reach the boundaries of the estates of St Osyth Abbey. By road the same journey is very much longer, but this makes a fitting climax to the exploration of the Colne.

St Osyth was originally known as Chich, an appropriate name meaning a winding creek. Here, according to a picturesque story the East Saxon king Sighere founded a nunnery for the benefit of his queen Osyth who became the first abbess. It was perilously near the sea, and Danes, raiding here in or about the year 870, sacked the place and took the abbess prisoner. When she declined to renounce her faith, they cut off her head; whereupon Osyth picked it up and walked with it to what was left of her abbey church. In due course she was canonized, and after the Conquest a new priory, following the Augustinian rule, was founded by the Bishop of London. This was later promoted to the rank of abbey. It was among the most prosperous of Essex houses. The last abbot was not of the calibre of John Beche and readily surrendered to the king in 1539; he was rewarded with a large pension. The treasures of the abbey disappeared into the Treasury, and the estate, originally granted to Cromwell, reverted to the Crown after his fall and became a favourite residence of the Princess Mary. Later it was sold to a local gentleman Sir Thomas D'Arcy, who became Baron D'Arcy of Chiche

The substantial remains of the abbey are often open to the public and less often the interior of the gatehouse, with its magnificent art treasures, may be visited. The abbey had been largely rebuilt shortly before the Dissolution during the abbacy of John Vyntoner and the great gatehouse is of this period. It is the finest part of the buildings and beyond question the most splendid abbey gate in the country. The decorative flintwork, with its slim vertical bands and pinnacles, shows this art at its most resourceful. Above the gateway there is a niche—formerly housing the image of St Osyth—with an exquisite canopy of which the pinnacle is extended almost the full height of the building. The spandrels contain figures of St Michael and the Dragon, very similar to those we saw at Fingringhoe church but with the figures reversed. Was the same sculptor responsible for both?

Within the abbey grounds, there is no sign of the church which straddled the area now occupied by a formal rose garden and a

30   Abbey Gate, St Osyth

opiary garden. Beyond this some of the conventual buildings urvive, but the most conspicuous feature is a tall flint tower with angle turrets, sometimes called the Abbot's Tower, but belonging to the house built by D'Arcy after the Dissolution. In the centre of the main block is Abbot Vyntoner's luxurious lodging, which has a most beautiful Tudor oriel window. The grapes which recur as a decorative motif are presumably a pun on the abbot's name.

St Osyth Abbey is at once magnificent and curious. The individual buildings are as fine as one could find anywhere. They make, however, no contribution to a general effect. This no doubt is due in part to the ravages of time, but some blame may be laid on D'Arcy, who had his share of Tudor pride but no feeling for the new spirit of his age. The main impression is mediaeval, without the controlling functional design which gave a satisfying pattern to the mediaeval abbey. D'Arcy, one must believe, was unaware of the Renaissance forces at work all around him.

A last visit might be made to a little battered thirteenth-century chapel behind the Abbot's Tower. Here a little of the spirit of the founders, forgotten in Abbot Vyntoner's day and irrelevant to D'Arcy's, persists with its affirmation of the validity of integrity, in faith and in design.

CHAPTER EIGHT

Stour

*Steeple Bumpstead—the Belchamps—Borley—Henny—
Little Horkesley—Langham—Dedham—Manningtree—
Harwich*

Those who, out of the fullness of their ignorance, condemn Essex
for a lack of natural beauty are forgetting that at least half of the
landscape that made Constable a painter belongs to Essex. The
Constable country spreads out from both banks of the Stour, and if
there is one scene which crystallizes Constable's vision it is the Essex
scene of Dedham Vale.

The Stour, which forms the county boundary from Sturmer to
the sea, is by birth a Suffolk river. It rises in the hilly open country
of West Suffolk towards Newmarket. It is still a small stream, however, when it meets Essex in the delectable surroundings of Sturmer
parish. Just beyond this it receives a little Essex feeder which gives
an excuse to start this journey in style at Steeple Bumpstead. Bumpstead has a charmingly bucolic ring about it, evoking visions of
bumpkins hitched around the knee dancing morris-fashion on the
green. In fact, the name seems likely to imply a homestead among
the reeds, probably a fair description in Saxon times. The 'steeple'
may refer to the church tower, but not the present sturdy no-
nonsense brick tower, of which only the base is Norman; alternatively, as has been suggested, the reference may be to a long-vanished
strongpoint in the neighbourhood. It is a pleasant place, town rather
than village, the distinction underlined by a moot hall which stands
as an island at a road junction. This is a two-storey timber-framed
building, of which the ground floor presumably stood open to the

weather to house market-stalls. Today the hall seems to lean for support on its massive brick chimney-stack. The origin of this attractive little building is obscure; it may have been the headquarters of a craft guild. In Elizabeth's reign it had become a school. Today it does a useful job in providing a home for the village library.

The church too reflects the former importance of this place. It is big, originally Norman, now mainly fifteenth century and later, showing an effective mixing of flint and brick. There are some good things inside, a fine timber roof, some Tudor benches and an unusual pillar alms-box protected by three locks. The showpiece of the church is the monument to Sir Henry Bendyshe. The Bendyshes lived at Bower Hall, a great house now rebuilt in the park just south of the village. Sir Henry died in 1717. The monument is a splendid example of the extravagant baroque of the day. Sir Henry lies in self-conscious elegance between twin 'barley-sugar' columns, with an infant at his elbow. This was the heir who died at six months and so the baronetcy lapsed. Above the canopy a tearful cherub mops his eye on a large handkerchief. So showy a piece comes very near to parody, but not quite; the proportions are so good and the portrait sculpture so convincing that laughter is silenced.

Essex is rich in good inn-signs. Opposite the Moot Hall there is a nice example, the Fox and Hounds; the pack go by in full cry, while the fox lies safely overhead along the branch of a tree!

A secondary road follows the brook from Steeple Bumpstead to where it enters the Stour. Beyond this, at Baythorn End, it pays to trespass briefly into Suffolk entering and immediately leaving the enchanting village of Stoke-by-Clare and so crossing back into Essex at Ashen. This is a pretty, and, like so much of North Essex, a friendly village. Roadside cottage gardens make a colourful show throughout the summer. There is nothing here to draw the curious, but perceptive visitors will enjoy the sense of remoteness and self-containment. The church looks well, its tall tower with contrasted brick stair turret dominating the street in proper style. It possesses one rarity, the back of the old churching stool, now set against the wall and declaring (prophetically?): 'This hath bin the churching the mearring stool and so it shall be still.'

There is no village on the Essex bank for the next six miles or more, and this gives us an excuse to strike inland to what is for me almost the best of this lovely county, the country of the Belchamps.

The quality of the landscape defies precise definition. It is open, n[o]
high—below 300 feet at its highest, and, although reasonably we[ll]
provided with good buildings, lacking any architectural feature [of]
the very first quality. It seems to me, nevertheless, to have th[e]
quality which one recognizes as Englishness. If I had to show [a]
visitor from overseas a scene which epitomized England I shoul[d]
take him not to Buttermere or to the Avon at Stratford but to th[e]
church of Belchamp St Paul and point across the rolling, fertile fiel[d]
to the distant line of the Stour. Here is a landscape busy with th[e]
business of producing food. Having no thought for beauty it co[n]
trives, by minding its own business, to be very beautiful.

Let us go then to Belchamp St Paul, an overlong journey fro[m]
Ashen because the old airfield has cut the road. There is not muc[h]
in the village and the church lies beyond with only the hall f[or]
company. It is an attractive group, the church massive and challen[g]
ing, the hall withdrawn and quietly perfect. The wide lawn whic[h]
flanks the drive has been left unfenced, a generous gesture whic[h]
shows confidence in the good sense of those who come this wa[y]
There are not many country churches in these parts which illustra[te]
so clearly the strength of the fifteenth century. It is not extravagan[t]
like the great wool-churches across the Stour, but massive. It loo[ks]
as if it could sit in this setting till Judgement Day. It has, like Cast[le]
Hedingham, its original stalls with their misericords. The carving [of]
these is conventional and unenterprising. The bench-ends are exce[l]
lent, however, with finely carved poppyheads and figures. A seate[d]
king, only a little mutilated, has a grave dignity which is genuine[ly]
moving.

Next comes Belchamp Otten, a small village with a very plai[n]
church, Norman in origin. It has retained its early Victorian (o[r]
earlier) fittings. Nearby is a Georgian hall with a good plain por[ch]
set asymmetrically.

Beyond this the lane drops down towards the Belchamp Bro[ok]
at Belchamp Walter and comes to an end just past the church a[nd]
hall. Paths radiate from here, tempting the traveller to a more i[n]
timate acquaintance with this country on foot. Belchamp Walt[er]
offers one of the most pleasing of the characteristic groupings [of]
church and hall which we have found everywhere in Essex. Th[e]
former is of mixed dates, from twelfth to fifteenth centuries. Th[e]
tower is tall but endearing rather than imposing—partly the effe[ct]

f a naïve little belfry turret. The church contains one of the most laborate mediaeval tombs in Essex. Here, according to the surviving eraldic evidence, lay a very tough warrior who played his part n the wars of Edward I and II, Sir John de Botetout. The tomb— o chest or effigy remains—is recessed into the north wall of the ave. There is an extravagantly rich canopy which may well have een the entrance to a chantry chapel, but of this no trace remains. ir John died in 1324, and his memorial represents the latest word n the Decorated style. It may seem surprising that the height of ashion should have been followed in so remote a spot, but here was o rustic craftsman but a sophisticated master of the art which had, ot so long before, produced the Eleanor Crosses. The wall-paintings re of this period too and of a high standard. The Virgin and Child s remarkably like that at Great Canfield. Had the painter, one won-ers, seen the older painting in the Roding valley, or did both turn o the same copy—perhaps a thirteenth-century Book of Hours— or their inspiration?

The most conspicuous monument from the eighteenth century is o Sir John Raymond. This elegantly formal work commemorates he builder, or rather rebuilder, of the Hall.

The first Raymond to come to Belchamp, another John, bought he manor from the spendthrift Sir John Wentworth of Gosfield, nd settled in an Elizabethan house. The Raymonds had come to tay! The present house is owned by Mr St Clere Raymond. It was uilt in 1720 in a style which was perhaps just a little old-fashioned n its day—Queen Anne rather than Georgian. It is Essex brickwork t its best. The façade is gravely formal, nine bays wide with a entral porch—a replacement but in the spirit of the original. The nain block of building is unchanged, except for the addition of harming overhung powder-closets on either side. In its exquisite etting, framed by superb trees and with a contemporary stone vase on the terrace enhancing the impression of classical dignity, it is as atisfying a house as we shall find in Essex. The owner generously hows the principal rooms by appointment. They contain Armada reasures—Sir William Harris, whose daughter married a Raymond of Charles I's reign, commanded a ship in the battle and brought home Spanish trophies, including an exquisite Flemish triptych— family portraits, including one of the founder, and a sweet-toned chamber organ associated, more probably than most, with Handel.

At the end of the raised grassy terrace flanking the house the
is a pretty 'Gothic' summer-house in the romantic tradition. It
not difficult for visitors to echo the motto carved thereon: '*Fortur*
mea in bello campo'—'My lot is fallen in a fair ground [or a *be*
champ]; yea, I have a goodly heritage'.

The Belchamp Brook, which provides the geographical justific.
tion for this excursion from the Stour, drops down through a woode
valley just below the Hall at Belchamp Walter and finds the Stov
at Brundon. This, although on the Essex bank, is in Suffolk, a
invasion made necessary by the expansion of Sudbury across th
river. It is not possible to follow the Brook closely by road, althoug
it can be done on foot. The quickest way back to the Stour is by wa
of either Borley or Bulmer. If you cut out the river above Sudbur
however, you will miss the lovely village of Pentlow, and this wou
be intolerable. It is well worth the extra miles to see this enchantin
place.

Pentlow is right on the river, with Cavendish just across on th
Suffolk bank. There is not a great deal here. Most of the houses a
at Pentlow Street. On high wooded ground a mile away the battl
ments of a slim tower show above the trees. This is Bull's Tower, a
agreeable conceit dating from the middle of the nineteenth centur
and illustrating a former rector's filial piety. The hall and churc
stand side by side with their backs to the Stour. The hall is amon
the best of these characteristic Essex buildings. It belongs to th
early Tudor period and was given a new look 80 years or so late
The centrepiece is in good plain half-timbering, the wings plastere
Centrally there is a really fine oriel window. All this can be see
from the churchyard, as can the remains of the moat—which ant
dates the present house—and a charming garden with a noble ceda

A half-turn from this extremely pleasing scene brings the churc
into view. Here is one of the Essex round towers and visually a ver
good one, a piece of virtuoso building in flint. The tower was a
afterthought in this predominantly Norman building. It was pu
across the front of an elaborate west door. The chancel is Norma
and is terminated by a singularly perfect apse. North of this is
small Tudor chapel, now filled half with the organ, half with a
exceptionally splendid Jacobean monument to members of th
Kempe family. George Kempe, a Judge, lies here with his son Joh
and the latter's wife. The costume is finely treated. Below kneel th

hildren, four sons facing ten crowded daughters. The other feature
f this church is the font, square Norman work with stylized decora-
on. On this there stands a most elaborate Tudor cover, elegantly
rched and pinnacled, so large that the panels may be opened to
ive access to the baptismal water.

Below Pentlow the journey is pleasantly uneventful. Near Glems-
rd station old gravel workings have flooded to form a chain of
nall ponds which attract wild life—as well as much dumped
ibbish. Foxearth has an evocative name and some attractive houses.
he church, however, was grossly over-restored. At Liston the church
ired better. It has a good brick tower. Much the best thing in this
eighbourhood, however, is the view across the Stour into Suffolk,
rith Long Melford's matchless church as principal eye-catcher sup-
orted by the brick turrets of the Tudor hall.

Next in this journey comes Borley. Not so many years ago the
ame was famous in psychic circles, for Borley Rectory was 'the
10st haunted house in England'. Much time was spent and ink
illed over the phenomena in this gaunt and unromantic building.
espite this the mysteries were still largely unresolved when the
ectory went up in flames, taking, one hopes, its troubled spirits
rith it. There are better things by which to remember Borley, the
iew from the churchyard for instance, which is the perfection of
nemphatic calm beauty. The low Suffolk hills close a scene which
epends for its effect on a complete absence of drama. Formally
lipped yews lead to the plain, well-lit church. Much the best of
1is building is a room-sized monument to Sir Edward Waldegrave
–of a family we met at Navestock. This has all the heraldic trim-
1ings. Sir Edward was one of those who found difficulty in adapting
ɔ the political and religious shifts of the Tudor age. He had been
ɔo faithful a servant to Princess and later Queen Mary to be left in
eace in the following regime. Evidence of superstitious (i.e. Catholic)
ractices was found in his house at Borley, and he and his wife
rere consigned to the Tower where he died in 1561.

Up to this point the Stour has been a little stream although a most
retty one. In 1706 the river was made navigable from Manningtree
p to Sudbury, and consequently for the rest of this journey we shall
ɔllow a controlled and substantial river.

One channel of the 'navigation' comes up to the road at Ballingdon
ɔuffolk), and just beyond this we enter Essex again and go up to the

little church of Middleton, in a remote, lovely and rather overgrow
site. From a distance this looks humble enough, although picturesqu
The south door, sheltered by a shallow wooden porch, corrects th
impression. This is an important Norman building. The doorway h
zig-zag decoration, but the general feeling is of some austerity. Th
is confirmed by the chancel arch, which has a grave majesty. Alt
gether a most impressive building.

The road past Middleton church comes down to the river ;
Henny Street. The old village—or rather the hall and its attendan
church, with an outcrop of new houses—is well inland and abou
200 feet higher. There is no tourist attraction at Great Henny, bu
lovers of quiet landscape will be rewarded. In the softly luminou
air which Constable found so inspiring and so challenging the field
and woods of these gentle hills take on delicate tints. Newl
ploughed, the earth is the palest gold. Set in the heart of this countr
is a severe hall, backed by the church in its frame of tall elms. Th
church is not an important building, but it has a queen-post roo
supported on corbels which are carved with musicians in pleasantl
homely dress. These are newly repainted. The double piscina in th
chancel is unexpectedly elaborate.

I leave this country with great reluctance, being most willing t
'waste my time in it'. Our route is by a narrow by-lane which crosse
the deep valley of a little stream and at last reaches the Stour ;
Daw's Hall. A nature reserve and bird farm have been establishe
here and visitors are welcomed. This is in the parish of Lamarsh an
the church (locked) is just down the road. This has the sixth an
last of the round towers which we have seen in Essex. It is o
Norman origin. A couple of miles further on the Suffolk village o
Bures is cut in two by the river, the smaller part called Bures Haml
being left on the Essex side. Hereabouts, in Henry VI's reign,
dragon—'*dente serrato*'—did much damage to crops and stock unt
he was scared off by a posse of local archers. Here the main roa
from Sudbury to Colchester crosses the river and must be followe
for a while. The village of Mount Bures stands back from the road
The 'mount' is the large motte of a Norman castle, and a crucifor
Norman church was built under its shadow. Much Roman bric
was re-used in the fabric.

A mile along the road a footpath leads through parkland t
Wormingford church, and the same point can be reached by roa

through the village. The church is much restored, but has some pleasing old houses for neighbours. The lane past these goes to the river and so into Suffolk. For our route we must endure the main road for a further mile and then, when it turns sharply right, continue straight on to Little Horkesley.

I have an inordinate liking for this small and quite unassuming village, not least for its inn—the Beehive—which has a real hive on a post for sign. There was a minor priory here, belonging to the Cluniac order, which was suppressed by Wolsey and entirely destroyed. It stood not far from the church. The mediaeval church was totally demolished in a bombing raid in 1940. A replacement in conservative style was completed in 1958. It may have been unenterprising to shirk the opportunity for a building reflecting the post-war image—whatever that may be. Certainly the new building, in a restrained Perpendicular idiom, is beautifully done. There is no fussy detail, but everything—panelling, screen, hangings, carpeting—is the result of good craftsmanship and good taste. The glass in the east window shows some of that inimitable peacock-blue which may in time come to be regarded as the hall-mark of mid-twentieth-century stained glass, as characteristic as was the deeper blues of the twelfth century.

Two important groups of monuments were salvaged from the bombed church. Three figures carved in oak now lie side by side on a brick plinth at the back of the south aisle. All belong to the second half of the thirteenth century and are perhaps just a little larger than life-size. They have not been identified. The carving is of strikingly fine quality, rendering faces and costume with a grave reverence which is strangely moving. The other restored monuments are brasses, notably Sir Robert Swynborne, who died in 1391, with his son, both in armour standing under canopies, and Lady Brygete Marney with her two husbands (1549).

The immediate surroundings of Little Horkesley church are most delightful. Beside the church stands a lovely plastered house, and on the other side the road drops down to give views towards Great Horkesley. Our way now is north, past a lovely half-timbered house called Josselyns, towards the river. A little short of the bridge into Nayland, we turn right and then left to follow a tangle of lanes towards Boxted. This is highly cultivated country with some parkland. For once the church is in the village, not next to the hall. Here lies a local worthy, Sir Richard Blackmore, who was royal physician to Queen Anne.

It is a complicated three miles and more from Boxted to Langham. Here we revert to the normal with church and hall well away from the scattered village. The church may look vaguely familiar at a first visit. It appears in Constable's painting of the Glebe Farm, the roofs of which are seen just beyond the church—but it will tax your ingenuity to work out from which viewpoint Constable worked. This was a favourite subject of his. He worked on the scene several times, moved, it may be, both by the charm of the buildings and their setting and by gratitude towards a one-time parson. For Langham was the 'poor bishop's first living'. John Fisher, rector of Langham and later Bishop successively of Exeter and Salisbury, was one of Constable's earliest and most loyal patrons, and his nephew, another John, was curate of the church. The younger Fisher played a vital part in Constable's complicated courtship of Maria Bicknell, they used to meet in the parsonage, and John set his professional seal on their runaway marriage.

The church is opulent, perhaps to excess. The decoration is well enough done, but all that lushness is distracting. Prosperity came from association with the adjacent great house, and the monuments recall in particular the Umfreville family who flourished hereabouts in Stuart times. The furnishings include benches with poppyheads, angels and leopards, and a singularly solid wooden alms-box.

The little brick box of a building just inside the churchyard is the village school and poorhouse, built by a rector in 1832. This, the church and the glebe farm stand within the park of Langham Hall. The gardens here are opened to the public occasionally in the summer. Their best feature is the brick terrace which looks across the Stour into Suffolk with a church tower (at Higham) in the middle, as essentially English a scene as one could wish. The hall was largely rebuilt about 1740, when it acquired the formal porticoed façade which faces the view. At Easter, with a cloud of daffodils in the grass, this is an especially delightful place.

A lane through Langham comes on to the busy Ipswich road on the steep slope of Gun Hill. Just past the old coaching inn, and a little short of the river, a lane right leads to Dedham. Very soon the most familiar of all Essex architectural shapes, the tower of Dedham church, is in view and holds the eye all the way to the best-preserved

f Essex high streets. By virtue of history and personality Dedham
s the capital of the Stour valley and a town which, for its size, can
tand comparison with any other in this country.

There is nothing, other than its situation, in Dedham as evidence
f the Saxon settlement and the succeeding Norman manor, unless
t is the fishponds whose outlines are said to be traceable and the
mill which is the latest—and the last?—of a long line. Dedham's
rosperity was founded in the reign of Richard II when Michael
e la Pole, the King's Chancellor and temporary favourite, granted
Fair to stimulate the cloth trade. For rather less than 300 years
he town was to make cloth, adapting itself resourcefully to chang-
ng technique and fashion and turning some of the profits into
tone, flint and brick. Its one principal street presents an anthology
f English domestic architecture in black-and-white, plaster and
rick. Of the first kind there is a splendid example in the Marlborough
Head, an inn on a corner site. This belongs to the beginning of the
ixteenth century and may have been a cloth hall originally. Later
private house, it turned inn in Queen Anne's reign and adopted the
ame of the currently popular hero. The formally fronted house
ext door (in High Street) is part of the same structure with a new
ace added in the eighteenth century. Two doors away there is a
all and handsome plaster-fronted house with a symmetrically exact
orch. There are other good examples from this period near the old
oaching inn, the Sun—which sports a fine sign. But Dedham is
ssentially a brick town, and there are many good examples, all
ouses of an essentially urban character. Two of the best have
ducational connections. East of the church, in the little square is the
ree Grammar School, founded in Queen Elizabeth's reign and rebuilt
bout 1730 under the inspiration of a formidable headmaster. A
ablet on the school reads:

THOMAS GRIMWOOD
Hujus scholae Magister. 1732.

t was his son who repaired some of the damage done to young John
Constable by a sadistic usher at the school in Lavenham, teaching
im a little Latin and French and at least not thwarting the boy's urge
o paint. The building, or rather buildings, for there are two distinct
tructures, make more than a little show with their white and red

bricks and tall flat pilasters. The school was reformed out of existence
in 1889. Opposite the church there is an even finer brick house o
about the same date which occupies the site of another Elizabethan
school, preparatory to the Grammar School across the road. This i
now a house called Sherman's. The founder of the school wa
Edmund Sherman, a woolman, who was an ancestor of the Genera
Sherman of American Civil War fame. Sherman's is curiously nar
row, but its face to the street is the handsomest in Dedham. A fligh
of steps rises to the door flanked by flattened Corinthian column:
above which an empty arched niche longs for a statue of the founde
in a toga! Above this again is a sundial. All in all an admirabl
composition, striking but not so rhetorical as to dominate the quie
street intolerably.

This dominance is the prerogative of St Mary's church. This grea
building stands, as a town church should, squarely in the middle c
its community. From almost any point in the town one is aware c
that majestic, almost magisterial tower, watching, like some spiritu;
Big Brother, over the activities of the parish. St Mary's is a tru
wool-church. The fifteenth-century woolmen made a clean swee
of the old church and replaced it with a building which would be :
credit to their devotion and their success. So they put it up in th
high fashionable style of their day, the soaring lines of English Pe
pendicular, much as we saw it earlier at Thaxted. The whole wor
was done by about 1520, a space of less than 30 years. This, the
is that rare thing, a mediaeval church conceived and made all of on
piece, and some at least of the founders lived to see complete th
work, if not of their hands, at least that of their purses. Two familie
the Gurdons and the Webbes, were foremost in the enterpris
Thomas and John Webbe in particular left their mark. The former
monument, in the Easter Sepulchre position, is the most prominer
in the church, and John's merchant mark is one of the devices use
to decorate the roof of a rich covered way under the tower; her
too are two heads which tradition identifies, very reasonably, wit
John and his wife.

The vicar of Dedham has one unusual distinction; he is vicar ar
lecturer. The lectureship was established in Elizabeth's reign. It w
not in the beginning necessarily combined with the office of vica
but the two offices have been joined since 1918. The most famous <
the lecturers was John Rogers, who died in 1636; his monumer

shows a severe Puritan divine but conveys no impression of 'Roaring Rogers' who put Dedham in fear of God for more than 30 years.

This is a very beautiful church. The ravages of the past have been well repaired, and all is immaculate. New heraldic shields have been placed in the magnificent roof, to illustrate the history of the town and its associations. The floral decorations are deservedly famous. Here for once is a church which enjoys the love and care which its age and its architecture demand.

Dedham is the best point from which to sample at close range the delights of the Stour. The town is the base for many walks, and no traveller should miss at least one. A short stroll, admirable for a summer evening if one is staying in the town, begins where the continuous row of houses ends on the western edge of the High Street. Here a path passes across National Trust land—with good backward glimpses of town and church tower—to reach the Stour a little short of Stratford bridge. The return journey is made on the Suffolk bank by a path which at times has difficulty—but not too much—in negotiating the drainage channels which cut the meadows into a watery jigsaw puzzle. All the way back Dedham tower is in view. The riverside path comes to the road at Dedham Mill, descendant of one which ground flour for a Norman knight and another built for the redoubtable Sir John Fastolf during Henry VI's troubled reign. It abandoned flour milling in favour of fulling cloth during the rich years of the cloth boom.

The other, and finer riverside walk is approached by a path going north at the corner of High Street and Brook Street. This quickly reaches the river and follows it all the way to Flatford Mill. By one of the inscrutable decrees of local administration the southern bank of the Stour here is in Suffolk and the county boundary follows the older stream. This need not deter us from the enjoyment of this mile or two of river walk, where the waterway is lined with the most contorted of ancient willows and the scene glows with what Constable saw as 'God Almighty's daylight'. This is still artist's country. Not even Constable has said the last word about 'willows, old rotten planks, slimy posts and brickwork' and these things are here in abundance, together with broad skies, low hills and Dedham tower visible at every turn of the river.

The return to Dedham may profitably be made by a simple retracing of steps—for this is scenery of a quality not to be exhausted at a single acquaintance. Alternatively a track south from the footbridge at Flatford might be taken to Jupeshill Farm, giving rather more than a mile of by-road back to Brook Street. A longer way round here would take in Castle House, a clothmaker's house near Dedham Heath which was the last home of Sir Alfred Munnings. This is opened frequently and much of his work is on show.

In most parts of the country anti-climax must follow a visit to a place as rich in beauty and interest as Dedham. By a happy chance we are let down gently from these heights, for the next village along the valley is Lawford. Lawford trails briefly along the main road out of Colchester, with the hall and church isolated half a mile away. Lawford Hall, a large Tudor house refaced in the eighteenth century, is now the headquarters of a research establishment. The church, halfway along the drive, is one of the Essex masterpieces and the finest representative in the county of the Decorated style. It would be good to know what access of prosperity or piety or what change of patronage prompted the rebuilding of a small village church on such an exceptionally lavish scale early in the fourteenth century. The work began with the chancel; by the time the restorers got to the nave the impetus had been lost or the money expended, and this part is ordinary enough. The best of it is in fact a slim pillar font added in the eighteenth century. The decoration in the chancel, although battered in places and partnered by an incredibly brash Victorian reredos, is inexhaustibly interesting. Around the windows twine luxuriant growths of branches and leaves, and birds and animals peep from among them. In one window men frolic and caper and play musical instruments. There is an infectious gaiety, almost frivolity, about it all. Below the windows the piscina, sedilia and priest's door are designed as a single unit. The carving here, being more accessible, has suffered more, and the figures are all headless; enough remains to show how fertile and individual was the imagination of this master carver, working away with sure hand and keen eye, love of fun and love of nature during the reign of that deporable—but fun-loving—king, Edward II.

The Stour is tidal to Manningtree, and this crowded town has a maritime air as well as a smell of malt. Some good houses, predominantly Georgian, survive among the traffic. The parish church is that rarity, a church rebuilt in Jacobean times, in 1616 but so much altered in early Victorian days as to show little of its origins.

or once, the Dissenters have the best of it, in architectural terms.

Manningtree has two memories that are worth pursuing, one pleasant, one extremely disagreeable. In Elizabeth's reign a regular attender at the market was a pioneer agricultural theorist, Thomas Tusser. Tusser, then farming just across the border at Cattawade, was of Essex stock. He had been born at Rivenhall, and after training as a musician tried his hand at farming, in Suffolk and Norfolk as well as Essex. He was, it seems, not too good at it. Fuller said unkindly: 'none . . . better at the theory or worse at the practice of husbandry'. His book *Hundreth Good Points of Husbandrie*, published in 1557, was a Tudor best seller, a most endearing verse medley of practical tips, folklore and common sense, shot through with the gentle personality of the author.

Matthew Hopkins, who practised law in Manningtree in the seventeenth century, is a minor contender for the title of Nastiest Man of Essex. The weakness of his case, as compared with, say, Richard Rich, is not lack of ill-will but the short term of his operations and their disastrous conclusion. For a brief three years he travelled the country as Witch Finder General. His territory included much of East Anglia, but he devoted himself especially to his own county, and in one year alone 60 women were humiliated, tortured and hanged as a result of his activities. At last someone asked the inevitable question: how did he know so much about the habits of witches? He was 'swum' as a sorcerer, floated and was hanged in 1647. A highly satisfactory conclusion. Butler in *Hudibras*, says gleefully that he

> . . . *after proved himself a witch*
> *And made a rod for his own breech.*

It would be a pity to leave Manningtree on such a sour note. We might therefore remember Prince Hal's word for Falstaff: 'That roasted Manningtree ox with the pudding in his belly.'

At Mistley there is the first view, and a good one, of the Stour estuary. The river is now more than a mile wide, and on the Essex shore there is a breezy meadow where the traffic of the river, and the flight of birds, can be watched. Mistley itself, once a mediaeval village, then a minor spa, later an industrial district, is now largely residential with much post-war housing. Of the third stage the building of the maltings, beside the river, are colourful and sensibl in design.

The old church lay inland, on the lane to Mistley Heath. It wa allowed to decay when a new church was built nearer to the ne centre in 1735, and now only the porch remains. If the rest was c this quality, it must have been a notable building. The porch is c flint, richly decorated with flushwork, including heraldic shielc and monograms, in the same manner as that employed in the towe at Dedham and perhaps from the same period if not the same hanc

The new church, a brick box, was enriched as part of ambitiou plans to develop Mistley in the second half of the eighteenth centur The idea came from Richard Rigby, the local Member and Paymaste to the Forces, one of those politicians whose public life was highl suspect but who seem to have had genuinely beneficent intentior towards their home town. Rigby lived at the hall. He engaged Robei Adam as architect of his plans. The full grandiose scheme was neve completed, but Adam remodelled the church. Churches were nc normally part of his activities, and his work was at least origina He built a tower at each end of the existing brick church and pr a new classical portico in the middle. Rigby's house has gone an so has the church, but Adam's two towers remain in their graveyar by the river. Perhaps their value as landmarks, rather than the fam of the architect, ensured their preservation, and the Ministry c Public Buildings and Works now has them in hand. There is littl enough left anywhere of the work of the greatest of eighteentl century architects, and we must be grateful. I must confess to fin ing these towers, with their colonnades and cupolas, rather mor curious than beautiful. The Adam church was superseded by Gothic Revival church with a tall tower; this remains.

From Mistley to the end of our journey, the road runs well bac from the estuary with only occasional glimpses of the water. Th countryside is pleasant enough but mostly disappointing after wha we have seen upstream. The villages, too, lack character. The fir is Bradfield which has grown up at the highest point of this main low country around a cross-roads. The large church is conspicuou Its most interesting feature is the pulpit, in which the Georgia carpenters re-used carved panels already a century and more ol Were they from an older pulpit, one wonders, or from some oth source? Seeing a priory not far off at Wix, it would be nice t

imagine that the panel portraying the Crucifixion was smuggled from there at the suppression, but the odds are against it. The local worthy of Bradfield was Sir Harbottle Grimston—delightful name—a politician who trod delicately during the Civil Wars and Commonwealth, supporting Parliament but well to the right of centre. He survived to support Monk's proposals for the Restoration and received a modest reward from the king.

There is nothing much to see at Wix. The priory has gone completely, and in its place is a house—Wix Abbey—of which the best feature is an Elizabethan porch with brick gable in the so-called Flemish manner. Wix is caught up in one of the sad strange legends of the middle ages, the story of the Green Children. Two children, with green skins, were found in Suffolk, it was said in Stephen's reign. They were brought before a knight of Wix for examination. The boy pined and died, but the girl grew up here, being 'rather loose and wanton in her conduct'. The two children had come from a twilit land beyond a great river, and had wandered by chance into a cavern giving entrance to this world. A similar story is told of some other places.

Over towards the river is Wrabness, a straggly village of no great charm. It does offer an opportunity to get down to the shore. A narrow lane through the village ends just below the sea-wall, from which you may take a walk on the wall or the shore, to enjoy the sight of sailing craft, decaying barges and numerous beach huts and to breathe the indefinable but unforgettable atmosphere of the estuary, composed of salt and mud and North Sea air.

The road from Wrabness to Ramsey is pleasingly wooded. There is much nondescript and ill-controlled building along the way. One cannot commend this, but I did see one admirable example of non-conformity, a front-garden folly, much larger and infinitely more individual than the usual gnomes. Ramsey has traffic troubles and has lost its leisured atmosphere. Exceptionally it has a church right in the middle of the village, while the hall and the Elizabethan Roy-don Hall are two miles away. The church has a commanding position and its brick tower—early Tudor—must make a useful mark for shipping. The building shows a variety of styles from twelfth to sixteenth centuries and has some good detail, notably a rich doorway on the south. Just beyond the church the entrance to Michael-stow Hall provides a brave flourish in a mainly dull route.

We are now within the influence of Harwich and it is bricks-and-mortar all the way. Dovercourt comes first, an ancient parish which came into its own halfway through the nineteenth century when an enterprising gentleman, the local Member, launched it as a seaside resort. This development took place along the North Sea shore, not on the estuary, and fanciers of mid- and late-Victorian Domestic will find something to interest them here as well as some later developments which may appeal less.

The old village, now Upper Dovercourt, has the parish church. Interest here is divided between an iron-bound alms-box of Elizabethan date and some melancholy memories of the Walcheren Expedition. An expeditionary force was sent to the mouth of the Scheldt in 1809 as part of the recurrent strategy of European wars to secure the Rhine delta. For a year the army sat here ineffectively, dying in their thousands from the fevers which lurked in the marshes. When the force was pulled out and brought back to Harwich many sick men died and were buried in the Dovercourt graveyard.

A glance at the map will explain the historic importance of Harwich. It occupies a little peninsula in the twin estuaries of Stour and Orwell, protected from the force of the sea by a tongue of land on the Suffolk side. It shared with Maldon the supremacy among the ports of mediaeval Essex, and unlike Maldon it did not lie at the head of a long and treacherous tidal river. The town gained its first charter from Edward II in 1318, by which time it had been a port of some consequence for at least a century; it returned two members to Parliament right up to the Reform Act of 1667. Walls were built around it in 1352. Today, in spite of innumerable changes, the town plan is still on the grid principle familiar in Edwardian new towns like Winchelsea. It had been a market town since 1253, but like other mediaeval new towns it was not an ecclesiastical parish. St Nicholas in Harwich was a chapel of Dovercourt. Here again there is a parallel with another south-eastern port; the Cinque Port of Hythe lacked independent ecclesiastical status throughout the middle ages.

These years of fame, of ships sailing out of Harwich to raid French ports and French men-of-war during the Hundred Years War and of French ships sacking the town in return, are gone. The opening of the railway in 1854 and the construction of Parkestone Quay n 1883 brought the town a renewal of prosperity. It has still, unlike most mediaeval ports, a part to play in traffic with the Continent, although air-travel and other technological changes have reduced its role. Today the town stands on the edge of change. It is half decayed, half in process of renewal. Much of the quaintness and picturesque messiness which gave it character until recently have gone, and so far not enough has been put in its place to reconcile us to the loss. Nothing significant remains of the mediaeval town. The church is early nineteenth century. The inn nearby, the Three Cups, is a good deal older, and in foundation may belong to the old town. A few Georgian houses still resist the demolishers. The persistent explorer will find rewards in some of the back streets. Most visitors however must for once forego the delights of the past and enjoy on the quayside the parade of craft in the river and the noise and colour of a still-busy port. For me this evidence of history in the making is not quite an adequate substitute for history past.

CHAPTER NINE

Western Boundary

Great Chesterford—Saffron Walden—Newport—
Clavering—Hatfield Forest—Harlow—Roydon—
Epping Forest—Waltham Abbey

On all sides except the north-west Essex has a natural boundary
water. Near Birdbrook, however, the Stour comes south out
Suffolk. From here to Great Hallingbury near Bishop's Stortford t
boundary line has historical validity but cannot be recognized l
any distinctive feature on the ground, except where it coincic
briefly with the Granta at Bartlow and follows the line of the Rom
road for a mile or two beyond Stump Cross.

One unifying factor in this north-western part of the county
the Cam which rises near Widdington, flows south-west for a fe
miles and then enters a narrow straight valley going north to t
Cambridgeshire border at Great Chesterford. This bright little cha
stream, which the main A 11 road follows closely, makes a co
tribution to this landscape quite out of proportion to its size. V
will follow the Cam up-stream to its source, and then go across
the Stort valley, following this along the Hertfordshire bounda
to its junction with the Lea. The Lea will take us inevitably in
London.

At Great Chesterford we are on the chalk, as a glance at t
scenery will confirm. The smooth contours of the skyline and t
gentle rise and fall of the ploughed fields are characteristic of cha
country. This is a land in which the sky assumes great importan
Its beauty vanishes when the mists roll in or one uniform gr
merges sky and skyline. On a day when huge billows of cumul

sweep across the sky the chalk downs of northern Essex are surpassingly lovely.

Great Chesterford, where the roads to Cambridge and Newmarket
part company, has been an important staging post throughout history and beyond. The area has produced some of the comparatively
few remains of Paleolithic man in this county, and it seems to have
been inhabited through most of the succeeding ages up to the arrival
of the Romans. The Romans built a fort to guard the crossing of the
river and this, as usual, provided the focal point for a sizable civilian
community. Of this town nothing stands above ground, at any
rate that the untutored eye can see, but plenty of relics have found
their way into museums.

The Saxon settlers followed their normal practice of setting up
their villages outside the Roman walls and this forms the basis of
the modern village. It is a complex and growing place, happily by-
passed by the main road. The best of it is in the immediate neighbourhood of the church, where there is an old inn and a half-timbered
house—dated 1674—by the churchyard gate. The church is large,
and seems once to have been larger. It is of thirteenth-century origin,
but much of its detail and nearly all its atmosphere have vanished
under a drastic restoration.

The church is only just off the main road, and it may be worth
going left here for a sight of the Cam and a large watermill. A lesser
road (A 130) to Saffron Walden offers respite from the main-road
traffic, and this will lead in rather more than a mile to Little Chesterford. The village street linking both roads bends sharply at the
church and hall. The church is locked, so we may say 'sour grapes'
and think that it does not look interesting. The hall cannot be seen
from either the road or the churchyard, but there is a good view of
it from the Cam bridge just down the road. This squat plastered
building, which looks like a hundred others in Essex villages, is a
remarkable survival from the thirteenth century. The oldest part is
of stone and is probably the oldest inhabited house in the
county.

As we are now close to the main road we may take this for a
few miles, gaining glimpses of the river and views across to woods
above the eastern bank. The next village is Littlebury, a place of
some size and of almost town-like character. The trunk road passes
through it, and it is wise to abandon the car in a side road in order

to look at leisure at the fine houses which flank it, some of them belonging to the great days of wool in the early sixteenth century others to the coaching age which brought a renewal of prosperity to Littlebury. Down by the river is a well-preserved millhouse.

The church stands just off the main road. It looks, and is, a mix ture, but one which produces good results. The oldest is the south doorway, late Norman and preserved when the wall in which it is set was rebuilt. It is protected by a most remarkable stone porch with an exceptionally tall arch and the remains of stone vaulting There is a similar one on the north. Inside it is very dark, and it may take a little time in the gloom to realize that the soaring splen dours of the chancel arch are Victorian, not fourteenth century They are not the less splendid. This chancel at Littlebury is among the best Gothic revival work in Essex. The screen is later still, early twentieth century and touched with a more classical restraint. The most conspicuous of the furnishings is a wooden font cover which entirely encloses the stone font; it has a fantastic canopy and elegant linenfold panels.

Our way lies straight down the road. If you would like a little taste of the chalk hill country you might turn right by a narrow lane rising above 350 feet on its way to Strethall, returning by an other, which as it descends towards the Cam valley, runs through a noble avenue, a foretaste of the landscaped delights of Audley End On the left, as we approach the main road again, there is a rounded hill with a crown of trees masking the earthworks of an Iron Age camp—Ring Hill. On the summit there is a round temple, one of the follies of Audley End, which was built to commemorate the end of the Seven Years War. A little domed drum is surrounded by an open arcade of Ionic columns.

We are now within the bounds of the greatest house in Essex Audley End presents a handsome face to the road with the widened waters of the Cam breaking the green lawns in the foreground. The house and grounds are now in the care of the Ministry of Public Buildings and Works and are open to visitors frequently.

The house dates originally from the beginning of James I's reign The land had belonged to the great abbey of Walden, founded— as a priory—by Geoffrey de Mandeville as a house of Benedictine monks. It had grown to become one of the more prosperous of the Essex abbeys. At the Dissolution the abbey was granted to Sir

homas Audley, for services rendered. He had been Speaker of the
eformation Parliament and was to become Lord Chancellor and
aron Audley of Walden. We have seen how many of those who
eered the English Reformation were from Essex. Audley, who was
f Halstead, was very much a man of this age, able, ambitious, pliant.
e destroyed the abbey buildings and built himself a house on the
te. This in turn was demolished by his grandson to make way for
 palace on the grand scale.

The creator of Audley End was Thomas Howard of Walden, Earl
f Suffolk, later Lord Treasurer of England, a man of character. As
 young man he fought against the Armada; in his later years he
ecame involved with an adventuress who helped to ruin him.
Ieanwhile he had built the largest house in England, about which
1e King had commented acidly: 'Too much for a King, but it might
o very well for a Lord Treasurer.' The present mansion, large as it
, is very much less than half the original, of which it formed the
entre. In front of the present entrance was a huge courtyard, en-
losed and with a gatehouse. The further courtyard was much
irger than it is now and was itself enclosed by a now-vanished range
f two storeys. So vast a house was a burden even to the Suffolk
imily, and at last in 1721 Vanbrugh advised some judicious prunings.
fter another reduction 30 years later Audley End was left about
1e size that it is now. Shortly afterwards the property passed to
1e future Lord Braybrooke who spent a fortune in restoring and
eautifying it.

John Evelyn observed that the house was 'twixt antiq and modern'.
he description is even more apt now that Vanbrugh's work of 1721
nd Adam's of about 1765 have underlined the contrast with the
lightly archaic great hall. There is a heavy richness about the great
arved screen in the hall which, for all its magnificence, is some-
rhat oppressive. The eye finds relief in turning from these deeply
arved arches and Jacobean caryatids to the clean soaring lines of
anbrugh's stone screen. Beyond this screen, however, all is light
nd grace. Even the most extravagant rooms, the Georgian saloon
nd the later dining room and library, have an architectural sim-
licity of outline which is not swamped by the ornamentation. For
1any visitors the most delightful experience will be the suite of
ooms decorated by Robert Adam, particularly the alcove room with
s formal panels and the dining parlour, successfully restored during

recent repairs. Then there is the chapel, a memorable essay in Straw
berry Hill Gothic.

When Evelyn visited Audley End in 1654 he found the garden
'not in order'. This was put to rights by Braybrooke who in 176
commissioned Lancelot Brown to devise a worthy setting for th
house. Capability Brown was at his resourceful best here, and w
are the beneficiaries. The noble house sits perfectly in the landscap
The lawns, the artificially lake-like river, Adam's exquisite bridg
on the approach road: these are matched by trees placed with ca
culated skill, glades and architectural conceits in the best eighteentl
century manner. Of these last, most visitors will find the fulle
satisfaction in the Tea House Bridge. Here, below the lake, the Car
is a modest stream again, narrow enough for a single span. This litt
stone bridge is topped with a quite delightful open pavilion supporte
on Ionic columns. Facing the house is the Ring Hill Temple, whic
we saw on the way in. Adam made a set of seats for this, and the:
have now been taken into the house for safe keeping. Behind th
house, in an effective position, is the Temple of Concord. This ha
a sublime uselessness. An open Greek temple, or the portico to
non-existent temple, not ideally suited to the English climate for a
the winds of heaven blow through it, this folly commemorates-
by a fitting irony—the recovery of George III from one of his bou
of madness. All these garden buildings, together with the colum
in memory of the Lady Portsmouth who demolished the easter
range and adopted Braybrooke, and the many ornaments distribute
through the grounds, add substantially to the delight of a visit t
Audley End.

Just outside the Lion Gate a little hamlet has grown up. The co
tages, all of one period, are exceptionally attractive. The lar
opposite leads to the College of St Mark, a group of almshouses no
used as a home for retired clergy. The Earl of Suffolk who buil
Audley End was responsible for this foundation. The building
laid out around two open courts with the communal rooms in th
centre. It makes a pretty group of gables and tall chimneys.

Saffron Walden, which begins just beyond the park of Audl
End, has grown in recent years just too much to retain its essenti
character. It is still the best of Essex towns—if we think of Dedha
and Thaxted as town-like villages—but in enjoying its finest qualiti
we have to blind ourselves to new blemishes and some old shabbines

34 Mistley Towe

A number of notable houses, including the *Sun Inn*, almost the most famous of all, seem in need of repair. There remains not merely a generous plenty of lovely houses but still more the indefinable but unmistakable atmosphere of a town with deep roots and a lively awareness of the modern world. It is an old settlement, inhabited during the Roman occupation and playing a strategic role before and after the Norman Conquest. The abbey brought additional fame, and the town grew, as witness the mediaeval earthworks of Battle Ditches. Later it shared in the boom of the wool trade in the fifteenth century, while the local production of saffron gave the town its distinctive name.

This long story is told most effectively in the Saffron Walden museum. I must admit to a general antipathy towards museums, finding that antiquities behind glass fail to stimulate my sluggish historical imagination. The museum in Saffron Walden is different. It seems to me quite the best of all small town collections and the best presented. In recent years the emphasis has been on selection and education; instead of ordered ranks of flints, pots and the like, a few characteristic exhibits have been carefully arranged and interpreted with maps and pictures. The display work is first-rate.

The museum is housed in a spacious brick mansion built in 1834, standing to the east of the church and close to the ruins of the castle. This is a late Norman building of flint and rubble, which formed part of the defensive system of Geoffrey de Mandeville, the ruthless and opportunist Earl of Essex. It seems not to have long survived the downfall of the Mandevilles, and became derelict at an early age. The remains, neglected and overgrown, are depressing rather than romantic, although they do afford a striking view of the church, which, because it is hemmed in by houses, cannot easily be seen in all its splendour.

Saffron Walden church is beyond question the finest parish church in Essex and can stand comparison with the best of East Anglia. It is indeed of the East Anglian school, a great Perpendicular building witnessing to the pride and wealth of the fifteenth-century woolmen and to the later acumen of Lord Audley. I find it, like most Perpendicular work, splendid rather than spiritual, but that may be merely the rationalizing of a prejudice. The church is beautifully light. The tall arcades of the nave are topped with clerestories which flood the wide building with a creamy glow. Some of this work is attributed to John Wastell, who was the last of the great masons in the tradition established by Yevele. He was concerned in the building of King's College Chapel at Cambridge and built the great Bell Harry Tower at Canterbury. The chancel arch and the nave arcades, with their nobly formal spandrels, are in his finest manner. The chapels in the chancel were completed after his death. The south chapel contains now, but not originally, the tomb of Henry VIII's pliant Lord Audley. The north chapel is exquisite in its grace and simplicity, my own favourite part of this great building.

Outside, the effectiveness of the church is much reduced by its position, which is lofty but confined. It is not possible to get back far enough to appreciate its scale and the beauty of its proportions. The tall spire, however, which was added in the nineteenth century, dominates the town from every angle.

The old town is concentrated in quite a small area, and every visitor should take at least a short walk to enjoy some of its charms. This should include the Market Place, where there is a fine inn older than its Queen Anne front and a comically showy Corn Exchange. Beyond Market Hill is Church Street which has on the corner the old Sun Inn (no longer an inn). Here is some of the most celebrated pargetting to survive from the seventeenth century. It is naïve but lively. The house was, it is said, the headquarters of the Parliamentary forces in the last stages of the Civil War. Down Church Street is Church Path—where there is the only uninterrupted view of the church—with its row of little cottages. In the High Street, which further on becomes Bridge Street, there are some good houses, some sixteenth century, some Georgian. The Cross Keys is the handsomest of the inns. On the corner of Castle Street there is a particularly lovely half-timbered house. Castle Street itself is less exciting, but it gives access to an unexpected pleasure, Bridge End Garden, a most satisfying piece of formal layout beside a stream. There is a summer house, a perilously rickety iron belvedere, and some nice garden sculpture. This walk can be concluded by following Museum Street back to the Market Place, or extended at will, always with profit.

Saffron Walden was the birthplace, and the home for much of his long life, of that pedant and poetaster—whose main function one might think was to correct the impression that the Elizabethan age was a nest of singing birds—Gabriel Harvey. Harvey played some part in local affairs and earned a certain notoriety by dabbling, with his brother, in the dubious science of astrology. A tedious man, he would have been quite forgotten but for the friendship of Spenser, who inscribed the introduction to the *Shepheardes Calendar* to 'the most excellent and learned both Orator and Poete, Mayster Gabriell Harvey' and wrote him into that work as Hobbinol.

Back across the Cam and briefly along the London Road there is a turning right—opposite an old inn with an amusing sign—to Wendens Ambo. The village is just beyond the railway. The original station-house, a little off the road, is a good example of the well-proportioned work of the golden age of railway architecture. Among Essex place-names Wendens Ambo stands high. Once there were two Wenden villages; they were amalgamated and so the parish became 'both Wendens'. The old village is very small, but it has—for me—the finest village street in Essex. Even the ubiquitous wires do not quite ruin it. On the left is a row of highly individual cottages, all different, all good. To the right a huge and ancient barn with hooded porches hides the hall. In front the picture is closed by the church with its squat tower, Norman or perhaps Saxon, and Hertfordshire spike—not an 'important' building but abundantly pleasing to the eye. Inside, the church is very dim, which makes it difficult to see the fragments of mural paintings which illustrate the life of St Margaret of Antioch. One small detail in the furnishings is interesting; on a bench there is an example of the confused natural history of the middle ages. A tiger—but it appears more like a bear—looks down on a mirror, in which it gazes entranced by its own beauty until, in its preoccupation, it will be taken by the hunter. This may be unsound zoology, but what a lesson against vanity!

The Cam flows east of the main road, and there lies our way. If you want to avoid two or three miles of heavy traffic, you might stay on this side and go a long way round to Newport, passing at Hobs Aerie a celebrated viewpoint and further on the pretty streamside village of Arkesden. At Wicken Bonhunt you will see another old inn with an attractive sign and, on the far edge of the village, the very old chapel of Bonhunt Farm.

Newport is spread out along and on either side of the main road. The High Street is very fine, and it is sad that so many heavy lorries shake the old houses during most of the minutes of the day. For this reason it is wise to see the little town on foot. There is much to see. Most of the buildings of the Grammar School are mid-Victorian and later, but the school is an Elizabethan foundation, by a bereaved lady who thus gained 'twenty good sons' to comfort her for the loss of one. Many of the houses which line the road are Georgian, or older with new Georgian faces. At the north end one displays good formal pargetting with the date 1692. The most conspicuous house is Monks Barn which looks just like a Kentish hall-house; it has bold half-timbering and a projecting oriel window carved below with figures of the Virgin and Child who are being entertained by angels performing on harp and organ. This fine house, which looks warmer than most through its use of red-brick infilling of the timbers, belongs to the very end of the middle ages. It makes a nice contrast to the noble five-bayed Georgian house just opposite, whose brick façade is broken with a generous growth of greenery.

The name of Newport may seem surprising as it is far from the coast or any navigable river. 'Port' is, however, commonly used to mean 'town', and this was one of the many market towns which grew up belatedly along the main roads of Essex after the main rural pattern had emerged.

From a distance Newport is quite dominated by its great church tower. When you enter the town you may have difficulty in finding it, for it is hidden away behind the west side of the street. Like Saffron Walden it is on an enclosed sloping site and cannot be well seen. It is a large cruciform building, suggesting something more than a purely parochial function. Was it connected with the mediaeval hospital in Newport? There has been much rebuilding, notably of the tower, but the new work blends well enough with the earlier, Early English to Perpendicular. The pinnacled two-storeyed porch is handsome. Inside, the building is light and spacious. The one undoubted treasure is a chest in the south chapel. This is a portable altar, its lid raised to display five painted panels making a ready-to-use reredos. This is contemporary with the earliest of the church's fabric.

South of Newport the Cam keeps close to the main road, and sometimes floods the side roads. Well to the east is the pretty village of Widdington. The church, hall and rectory make a fine group. For me Widdington is most memorable for Mole Hall, a moated house lying a mile along a narrow lane to the south-east. This would be delight enough in itself, for Mole Hall is a singularly perfect

xample of the Elizabethan Essex hall framed by trees. The owners
ave however established here one of the most agreeable of small
vildlife parks. (The word 'zoo' with its implication of cages and
arriers is inappropriate.) At Mole Hall you may stumble over a
ocile deer, come face to face with a pelican, or be assaulted by a
igh spirited and friendly young chimpanzee. There are enclosures,
or sensible practical reasons, but these are largely for the benefit
f the inmates—mostly birds but with a leavening of monkeys,
vallabies, otters and the like. Many right-minded people dislike the
dea of animals in captivity. At Mole Hall one does not often think
f captives and captors; this seems for the most part to be a satis-
actory partnership of which we are privileged to be spectators.
here are few better ways of passing a sunny afternoon than in
trolling about this friendly park.

The lane past Mole Hall peters out fairly soon in high country near
he source of the Cam. Our way must be back westwards across the
iver—if the floods allow—and so down a lane turning south and
ast to Henham. This is near enough to the infant Cam to make a
ood conclusion to this journey up the river. Henham is a 'picture'
illage, which is no bad thing if it neither produces a rush of precious-
ess to the villagers' heads nor attracts visitors in such numbers as
o destroy the peace they come to enjoy. Henham does not do badly.
t has a long winding street with a large green at the centre. There
s much half-timbering and thatch, and a general impression of
vell-being—clearly a good place to have a stake in. At a bend in
he road the church stands well back. It is an effective building with
neat spire of the Hertfordshire pattern. There are some fearsome
argoyles, one with a little man perched head-down between his
orns, halfway to hell. The screen is handsome and so is a lectern
vith Jacobean panelling. The most attractive feature of the interior
s a capital in the nave, on which the Virgin sits attended by angels.
like too, for different reasons, the elegant abstract classical monu-
nent to Samuel Feake, who lies here far away from the scene of
is terrestrial activities; he was Governor of Fort William in Cal-
utta in the days of John Company.

We have now to get across from the Cam valley to the Stort. One
vay of doing this would be to drop down to Elsenham, a large
illage where they make, most successfully, 'the most expensive
am in the world' and I daresay the best. Here there is a generous

plenty of fine houses, a church with Norman chancel-arch an
double piscina, and a welcoming inn—the Crown—at the cross
roads. Beyond the railway-station is Ugley—whatever does th
Women's Institute call itself?—which quite belies its name, an
after a run north along the Cambridge road a lane goes left throug
Rickling to Clavering. Here we are close both to the Hertfordshir
border and to the source of the Stort, and, moreover, in country o
especial excellence.

The Stort is a tiny trickle of water here, but it plays a part i
the defensive system of Clavering. From a back lane north of th
village you can cross a stream and walk among the low embank
ments of Clavering Castle. This, it is generally accepted, was tha
rarity, a pre-Conquest castle, established by Norman immigrant
during their temporary ascendancy under Edward the Confessor an
used by them as a refuge after Godwin's return from exile. Whethe
or not this was so a Norman castle followed the Conquest. The wall
which topped the earthworks have now quite gone.

The castle made Clavering a place of importance through th
Middle Ages. It is a large village but scattered. It has two principa
accents today, one by the church and the other in Middle Street
where a double row of admirable houses runs down to the Stort
The lane leading up to the church makes one of the best villag
scenes in the county. There are better cottages than these, but fev
which sit in their setting with such quiet assurance. One of them i
very long and its overhung face undulates gently. The church make
an effective close to the picture.

This is a large and elaborate building, reflecting the status of th
parish. Mr C. C. J. Simmonds, in an excellent brief guide, puts i
among the first four churches of north-west Essex and the claim i
just. It belongs to the second half of the fourteenth century, in th
first fine flourish of English Perpendicular, and it illustrates the spiri
of an age which, despite plague and labour unrest, was confiden
and prosperous. It has one of the best of Essex roofs and a scree
of outstanding loveliness, light and graceful and—dare one say it?—
all the better for the destruction of its loft and rood. In front o
this is an elegantly poised Elizabethan pulpit. There are two notabl
monuments: one commemorates a local benefactor, Haynes Barley
and his two wives, the other an unknown knight who must hav
been brought from the earlier church. It would be nice to believ

he tradition that this was John's mentor and Henry III's regent Iubert de Burgh.

From Clavering the Stort flows parallel with the County boundary nd a road keeps close to its western bank. Berden, where there vas an Augustinian priory and a mediaeval mound of doubtful •urpose and where the church has an unexpectedly luxurious hancel, lies off to the west. The next village on the river is Manuden. This is a charming place with many good cottages around he cross-roads. There is a delightful row backing on to the church- ard. Restoration, or more correctly rebuilding, has left little of nterest in the church, except for the rescued rood-screen. Manu- en is the starting-point for some good walks in this gently pleasing ountry.

Beyond Manuden both river and road meet the Hertfordshire •order. To avoid this trespass, you may turn east over the Stort nd come in three winding miles to the main road at Stansted. tansted—its full name Stansted Mountfitchet commemorates a .night from Normandy—has won an unenviable fame since the Var, first for its minor but still busy—and noisy—airport, then as he chosen site for a London Airport. Apart from the existence of runway here, the choice could hardly have been less apt. Stansted ies at the heart of the least spoiled part of the Home Counties and mong rich cornlands. Although it is served by road and rail, no one ould pretend that either is adequate even for existing demands. 'olitical decisions rarely take account of such factors as rural ameni- ies or food production and Stansted and the lovely countryside round seemed doomed, but a vigorous and concerted protest rought at length an almost unprecedented action. Government onceded not that it was wrong but that it might have been wrong, nd Stansted was temporarily reprieved. The threat has now passed lsewhere, but the airport, even in its present restricted area, ontinues to grow alarmingly.

Stansted has been a place of some importance at least from Norman times. The early mediaeval town was dominated by a :astle. The masonry has vanished completely, which is hardly sur- •rising as the castle is said to have been abandoned after receiving lamage in the troubles of King John's reign. If you stand on the ·ailway bridge, just off the town centre, you will see clearly the umbled earthworks of the motte and bailey.

There are really three parts to Stansted: the old town street nea
the castle with one or two fine houses, a long straggle along th
coaching road, joined to the other by a connecting street at th
head of which stands an iron fountain, typically mid-Victorian i
its unconscious silliness, and the church end a mile away. Th
church, famous for its monuments, sports locked doors, and mo
visitors will have to make do with seeing the exterior, dull but fo
two magnificent Norman doorways.

Just north of the town, at Norman House, is the Wildlife Par
established by Aubrey Buxton. Here one can go for a country wal
and see on the way, in conditions simulating complete freedom,
large collection of birds, largely ducks and geese but with a generou
number of more exotic animals, flamingos, cranes and som
gorgeously coloured pheasants. Part of the route is through an olde
landscaped park in which the birds are set off against a backgroun
of formal lakes and fine trees. This sanctuary, which is opene
regularly to visitors, is as delightful, in its different way, as Mol
Hall.

The county boundary, which follows the Stort briefly near Star
sted, now makes an abrupt bend to leave the eastward sprawl c
Bishop's Stortford in Hertfordshire. This necessary departure fron
the Stort provides an opportunity for a visit to the second larges
of the surviving fragments of the great Forest of Essex. Perhaps th
easiest way to reach Hatfield Forest from Stansted is to take the roa
south almost opposite the church, which in three miles crosses th
Dunmow road near the site of Thremhall Priory. A mile and a hal
east along this road brings us to Takeley Street—Takeley, where th
church has an elaborate font cover, is further on—and a turnin
right leads to one entrance to the Forest.

Hatfield Forest came to the National Trust in 1924 as a gift of E
North Buxton. It is always open to the public. Rather surprisingl
cars are admitted and these can be driven right through the fores
from Bush End to Lodge Farm near Woodside Green. I must confes
to thinking that in a forest, if anywhere, one ought to be able t
escape from the motor car. Happily there are many parts whic
the car cannot penetrate, and in wet weather—of which this are
has its share—even the main rides become impassable. A few peopl
perhaps, the disabled, the aged and the chronically lazy, might othe
wise be deprived of the charms of Hatfield Forest; for my part

prefer to see it on foot, seeing what the motorist misses, the narrow forest paths, the birds and the flowers.

Motorists and walkers alike are likely to find themselves at the ornamental lake on the eastern edge. Anglers come here in hundreds to try for the tench and pike. Beside the lake there is a little lodge ornamented, in the eighteenth-century fashion, with shells. On the lake front these form what I take to be a spread eagle.

Visitors will notice particularly that most of the forest consists of young trees. The whole tract had been sold for its timber when Mr Buxton took vigorous action in 1923. He managed to save a few old trees, but the rest were felled. It is an interesting exercise to identify the survivors, mainly oaks and hornbeams. The new plantations are mixed, with a good sprinkling of silver birch. Between the dense coppices are open chases typical of the Essex forest lands. Two detached areas of forest, near Woodside Green, were added to the National Trust land in 1933.

The most famous tree in the forest was the Doodle Oak which is said to have been 60 feet round at the base. It may have been one of those legendary oaks 'mentioned in Domesday Book'! Whether or not this was so, and the tree must certainly have been there at the time of the Conquest, this may well have been the Broad Oak which gave the neighbouring village of Hatfield Regis its ancient nickname. This may seem far from the Stort, but the Hatfield stream, here Pincey Brook, drains to the Stort, and we might visit it now.

I call it village, but there is something of a town character about Hatfield Broad Oak. One might expect a place of some substance to grow up at the gates of a priory. There was a Benedictine house founded at the end of Henry I's reign by Alberic de Vere, the builder of Hedingham Castle. It had some importance but by the time that Henry VIII's Commissioners turned their attention this way it was in decline, and the foundation was suppressed among the minor monasteries of 1536. Every trace of the conventual buildings has vanished, but the nave of the priory church was claimed by the parish. This is still there, a noble fragment but not so big as to be a serious embarrassment to the modern parish. Little remains of the original church. It was largely rebuilt in a period of prosperity in the fifteenth century, when it acquired the tall flint tower—which looks equally good from a distance dwarfing the village and at close range—and an equally striking south porch with slim stone pinnacles. Hatfield must have enjoyed a revival too in the eighteenth century, to which period many of the internal fittings belong. These include the four Evangelists which—perhaps not in their original position—sit on the ends of pews in the nave. These are all vigorously carved, and Luke's ox and John's eagle are especially impressive. Most of the monuments are typically Georgian, and there are rather too many of them; one is a Flaxman with angels. In the middle of the chancel lies a battered knight. He ought, in this position of honour, to be the founder, but the armour is a century too late for this. He is doubtless another de Vere, probably Robert who was one of the barons who forced the Great Charter on King John.

The village has some attractive houses along two streets, though nothing of the first order—by Essex standards. There is a curious gabled entrance to a driveway almost at the road junction which has a memorable eccentricity.

We must return to the Stort, not following Pincey Brook which goes too far south, skirting the parkland of Down Hall, the home of Matthew Prior, the poet and politician who won some fame or notoriety for his part in the negotiation of the Treaty of Utrecht. Our way lies north and west to Great Hallingbury, close to Bishop's Stortford. This is a well-wooded district with a great deal of charm, another place where the walker will be rewarded for his exertions. The church lies well away from the village, with a tall spire as a landmark. It is a strange building, so obviously Victorian that you will not be prepared for the early Norman chancel arch, a singularly perfect feature retained, with rare perceptiveness, by the restorers. The modern work is not unsatisfactory, and the patron saint, Giles, is portrayed pleasantly in wood on a choir stall and in stone above the south door.

The Stort, a mile away, has now become a 'navigation', with a towpath which offers the longest walk in Essex, all the way from Bishop's Stortford to the London boundary. While I would not suggest that you undertake this, a small part of it might be worth doing, perhaps from Great Hallingbury to Little Hallingbury or to Sawbridgeworth. Here the river is the county boundary, and the path is alternately in Essex and Hertfordshire. Within the first two miles the river passes below the earthen ramparts of Wallbury Camp, the most striking of the Iron Age hill-forts of Essex. The Stort is here a quiet canal, not excessively popular with anglers, with enough places in which to picnic, find wild flowers or watch birds.

Little Hallingbury is close to the river. There is not much to see, but the houses near the church, with a great willow, make an attractive scene.

The choice of route here is not entirely clear. A lane keeps close to the river, but it has no special attraction. The main road swings eastwards to Hatfield Heath, where there is nothing of historical or architectural distinction but where you may find refreshment in several inns. If you go this way, you may take in Sheering, a village close to the Pincey Brook. This is worth the diversion because of some good stained glass in the church and, better still, a fine collection of grotesques carved on the porch. The gargoyles are conventionally horrid, but on the angle of the wall is something special, a struggle—to the death—between a hairy man and a lion. That this energetic piece may be renewal work—it is in very good condition —is no detraction.

If you take the lane towards Sawbridgeworth and then turn left you will come to two houses of quite outstanding quality. Right beside the road is Aylmers, a tall and noble half-timbered house with projecting porch, fine Tudor work and beautifully maintained. It makes a sharp contrast to Durrington House, which stands opposite but behind a wide lawn and ornamental pond. The gardens are shown sometimes in the summer. The house is late Georgian, perfect in its restraint; none of the bluster of the new-rich here, but a quiet grave self-containment. Even the fine pillared portico invites more than it impresses. The gardens are in keeping. There are no real highlights, but everything is designed to lead the eye to the house and to give it a worthy frame.

Here we are on the edge of Harlow, which is approached through the old town gathered around the church. The church itself is imposing but damaged beyond repair by drastic restoration. The town is quite delightful. There are individually fine houses like Mulberry Green, a modest product of the age which gave us Durrington, but it is the general effect that is important. It is not often that a place as large as this has so few unworthy buildings. There are two rows of almshouses.

The old manor was at Harlowbury, nearer to the main road and the river. Here there is a little Norman chapel, in a fair state, which belonged formerly to the abbey of St Edmundsbury. The river is very pretty here.

Harlow is an ancient place with Roman associations. It has stepped boldly into the twentieth century with one of the first and the most successful of New Towns. This was established in 1947 under the guidance of the distinguished architect and architectural historian Frederick Gibberd. The area is large and takes in four old villages and several hamlets. Part of the interest of the scheme is the way these settlements have become neighbourhood units of the new town. I have found most of the modern domestic architecture of Essex dull or timid, but at Harlow there is much that is exciting and little which is wholly unsuccessful. There are great towers, like the town hall and Gibberd's noble Lawn, clusters of modest houses, some imaginatively conceived public-houses—all named after butterflies and with appropriately colourful signs—and plenty of open spaces. In fact the first criticism must be of the sprawling nature of the community. Like New Delhi it has been designed for Carriage Folk! It is good to see so much green, but will the people of Great Parndon and Burnt Mill get to know their fellow townsfolk in Mark Hall North or Hare Street? Harlow may become, like London, a collection of villages.

These are questions for the sociologist. The visitor who comes to Harlow to discover what contribution the twentieth century has to make to the Essex landscape will find much to please him. Apart from the architecture there is a generous amount of sculpture, carefully sited. It is pleasing to see how a few old buildings, churches and barns, have been incorporated, and even integrated, into their new settings without too much self-conscious olde worldiness. Of these old buildings Netteswell church is perhaps the best I remember it for its homeliness, for an interesting inserted panel in brick with the rebus of Abbot Rose of Waltham Abbey, and for the friendliness and good manners of the children waiting for morning service. Nearby the village pond makes the centrepiece of an open space beside one of the radial roads.

Harlow is a place to live and to work in. On the whole the industrial buildings are less interesting than the domestic—the reverse of the normal condition in Essex—but the office block of Gilbeys is a forceful design and some of the factories in Pinnacles are dramatic.

One may or may not think that at Harlow we have a wise
penditure of six thousand or so acres of good land. What can be
mmended without reservation is that the New Town has clearly
fined limits. There is none of the messy no-man's-land which
sfigures the edges of most towns. We are in Harlow—and then we
e back in the country, across the Stort into Hertfordshire or down
e winding leafy lane which leads to Roydon. This is a border vill-
e with that indefinable air which marks the frontier community,
en when the boundary is the gentle Stort and the enemy Charles
amb's 'happy homely loving Hertfordshire'. The church indeed
ems stylistically to have one foot in foreign territory. It sits well
1 the bend of the main street leading down to the river. There is a
iangular green opposite with some undistinguished but satisfactory
ouses around. The best visually is a long low plastered cottage half
cross the front of the church. There was a market at Roydon at one
me, which accounts for a certain urban character, and accounts
10 for the stocks and lock-up on the green, provided not for the
ood citizens of Roydon but for unruly characters come in for the
ir.

I have long cherished the memory of a romantically ruined house
ere. Visiting it again recently after 40 years I have found that the
omance has worn thin, but it is still probably worth the journey
own a side lane towards the Lea to see the battered gatehouse of
ether Hall. (Where was Upper Hall, I wonder?) This must once
ave been a towered gatehouse in the grand Essex manner, like
eez Priory. It is of red brick patterned in blue. Age and neglect
ave brought it into ruin of a distinctly picturesque kind. Dim recol-
ctions persist of a connection between the Hall and Rye House
cross the Lea with—of course—underground passages. Alas, highly
nprobable.

Near Nether Hall a byway and track lead to the confluence of
tort and Lea at Rye House. The Lea, which has come out of Bed-
ordshire and right across Hertfordshire, is the senior partner. The
ea valley has long been a muddle of outer suburbs, market gardens,
idustry, rubbish tips and reservoirs, in which the undoubted charms
f the river have tended to get lost. The first gleams of hope for a
etter future appeared in the imaginative idea of a Lea Valley
egional Park. This came originally from Sir Patrick Abercrombie,
ollowed in 1964 by a report of the Civic Trust. The Lea Valley

Regional Park Authority was set up three years later, and plans f
bringing the dream to reality are now in preparation. It is a lon
term project, difficult and costly, but out of it may come somethir
new in this country, a linear park coming out of the country ar
penetrating deep into a densely populated urban area. It would pr
vide for sporting and other communal and semi-communal activitie
and inevitably would cater mainly for the needs of large numbers
people. Maybe room might be found too for the minority who lil
to be alone.

One hopes that the Park, while cleaning up the present mess, w
not be too clinically tidy. The present situation is not all loss. Th
great reservoirs between Waltham and Walthamstow have becon
a major bird sanctuary and must remain so. Some of the industri
buildings beside the river, like the power station at Brimsdown, ha·
a grandeur which would not be enhanced by a sprinkling of law·
and formal gardens. For all its present squalor, this is a fascinatir
area, particularly for the industrial archaeologist, and some of ı
unsuspected assets might too easily be squandered.

This is for the future. At present we will turn away from the glas
houses and the bungalows of the valley for a last look at rural Esse·
Much of modern Nazeing lies on the low ground towards the rive
but the old village is two miles away and a hundred feet or mor
higher. The church of All Saints has as fine a position as any in th
county. The tall tower looks across a valley gleaming with wate
and glass to the hills of Hertfordshire. It is a crowded scene, yet th
immediate surroundings of the church are most green and peacefu
So (comparatively) lofty a site suggests that this was an earl
Christian foundation, possibly superseding a pagan shrine, and ce
tainly there was a church here before the Conquest, belonging to th
Abbey at Waltham. Rebuilt in stone a century later, this forms th
nucleus of the present building which includes additions made ove
at least seven centuries. It is not a church of great architectur.
pretensions, except for the fine Elizabethan brick tower, but it ha
the atmosphere of a building whose roots go deep.

South of Nazeing church is an area of quite remarkable remot
ness, considering the nearness of London. There is only one motc
road between Nazeing and Upshire, but this rolling land is cris
crossed by farm tracks, bridle paths and field paths. It is good countr
for those with leisure and a fair supply of energy. It can be muddy

have an indelible memory of an attempt, in boyhood, to cycle
oss-country from Epping Upland to Waltham, one which ended
nee-deep in rich black mud on what my map assured me was a road.
his would not happen now, but you would still need strength and
difference to surface dirt to make the journey.

By road the route from Nazeing goes by way of Broadley Com-
on to Epping Upland, the parent village of modern Epping, high
p on a long ridge and, like Nazeing, commanding wide views. Here
o there is a well-placed church with a dominant brick tower. This
as another manor of Waltham Abbey. Much of the building was
newed in the nineteenth century, but it is not without charm.
he memorial altar table and reredos are good modern craftsman-
iip from between the wars.

From the churchyard Epping itself is conspicuous on a neighbour-
ig ridge. The town has grown greatly in recent years, with some
oss of character, but it is still a clean and breezy place. The high
reet rises to 300 feet, making it one of the highest towns in Essex,
nd this is the impression one gets. The houses are a mixed lot, with-
ut any of outstanding quality, but there is less superficial gloss or
ipermarketry than one might expect. Architecturally much the
est thing in Epping is the tower of the modern church, a superb
ssay in the East Anglian manner by Bodley. This will please even
iose who are normally resistant to the appeal of neo-Gothic.

Epping has given its name, comparatively recently, to the largest
f the surviving fragments of the great Forest of Essex. Epping
orest, which narrowly escaped complete destruction in the nine-
eenth century, is one of the greatest treasures in the county and the
iost precious to the teeming thousands of east London who have in
 the loveliest of back gardens. Motor transport, which has brought
 nearer to more people, has also shrunk it. One can drive the entire
ength of the forest, provided the usual traffic jams are—by some
iiracle—missing, in a few minutes. Seen on foot, its right propor-
ions return. Although the walker is seldom out of sound of a road
e can walk for hours in peace and in the most lovely surroundings.
he forest is beautiful in all seasons. Many would prefer autumn,
ut there is a beauty in the frost-bound glades in deep winter when
he superb architecture of each tree can be seen unencumbered and
ach twig is outlined in rime.

Epping Forest is a bit of true forest, not Forestry Commission forest. That is, it was an area deliberately kept waste for huntir It would have made poor sport if the whole tract had been dense wooded. There were wide plains for galloping free and copses give shelter to the deer. So the forest is still, although new plant tions have filled in some of the open land. There is a wide varie of trees, with many oaks and silver birches. The characteristic tr of Epping however is the hornbeam. Over the centuries commone exercised their right of lopping these trees, and the ancient hor beams have assumed as a result the most fantastic shapes. In tl dusk some of these groves seem peopled with monsters. Beside tl slim beauty of birch and beech they have much the same fascinatic as gargoyles.

Before looking closely at Epping Forest, it is well to visit the fore museum at Chingford. To reach this one must traverse the ma forest road, which is the busiest as it is the most beautiful ma road in the county, turning right towards Chingford town. Short the wooded area falls away and the landscape opens up at Chin ford Plain. On the right, dwarfed by the huge mock-Tudor of tl Royal Forest Hotel, is Queen Elizabeth's Hunting Lodge. This tal slim building, timber-framed and picturesque, was designed as grandstand from which the delicate and the idle might watch tl hunt on the plain below. It was originally open to the weather fc better viewing, but the walls have been closed to make three goc rooms, one above the other. This most interesting building, earl Tudor, is owned by the Corporation of London and provides a hom for a small museum of forest science and history. Here, before see ing them on the ground, one may identify the animals, trees, flowe and fungi to be found—or once found—in the forest.

Everyone has his favourite walk in Epping Forest, and the expert would claim that there is no alternative to walking it all. It might b profitably sampled around High Beech church, where Tennyso heard the bell of Waltham Abbey.

> *below the hill*
> *. . . pealing folded in the mist.*

This, although attractive and with good views, is an accessible an consequently crowded part of the forest. Further north, by th Wake Valley ponds, it is lonelier despite the clamour of traffic o

ιe road. Across this road there is a heavily wooded area in which,
' you are skilful or lucky, you may come upon the ramparts of an
·on Age camp above Loughton and perhaps see some of the shy
ιllow deer. Further on still there are beautiful glades beyond the
ɔmmuters' estates of Theydon Bois and, close to the main road,
ιe second camp in the Forest, Ambresbury Banks. Persistent tradi-
·on, in the face of probability, claims that this was the scene of
·oadicea's last stand. Then, beyond Epping, is the detached triangle
·f the Lower Forest which has its distinctive character.

Epping Forest—a precious possession indeed. It adds something to
ne's feeling of possessiveness towards these lonely thickets and
ɛmote sun-soaked glades to know that the packed houses of Lough-
ɔn and Debden, however near, are here held at bay. However much
ιe crowds pack the roads and clutter up the fringes of the forest,
ιere is in these 5,500 acres a secret place for everyone who wants
ɔ find it.

The old name was Waltham Forest, derived from the ancient
ɔwnship on its western edge. To reach Waltham, you drop down
·om the forest ridge at Wake Arms, having a last delectable glimpse
·f the forest at Honey Lane Plain, then through increasingly built-up
·treets to the abbey church in the water-meadows of the Lea.

After Bradwell and Greensted this is the holy place of Essex. The
·orrect name of the town is Waltham Holy Cross. It comes from the
·ossession of a rood found, according to a beautiful tradition, on
ιnd at Montacute in Somerset belonging to Tovi, standard-bearer to
ιe great King Canute. Tovi decided to give it to the abbey of
·lastonbury, but the oxen chosen to draw it there refused to budge.
ʌfter further abortive attempts to take it to west country shrines,
·ovi decided on Waltham, where he held land. The oxen went there
·villingly, and Tovi built a church to contain the cross. Later the
ιanor came to Harold Godwinsson, who rebuilt the church and
·ounded a college of secular canons, bringing in a famous scholar,
ʌdelard of Liege, as the first chancellor. When Harold returned
·rom his pilgrimage to Rome in 1060, the new church was dedicated
·y the Archbishop of York—Stigand, the Archbishop of Canterbury,
·vas unpopular with the Godwins—on 3rd May (Holy Cross Day). It
·vas a great occasion and the King, Edward the Confessor, was
·resent. If anything is clear about those distant and troubled times,
·t is that Harold, a man of many contradictions, was deeply attached

to Waltham. He came here, according to another story, befor
Hastings, and the war cry of the English in the battle was 'Hol
Rood'. Opinions vary as to whether he was buried here or on th
foreshore at Hastings, but the Conqueror was a religious—or supe
stitious—man and it seems likely that he approved the prayer of th
Waltham canons, on the battlefield, and allowed the body of h
enemy to be buried in his own church. Henry II dissolved Harold
foundation and replaced it with an abbey of Augustinian canor
which became one of the most powerful in the country. The Abbc
held great state and sat with the Lords in Parliament. Unlike mos
of the Essex houses it remained prosperous to the end and was th
last English abbey to surrender to the King in 1540. According t
one proposal Waltham was to be given cathedral status after th
Dissolution, but this idea was abandoned and the abbey destroye
systematically. Only the nave of the abbey church remained, save
at the last moment by the parish who claimed that it had been fror
time immemorial their parish church.

It is tempting to think of this noble fragment, much the fines
Norman church in Essex and, even in its incomplete state amon
the best in the country, as the church of Harold's foundation. Bu
these vast pillars, with their deep zig-zag and spiral decoration, b
long to the fine flowering of Norman architecture in Henry II's reigr
not to its seed-time before the Conquest. It is strongly reminiscent o
Durham. It is a singularly perfect nave, apart from a nearly di:
astrous attempt to bring the western bays up to date in the thirteent
century, but one has to assess it bearing in mind that the buildin
now goes only as far as the western arch of the crossing below
great central tower, and that two-thirds of the church lay beyon
this. The white western tower, put up hastily in Queen Mary'
reign, using materials from the demolished buildings, to house th
bells and to prop up the sagging building, is equally out of scale. Th
Lady Chapel, however, on the south side, is a very lovely piece o
late thirteenth-century work and so is the crypt below it.

We may well curse the greed of Henry VIII and of Sir Anthon
Denny, who acquired the abbey on its suppression, for destroyin
the proportions of this great building. What remains is imperfect
like an illuminated copy of the Gospels with the cover and half th
pages missing, but like the Gospels the fragment is priceless. Durin
recent restorations, undertaken more than nine centuries after th

foundation, the church was put into very good repair, and one omission made good. On a buttress was set a statue of the founder, King Harold, carved in the mediaeval convention with one hand on his sword, one arm cradling his church. This excellent modern work is by Elizabeth Muntz, whose sister wrote, in *The Golden Warrior*, the finest fictional portrait of the King.

The town of Waltham Holy Cross has suffered from recent rapid growth and from an intolerable increase in through-traffic. It is still a place of character, with a lively street market and a cattle market in the ancient square known as Romeland. There are a few attractive houses, an ancient inn, and, next to it, the Elizabethan Lichgate House which gives a home to a small local museum. Of the abbey buildings there are a few scraps of wall, the battered gatehouse and a nice vaulted building standing in a corner of the vanished cloister, perhaps the entrance to the Abbot's Lodging.

The remaining charm of Waltham is in its riverside. The abbey stream, later a mill stream, is a leat from the Lea which flows through meadows as yet unspoilt although they are so close to the town. At one point the stream is crossed by a single-span mediaeval bridge called, anachronistically, Harold's Bridge. The scene is one of great charm, precariously preserved in the face of many pressures. Like so much of Essex, as we have seen, here in the meadows of Waltham we enjoy a landscape of quiet loveliness, which owes much to nature and as much to the men who, for practical reasons, diverted the stream, planted the trees, and built the bridge and the stone walls. Closing the view southwards is a great and beautiful church, enriched by centuries of patrons and craftsmen and damaged by a single generation of predators. To left and right we see mean houses and festoons of wire, the legacy of a civilization which, unlike most of those of the past, has found it difficult, or perhaps not worth while, to give an individual quality to ordinary things. The wounds of Waltham Abbey have healed, although the scars remain. Perhaps the damage so cruelly done here and throughout this lovely county by our greed-ridden century will be repaired by time, aided by another generation which has renewed its faith in beauty and integrity.

Index

Index

Index

Canute, King, 137, 241
Canvey Island, 53
Capel family, 153
Capon, Kenneth, 190
Caractacus, 20
Carausius, 159
Caroline, Queen, 56
Carpenter, Reverend William, 125
Cassivellaunus, 20
Castle Hedingham, 21, 169 : **26**
  parish church, 171
  sheepcote, 170
Castle House, 208
Castles, 21, 80, 90, 120, 169, 184, 202,
  228
Cattawade, 209
Cavendish, 200
Cedd, Saint, 21, 45, 49, 160
Celts, 19, 20, 182
Central Electricity Board, 102
Chad, Saint, 21, 50, 160
Chadwell, 49
Chalkwell, 59
Chappell, 178, 181
Charles I, 22
Chaucer, Geoffrey, 112
Chelmer and Blackwater Navigation,
  130
Chelmer, River, 32, 79, Chapter 5
Chelmsford, 20, 104, 120, 122ff.
  Cathedral, 123 : **23**
  Marconi factory, 124
Chich, 192
Chickney church, 79
Chignall St James, 119
  Smealy, 119
Chigwell, 15, 99, 100, 138
  Harsnett's Grammar School, 100
  King's Head Inn, 100 : **19**
Child, Sir Josiah, 101, 102
Childerditch, 63
Chingford, 238
  Forest museum, 238
Chippinghill, 150
Chipping Ongar, 89, 90, 91
  Castle, 90
Christopher, St, wall-painting of, 99
Church, Richard, 137
Churches, 25, 26
Churchill, Charles, 38
  Sir Winston, 101
Cistercian Order, 108, 147
Civic Trust, 235

Civil War, 22, 23, 138, 188, 224
Clacton, 19, 27
Claudius, 20, 182
Clavering, 19, 31, 228 : **37**
  Castle, 228
Cloth trade, 23, 24, 205
Coalhouse Fort, 45, 46
Coggeshall, 109, 146
  Abbey, 147
  Market Street, 147
  Paycocke's, 148 : **24**
  Woolpack Inn, 147
Colchester, 19-22, 23, 163, 183ff.
  All Saints' Church, 186
  Balkerne Gate, 183
  Castle, 184 : **28**
  Castle Museum, 185
  Dutch Quarter, 184
  Holly Trees Museum, 186
  Holy Trinity, 187
  Hythe, the, 189
  King's Head, 188
  St Botolph's Church, 27, 186, 187
    Priory, 186, 187
  St James's Church, 186
  St John's Abbey, 187
  Siege House, 181
  Town Hall, 184
  Walls, 183
  Water-tower (Jumbo), 183
Cole, Hubert, *Hawkwood*, 172
Cole End, 137
College of Physicians, 138
Colne Engaine, 178, 179
Colne Priory, 149, 171
Colne, River, 22, 24, 32, Chapter 7 :
  29
Commuters, 24
Conrad, Joseph, 44
Constable, John, 19, 149, 196, 202, 204,
  205
Copford Church, 189
Corringham, 50, 51
Coryton, 50
County Record Office, 31
Courtauld family, 37, 144, 178
Courtaulds, 144, 177, 178
Cowdray, Lord, 185
Cox, Dr Charles, 62, 70, 81, 136
Cracknell, B. E., *History of a Marshland
  Community*, 53
Craftsmen, 28
Cressing, 154

247

Index

Index

Hatt, Sir John, 42
Haverhill, 163, 167
Havering, 19
Havering-atte-Bower, 37
Hawkwell, 71
  Church, **14**
Hawkwood, Sir John, 172
Heckfordbridge, 189
Hedingham ware (pottery), 170
Hempstead, 138
  Church, 138
  Winslow House, 138
Henham, 227
Henny Street, 202
Henry I, 231
  II, 90, 242
  III, 55
  V, 69, 89
  VI, 202
  VIII, 37, 45, 108, 115, 129, 224, 242
Herbert, George, 101
Hermes, Gertrude (sculptor), 106
Herongate, 62
Heron Hall, 63
Heybridge, 156
Higbed, Thomas, 43, 44
High Beech Church, 238
Higham, 204
High Easter, 26, 120
  Ongar, 89
  Roding, 82, 119
Highwood, 130
Hill Pasture, 80
Hobs Aerie, 225 : **2**
Hockley, 71
Hogan, Robert, 164
Hole Haven, 54
  Lobster Smack Inn, 54
Honey Lane Plain, 241
Hopkins, Matthew (Witch-finder), 209
Horham Hall, 108
Hornbeams, 238
Hornchurch, 37
Horndon-on-the-Hill, 43
  Bell Inn, 43
  Church, 44
Hospitallers, 155, 174, 177
Houses, historic, 25, 28
Howard of Walden, Thomas, 219
Howe Street, 117, 118
Howlett, Sarah, 168
Hoxne, Battle of, 92
Hubba, 92

Hullbridge, 68
Humphreys, Edmund, 68
Hundred Years' War, 23, 70, 215
Hylands, 125
Hythe, the, 189

Industry, 24, 36, 44, 105, 144, 170, 177
  178, 205, 223
Ingatestone, 25, 62, 126
  Bypass, 125
  Hall, 127
Inglebourne Brook, 37
Ingrave, 27, 63
Ingwar, 92
Inworth, 149
Iron Age, 20, 218, 232, 241
Ithancester, 160, 161

Jericho, 129
John, King, 22, 55, 122, 125, 232
Johnson, John, 123
Josselyns, 203
Julius Caesar, 19
Jupes Hill Farm, 208

Kelvedon, 148, 149, 167
Kelvedon Hatch, 93
Kempe family, 142
  monument, 200
Knight, John, 180
Knights Hospitallers, 155, 174, 177
Knights Templars, 155, 174, 177
Knowles, D., and St Joseph, J. K.
    Monastic Sites from the Air, 147

Laindon Church, 52
  Hills, 13, 39, 52, 63 : **12**
Lake village, 20
Lamarsh, 202
Lamb, Charles, 235
  Lynton, *County Town*, 122
Lambourne, 27
  Church, 98, 99
  Hall, 99
  Place, 98
Langford, 156
  unique church at, 156
Langham, 204
  Hall, 204
Langleys, 118
Latchingdon Church, 72, 158

250

Index

Index

Index

Index

Index